THE HENRICIAN REFORMATION

A sixteenth-century bishop, possibly John Longland, from a missal certainly belonging to him. (B. M. Add. Ms. 21974; reproduced by permission of the British Library.)

THE HENRICIAN REFORMATION

THE DIOCESE OF LINCOLN UNDER JOHN LONGLAND 1521–1547

MARGARET BOWKER

Reader in History
University of Lancaster

CAMBRIDGE UNIVERSITY PRESS

Cambridge
London New York New Rochelle
Melbourne Sydney

Published by the Press Syndicate of the University of Cambridge
The Pitt Building, Trumpington Street, Cambridge CB2 1RP
32 East 57th Street, New York, NY 10022, USA
296 Beaconsfield Parade, Middle Park, Melbourne 3206, Australia

First published 1981

Printed in Malta by Interprint Limited

British Library Cataloguing in Publication Data

Bowker, Margaret
The Henrician Reformation.
1. Lincoln, Eng. (*Diocese*)
I. Title
262.2'0942534 BX5107.L5 80-41655

ISBN 0 521 23639 8

TO JOHN AND DAVID

Qui domi moras, auxilium studiis
attulerunt non sine dolore ac
risu mutua vice inter se coniunctis.

CONTENTS

TABLES AND GRAPHS

ILLUSTRATIONS

MAPS

PLATES

PREFACE

This book has been an intolerably long time in the research and the writing: not only did I bite off rather more than could be easily chewed and digested, but the move of my family to Lancaster put more than 200 miles between myself and my sources and required of me wholly new lectures and skills. The research loaded into the removal vans in 1973 has only really been able to come out over the last year and much of it has looked faded or incomprehensible. I should have burned it all by now were it not for the persistent and sympathetic help of a number of research foundations and the conviction shared and facilitated by my husband that 1979 was to be 'make or break' year in my long involvement with the diocese of Lincoln. The willingness with which he has talked through the problems, tried to correct the style and cooked the supper makes the feminism of some of my contemporaries sound a deal too shrill.

But I have also been helped with access to my sources: first when my son was too young to allow me to reach them and thereafter when distance made travel expensive and often impossible. I am most grateful to the Leverhulme Foundation, the British Academy and the University of Lancaster for the generous help they have given to me in overcoming some of these problems, and to the patience of archivists at Lincoln – where they must have wondered if I would become part of the furniture – Leicester, Bedford, Buckingham, Huntingdon, Northampton, Oxford, the British Library, Lambeth and the Public Record Office.

The volume of the material which this research produced necessitated the use of a research assistant. Miss Susan Hunt has looked up more than 2,000 clergy in Emden and other volumes. I am grateful for her good-humoured patience and for the support of the Leverhulme Foundation in paying her. The pure business of transcribing so much material had me all too frequently flat on my back. My late mother-in-law, a highly skilled calligrapher, wrote and wrote to my dictation with much humour and even more compassion. The results of her labours and mine we realised would, in card form, put the dining-room table almost indefinitely out of commission. I decided that no sample would do justice to the subject, and all the clergy, their patrons, their incomes and their parishes were put on computer tape. I am grateful to Dr Martin Porter and the Institute of Applied Linguistics at Cambridge for their help in this regard.

Much of the material for the investigation was in difficult Latin. Longland's sermons were translated from English into an Erasmus-type Latin which often nearly defeated me and certainly would have done so had not Mr James Hunt, formerly of Rugby School and now of Magdalene College, Cambridge, borne with my ignorance, translated what I could not and conveyed to me the 'Churchillian gusto' (his words) of the original.

I am grateful to the British Library for the reproduction from Longland's missal of which the wood cut of the bishop is thought to portray some likeness to the owner. I am also greatly indebted to Mr C. V. Middleton of Lincolnshire Press and Television Services for his photographs of the Cathedral and bishop's palace and to Mr A. P. Moore of Bishop Grosseteste's College for his picture of Longland's chantry.

After so much help, one would hope that the book would be worthy of the generosity accorded it. I know it is not. It would be worse if Dr Christopher Haigh and Professor Kathleen Major had not pruned it of its more elementary errors. I am profoundly grateful to both and to Dr and Mrs John Nurser who have cherished me at Lincoln. It will, no doubt, be a relief to everyone – not least myself – that my long association with the diocese of Lincoln is now at an end.

Finally, I would like to thank Mrs Deirdre Grant for her feats of typewriting, performed after long days in the university. My mother, after retiring from a medical career, took on the onerous task of indexing. Such maternal devotion goes well beyond the call of duty. To her and to the staff of Cambridge University Press I owe much for their meticulous correction and kindness.

Copies of the data base of research material are available. Approval for receiving a copy should first be sought from Mrs M. Bowker, Department of History, Furness College, University of Lancaster, Bailrigg, Lancaster LA1 4YG, UK. Details of costs will be sent with the approval. Payment should then be sent to Mrs Bowker, and a 2400-foot 9-track magnetic tape should be sent with a copy of the approval and details of the tape format required to the Literary and Linguistic Computing Centre, University of Cambridge, Sidgwick Avenue, Cambridge CB3 9DA, UK.

Margaret Bowker
Michaelmas 1980

The Cottage,
Bailrigg, Lancaster

1. The dioceses of England and Wales in 1521

2. The diocese of Lincoln in 1521

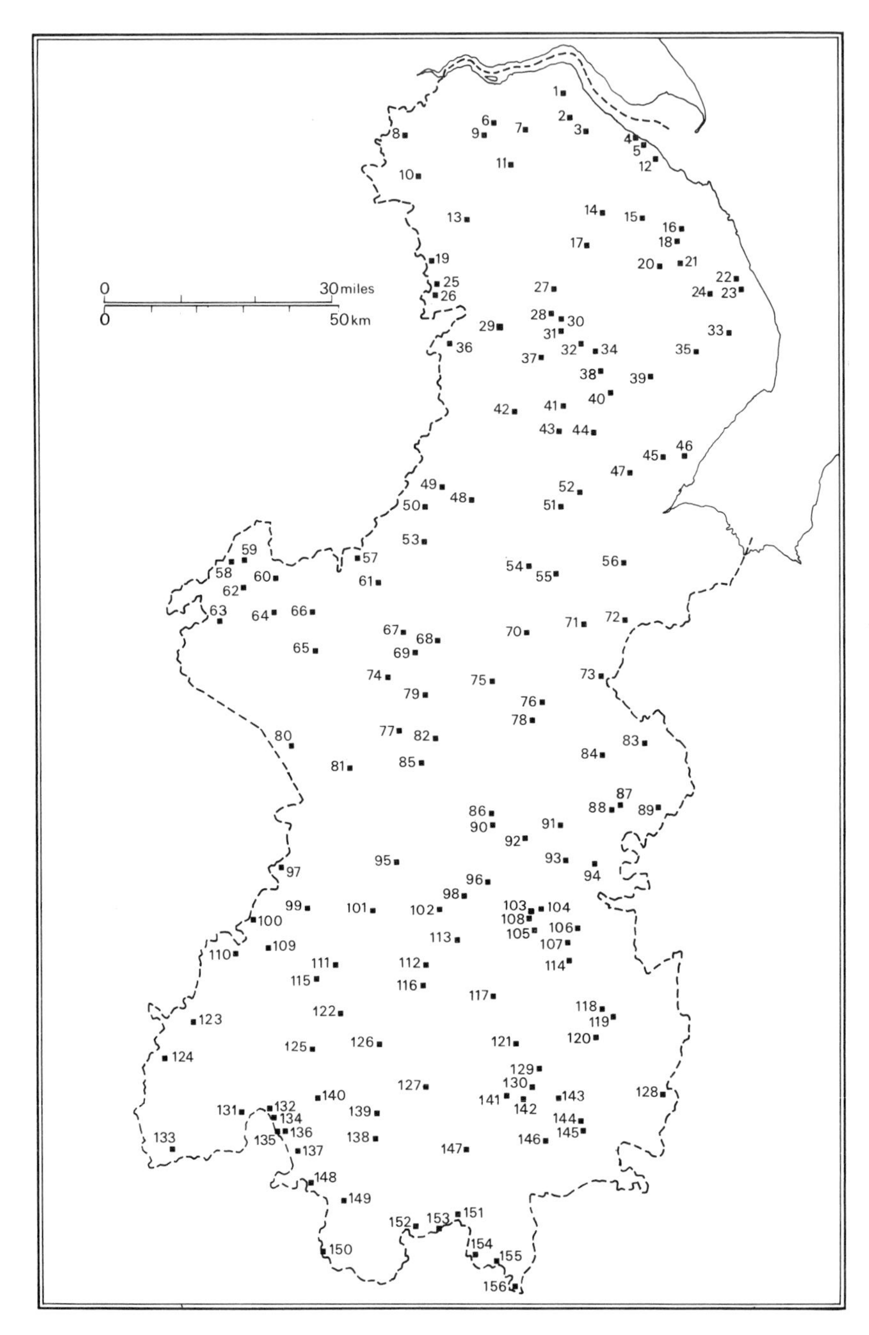

3. The religious foundations of the diocese of Lincoln

KEY. The order to which each foundation belonged is given in the Index.

1 Thornton
2 Newsham
3 Nun Cotham
4 Grimsby
5 Wellow
6 Thornholme
7 Elsham
8 Hirst
9 Gokewell
10 Axholme
11 Newstead
12 Humberston
13 Willoughton
14 Orford
15 North Ormsby
16 Alvingham
17 Sixhills
18 Louth Park
19 Heynings
20 Maltby
21 Legbourne
22 Hagneby
23 Markby
24 Greenfield
25 Torksey
26 Fosse
27 Bullington
28 Barlings
29 Lincoln
30 Stainfield
31 Bardney
32 Tupholme
33 Thwaite
34 Stixwold
35 Spilsby
36 Eagle
37 Nocton
38 Kirkstead
39 Revesby
40 Tattershall
41 Catley
42 Temple Bruer
43 Haverholme
44 Kyme
45 Boston
46 Freiston
47 Swineshead
48 Grantham
49 Newbo
50 Belvoir
51 Sempringham
52 Bridge End
53 Croxton
54 Vaudey
55 Bourne
56 Spalding
57 Dalby
58 Breedon
59 Langley
60 Garendon
61 Kirby Bellars
62 Gracedieu
63 Heather
64 Ulverscroft
65 Leicester
66 Rothley
67 Owston
68 Brooke
69 Launde
70 Stamford
71 Deeping St James
72 Crowland
73 Peterborough
74 Noseley
75 Fineshade
76 Fotheringhay
77 Dingley
78 Cotterstock
79 Bradley
80 Lutterworth
81 Sulby
82 Pipewell
83 Ramsey
84 Sawtry
85 Rothwell
86 Irthlingborough
87 Huntingdon
88 Hinchingbrooke
89 St Ives
90 Higham Ferrers
91 Stonely
92 Melchbourne
93 Bushmead
94 St Neots
95 Northampton
96 Harrold
97 Catesby
98 Lavendon
99 Canon's Ashby
100 Clattercote
101 Sewardsley
102 Ravenstone
103 Bedford
104 Newnham
105 Elstow
106 Northill
107 Warden
108 Caldwell
109 Chacombe
110 Wroxton
111 Biddlesden
112 Bradwell
113 Tickford
114 Chicksands
115 Brackley
116 Snelshall
117 Woburn
118 Hitchin
119 Wymondley
120 Temple Dinsley
121 Dunstable
122 Chetwode
123 Cold Norton
124 Bruern
125 Bicester
126 Hogshaw
127 Aylesbury
128 Hertford
129 Markyate
130 Flamstead
131 Eynsham
132 Godstow
133 Clanfield
134 Rewley
135 Osney
136 Oxford
137 Littlemore
138 Thame
139 Notley
140 Studley
141 Ashridge
142 St Margaret's
143 Redbourn
144 St Albans
145 Sopwell
146 Kings Langley
147 Missenden
148 Dorchester
149 Ewelme
150 Goring
151 Little Marlow
152 Medmenham
153 Bisham
154 Burnham
155 Eton
156 Ankerwyke

ABBREVIATIONS

Full details of the manuscript or secondary sources will be found in the bibliography. Manuscripts are in the custody of the Lincolnshire Archives Office, the Castle, Lincoln (L.A.O.) unless otherwise stated.

A.A.S.R.P.	*Associated Architectural Societies Reports and Papers*
Bodl. Libr.	The Bodleian Library, Oxford
B.L.	British Library
Bucks. R.O.	Buckinghamshire Record Office
Emden, *Oxford*	A. B. Emden, *A Biographical Register of the University of Oxford to A. D. 1500*, 3 vols. Oxford, 1957–9
Emden, *Oxford*, n.s.	A. B. Emden, *A Biographical Register of the University of Oxford to A. D. 1500*, 3 vols.
Emden, *Cambridge*	A. B. Emden, *A Biographical Register of the University of Cambridge to A. D. 1500*. Cambridge, 1963
Hunts. R.O.	Huntingdonshire Record Office
L.A.O.	Lincoln Archives Office
Leics. R.O.	Leicestershire Record Office (Leicester Museum, Department of Archives)
L.P.	*Letters and Papers Foreign and Domestic in the reign of Henry VIII* ed. J. S. Brewer, J. Gairdner and R. H. Brodie. London, 1862–1910
L.R.S. 5, 10.	*Lincoln Wills 1271–1530*, ed. C. W. Foster. Lincoln Record Society vol. 5, 1914; vol. 10, 1918
L.R.S. 12, 13.	*Chapter Acts of the Cathedral Church of St Mary of Lincoln*, ed. R. E. G. Cole. Lincoln Record Society, vol. 12, 1915; vol. 13, 1917
L.R.S. 33, 35, 37.	*Visitations in the Diocese of Lincoln 1517–*

	1531, ed. A. Hamilton Thompson, 3 vols. Lincoln Record Society, vol. 33, 1940; vol. 35, 1944; vol. 37, 1947
Longden I–XVI	H. I. Longden, *Northamptonshire and Rutland Clergy*, 16 vols. Northampton, 1938–52
Northampton R.O.	Northampton Record Office
O.H.S.	Oxford Historical Society
P.R.O.	Public Record Office
S.R.	*Statutes of the Realm*, 11 vols. 1810–28
Valor Ecclesiasticus	*Valor Ecclesiasticus*, 6 vols. Record Commission 1825–34
Venn	*Alumni Cantabrigienses*, Part I, J. and J. A. Venn, 4 vols. Cambridge, 1922–7

INTRODUCTION

The Henrician Reformation has received much attention from scholars in the last twenty-five years. Professor Knowles completed his monumental work on monasticism with a volume on the Tudor age[1] and Professor Dickens has brought a new insight to bear on the interaction of the royal will and the demand for reform in the country;[2] there have also been a number of brilliant studies which have taken us nearer to understanding how the break with Rome was enacted[3] and how Henry VIII and his ministers proposed to enforce change by means of legislation and propaganda as well as by intimidation and brute force.[4] All this work has revealed the need for more. How far was the will of the government enforced in the provinces? Did enforcement vary from place to place? What were the factors determining whether a county or a diocese acceded to the royal will or blocked it? Was a groundswell of already committed Protestantism necessary for even the modest requirements of the royal articles of 1538 to be accepted? Did Henrician England undergo a change from Catholicism to Protestantism? Was the faith of the statute book successfully translated into conviction at the level of the parish?

These questions and others like them have resulted in a detailed probe into some dioceses and in a growing awareness that the picture which emerges from Ely is distinct from that which we encounter in Lancashire and different again from that of Kent and Gloucestershire.[5] But so far the local studies have been limited to small areas of England as a whole, and the repetitious nature of the evidence contained in bishops' registers and court books has made studies of the larger dioceses a formidable undertaking. Dr Haigh has suggested some of the salient characteristics of the reformation in the north,[6] and a number of other scholars have concentrated on certain problems and certain areas.[7] For the huge medieval diocese of Lincoln which ran from the Humber to the Thames and comprised eight entire counties (as well as Rutland and parts of Hertfordshire), we have had some important contributions: the Lincoln Record Society has made available some critical manuscripts on which any estimates of the effect of the reformation must be based;[8] Mr Hodgett has made an invaluable study of the religious and ex-religious;[9] and Dr Walker in an important dissertation has tried to show the effects of religious legislation throughout the sixteenth century on the two archdeaconries of Lincoln and Stow.[10] But the detailed study of the whole diocese of Lincoln has so far defeated us. I have previously attempted to show the state of the secular clergy in the diocese in the first two decades of the sixteenth century, but the picture which I gave in *The Secular Clergy in the Diocese of Lincoln*[11] was, broadly speaking, a static one. In that earlier period there was little innovation emanating from Pope, king or convocation, and the modest changes which I detected look as though they were the work of an unusually conscientious and devoted bishop, William Atwater. Many of the clergy whom he visited or collated to livings were still alive in 1534 when the break with Rome occurred; some of them joined in the Lincolnshire rising and some lived on to receive the order for an English Bible in every church and for the instruction of all parishioners in the Lord's Prayer, the Hail Mary and the Apostles' Creed. How did they react to change? When, if ever, did they become Protestants, and how was innovation achieved?

It is in the hope of answering some of these questions that I returned to the clergy of the medieval diocese of Lincoln in an attempt to trace them through the innovations of the Henrician Reformation. My task was a difficult one because the diocese had nearly 1800 parishes and many more clergy. I found that the only way to gain a plausible insight into them was not by choosing the odd and entertaining example, nor even by sampling, which can prove arid where information is scant, but by indexing them all with the help of a computer programme which worked splendidly for the kind of data I was studying. This has meant that whatever my own errors of interpretation will prove to have been, at least the reader will find some detailed statistical information from which he may proceed. But the voluminous extent and repetitious nature of much of the evidence, and the incomplete nature of the more interesting parts of it, were not my only problems. In February 1521, the diocese of Lincoln received a new bishop, John Longland, and it became important to see whether that event did anything to change the picture which I had already described before it was necessarily affected by legislation. I have had, therefore, to look at the state of the diocese before the break with Rome. Much of what I have discovered about it does not differ very greatly from my earlier findings and so I have not outlined again the constitution of the diocese and the particular pattern of delegation which emerged under successive bishops of Lincoln. Nor have I sought to retrace the path by which an ordinand came to the priesthood and to a benefice, until it changed; nor have I much to add about his financial situation – again until it changed. These subjects have not only been studied by me but, independently, by Peter Heath, whose conclusions differed little from my own.[12] I have, therefore, tried to isolate the changes which were occurring in the diocese under a new bishop, and to assess his particular impact, if such there was, before considering how he and his people reacted to the changes which came about in the Reformation Parliament and thereafter. Inevitably this has meant a somewhat arbitrary division of my subject matter. The finances of the bishop and the dean and chapter reached a crisis point in the 1530s; I have, therefore, looked at their assets in the period 1521 to 1529 in the second part of the book so that the full force of change can be illustrated. Equally, the monastic orders changed little between 1530 and their dissolution, so it seemed best to deal with them mainly in the first part of the book. Finally, the bishop himself succeeded to the bishopric at a time which is not particularly significant in any other sense, so the dating of all sections has to be arbitrary. Longland conveniently died a few months after Henry VIII. To stop at that point will seem to some like stopping a match when it has just begun. I have some sympathy for that sentiment, but the surviving records for the Lincoln diocese are very thin indeed between the death of bishop Longland and the translation of Thomas Cooper to the diocese in 1571. Moreover it would be absolutely impossible to use a similar research strategy for the period 1547–71. Though some of the institutions and court proceedings survive for this period, they are incomplete and are not adequately supported by visitation material.

Dates are corrected to a year beginning 1 January and not 25 March. No attempt has been made to convert pounds, shillings and pence into pounds and new pence, and all the old county boundaries used in E. Ekwall, *The Concise Oxford Dictionary of English Place Names* (Oxford, 1936), have been preserved, including Rutland, since commissions and appointments were made to them, and to fragment these divisions into their modern equivalents would be to bewilder and mislead. Direct quotations given in *Letters and Papers* have been preserved in their modernised form but all other quotations from original sources have been kept in the language in which they were written.

I

THE DIOCESE OF LINCOLN: THE INHERITANCE OF A NEW BISHOP

John Longland succeeded William Atwater as bishop of Lincoln in May 1521. The extent of the area under his responsibility was daunting. The diocese of York was greater in square miles but it had fewer parishes than that of Lincoln. Lincoln had 1,736 parishes in 1535, and covered an area of 7,265 square miles. In contrast York covered just over 8,000 square miles but only had 694 parishes. The diocese of Norwich resembled Lincoln more closely in the number of parishes, but it was only half the size.[1] This meant that, administratively, the diocese of Lincoln presented an enormous problem. There were a large number of parishes to visit, scattered over a huge area. Nor was that area always easy of access. The floods in the fens were apt to isolate Lincolnshire, and the journey from Lincoln to London took three days' hard riding even on the Great North Road; but only a tiny fragment of the diocese could be seen from that highway, and a bishop eager to explore the diocese would have to contend with the mud and water of the country lanes.[2] There were a number of episcopal residences which facilitated travel and communication a little; in Huntingdonshire, and on the north road, was the manor of Buckden, and further north and a little west of the road was Liddington in Rutland which was the favourite resort of Bishop Atwater. In Lincoln itself the bishop had a palace, and in the extreme south-westerly point of the diocese there was a manor at Wooburn which Longland often found convenient, in addition to manors at Sleaford, Louth, Stow and Netteham. When in London the bishop stayed in his residence at Holborn, and elsewhere in the diocese there were manors which were leased, but which might provide the bishop with hospitality, or religious communities who would do the same. If a bishop had the energy and will to travel, he could do so; but if he was required at court, he would have had difficulties if he was summoned rapidly from the northern parts of his diocese.

A diocesan population return of 1563 gave the number of households in each deanery of the archdeaconry of Lincoln. We know that the

1. The cathedral church of St Mary of Lincoln

population had increased between 1521 and 1563,[3] but whether this came about through rising numbers within a household or by an overall increase in the number of households is highly problematic, particularly before 1538, when the keeping of parish registers was ordered for the first time. In 1563 in the same archdeaconry there were 22,505 households; by the same date and in the same area, there were 438 parishes, suggesting an average of one parish to every fifty-one households.[4] The increase in population between 1521 and 1563 had been accompanied by a decrease in the number of parishes and chapels, particularly chantries which communicated parishioners, so the favourable ratio of parishes to households in 1563 would have been even more marked in 1521; there were certainly more churches and probably fewer households making use of them.

The parish churches of the diocese had experienced some modest reforms in the six years before Longland came to the see of Lincoln. Atwater had personally visited many of them, assiduously checking up on non-resident priests and seeing to it that their dispensations were in order and that their deputies were adequate.[5] Careful investigation by the bishop revealed a number of clergy who found the requirements of celibacy too much for them and who had, under the guise of servants or relatives, ladies whom the scribes called suspicious women (*mulieres suspectae*). The ladies did not, however, detract from the devotion of the clergy; nor did the penance performed by the erring priests result in a change of life-style. At the next visitation the same women were likely to be in residence. But if chastity was a heavy burden for some, the duties of saying mass and the offices, of hearing confessions and visiting the sick, were not, and very few clergy in the diocese failed in their liturgical and pastoral obligations, either in the Lincoln diocese or in Lancashire and elsewhere.[6] The education of most priests was a chancy affair, and though many were unable to distinguish a Biblical story from the lives of the saints (both seemed to possess an equal authority), they were nevertheless instructed enough to know what was expected of them – even if they would be in difficulties trying to explain the *rationale* behind the teaching of the church and its ceremonial.[7] Many of the clergy and chantry priests were poorly paid and badly housed, and though stipends of rectors were only marginally higher in many cases, the rector usually had glebe which could be farmed to his profit or for his own use.[8] The fabric of many churches had long been neglected, and monastic houses which had been allowed to appropriate the greater tithe and become responsible for the chancel often ignored appeals to repair. But in spite of celebrating all too often beneath a leaking roof – which if it did not drench the incumbent might distract him or his congregation (as happened at Humberston[9]) – the majority of the clergy seem to have been acceptable to their parishes; and this was so despite the inevitable friction which arose from time to time about tithes and fees.[10] There were few signs of anti-clericalism, and Lollardy seems to have been confined to Buckinghamshire.[11]

The collegiate churches, however, were giving rise to gossip. There were nine in the diocese, the greatest being of course the cathedral church of the Blessed Virgin at Lincoln. The cathedral differed from the churches where groups of priests lived together to fulfil a common purpose in that it was not a chantry, though many chantries were located in it. It housed a number of residenciaries in the close, and absent canons substituted vicars choral as their deputies for purely liturgical functions. The other churches (of which the greatest was the college at Newarke in Leicester) were chantries of various kinds and were particularly prone to disorder. At Newarke there was brawling, hunting and neglect of the offices, which suggested that the canons had a cynical contempt for the wishes of their founder.[12] In contrast, the canons in residence in the close at Lincoln were devoted and rarely quarrelled (and then only on matters which touched their pockets), but they were quite unable to control the vicars choral and poor clerks whose correction was their responsibility. The poor clerks in particular were apt to neglect offices and take themselves to the nearby pub or brothel. They were, like their brethren at Newarke, using the endowment of the foundation as a passport to a life of pleasure, limited though this might be by the meagre stipends which they received.[13] Longland was likely to be scandalised by their life-style. He had preached before the monks of Westminster in terms which left few doubts about his attitude to the vices of drunkenness and fornication. He told them

> Woe unto them who do not devote themselves to prayer and reading ... but rather long for public assemblies and public places and drink in fabulous and absurd stories. They do not utter sighs through love of Christ ... they do not sob bewailing their own sins, they do not grieve for the sins of others, but they give themselves over to gourmandising and self-indulgence. When they have filled their bellies they belch, they sit idle, they laugh and pass most of the time in relaxation and idle vanities ... The pure will see God and rejoice in the sight; the impure will neither rejoice nor see ... Everywhere the company of women is to be avoided lest their beauty cleave to your heart ... Among them the purest flower of chastity will quickly fade, among them the lily of virtue will fall.[14]

Longland's words were prompted by a Trollopian observation of collegiate life, whether that of the university college or the cathedral close, and in the ensuing years canons and religious alike would live to regret the particular slant on affairs that years of life at a university had given to their scholarly bishop.

Like most of his colleagues on the bench, Longland's origins were relatively humble.[15] Born in 1473, he was appointed to the see of Lincoln when he was still under fifty – in marked contrast to his predecessor.[16] His family were of yeoman stock and lived in Henley-on-Thames where Longland may well have gone to school.[17] It is also possible that, like his predecessor, he won a place at Eton, but this is not recorded. In any event he formed an attachment to the college and asked that, if he were to die in the southern part of his diocese, his body should be laid to rest in the college chapel – as indeed it was to be.[18] Like Atwater and Wolsey, his advancement came through Magdalen College, Oxford, and through a doctorate in theology. It is probable that he stayed in the university with visits to the court until 1514. His experience of Oxford made a deep impression on him which he records with characteristic pessimism but with considerable gratitude to his parents:

> But I tell you how my parents sent me to Oxford to undertake the *study of death* ... I was entrusted by my parents to a school of good and sound learning ... through which I might live a good life chastely and studiously and instruct others in the same way, for I know that this was the wish and prayer of my virtuous parents.[19]

It is unlikely that he resided at any of the three west country benefices which he had acquired between 1505 and 1513. In 1514 he became first a canon of Salisbury and then its dean (again as Atwater had done before him), and to this preferment he added a Lincoln canonry and a canonry and prebend of St George's Windsor. There is no evidence of his residing in either.[20] His career was apparently centred on Oxford and far from any political and diplomatic imbroglio. This was gradually to change when his gifts as a preacher were brought to the king's attention. Payments to him for preaching at court occur regularly between 1518 and his translation to the bishopric of Lincoln.[21] In this period he seems to have been at court regularly, and he was amongst those present at the Field of Cloth of Gold.[22] He and John Clark, the future bishop of Bath and Wells, were present with the king at the consecration of the abbot of Reading.[23] It has been assumed that Longland became confessor to Henry VIII in about 1518, but this is not so: John Stockesley seems to have had this unenviable privilege at that date,[24] and it was not until after his appointment to Lincoln that Longland succeeded him, and unwittingly stepped into the political limelight.[25]

Longland's early career is a reminder that Tudor bishops were not all drawn from the same stable: they were not all diplomats like John Veysey of Exeter, nor were they all lawyers like Tunstall of London (and then Durham), or William Warham, the archbishop of Canterbury. In the southern province of fourteen sees beside that of Lincoln, there were only two theologians (beside Longland himself) and one doctor of medicine. The law dominated the bench and is so doing placed a singular responsibility on the theologians.[26] Longland's ability to unpack his theology for a wider audience by preaching and his reputation for practising what he preached made him a force to consider.

It was, therefore, as teacher and scholar but above all as inspiring preacher that Longland commended himself as successor to Atwater. Not for him the diplomatic scheming which brought Tunstall and eventually Gardiner (to say nothing of Wolsey himself) to prominence; Longland's career shows some similarities with that of John Fisher, and until the king's intended divorce strained friendships in England, Longland seems to have been accepted among humanist scholars and churchmen as an intellectual equal, and as an eloquent spokesman for catholic reform. The asceticism which ran through his sermons appears to have been no mere affectation: Sir Thomas More, no profligate courtier himself, likened Longland to a John Colet and remarked on the brilliance of his sermons as on the purity of his life.[27] Erasmus praised Longland's understanding of the psalms (to which he devoted several sermons) and he went so far as to dedicate his work on the fourth psalm to the bishop.[28] Longland frequently sent money to the indigent scholar,[29] but it is clear that the bishop, like More and Tunstall, thought Erasmus' remedies for the church more dangerous than the sickness which he diagnosed. In the event, More took issue with one of the first attempts to bring about Erasmus' dream of the vernacular scriptures on the lips of the servant as well as his master,[30] and Longland and Tunstall rebuked Erasmus for ridiculing time-honoured ceremonies in his *Colloquies*. In vain Erasmus wrote that he was only castigating the superstition which surrounded ecclesiastical ritual; 'Ecclesiasticas ceremonias nec ibi nec usquam damno, sed quomodo illis utendum sit indico et ad meliora provoco'.[31] But the subtlety and irony of the *Colloquies* were lost on Longland, who, for all his virtues, never seems to have displayed a sense of humour. The analogies in his sermons, the message he was trying to impart, and the rhetoric he used to convey his convictions all show a grim sense of urgency guaranteed to make his congregation quake but not smile. It is indeed unfortunate that only two of his sermons survive in the English form in which they were given, and that for the impact of the rest we have to rely on the printed translation into Latin of Thomas Key. But even through the laboured style of the translator, we can hear the future bishop of Lincoln conjuring up the devil, and turning forbidden fruit sour:

> The body is the food of the Devil; the body is the snare of the Devil, the body is the trap of the Devil, with which he sets an ambush for souls which latter he catches as with a hook. The body is an engine with which he throws to the ground the soul's virtue; it is a battering ram with which he stoutly shakes the soul's walls.[32]

Metaphor and allegory feature greatly in Longland's sermons, and he did not apply a literal interpretation of Scripture very often in them. Indeed he frequently argued that the literal use of scripture can be positively harmful:

> If you follow only the grammatical sense (of Scripture) which appears on the outside surface like the rind, you will find no profit and no sweetness.[33]

Scripture was to be interpreted by the church, and Longland, in his own sermons, suggests that it should be interpreted allegorically.[34] The visit of the Queen of Sheba to Solomon prompted Longland to ask:

> Who then is that queen making so long a journey to hear the wisdom of Solomon? If someone considers this carefully, he will find that she is the soul of man, which, coming from the world to Christ, from the flesh to the spirit, from sin to penitence, from faithlessness to the church, hears the wisdom of Christ, which bears out the evidence of Holy Writ.[35]

Longland seems to have achieved effect in his preaching by using the device of the rhetorical question. Preaching on Good Friday at Greenwich in 1538 his prose (on this occasion we have the original and not a translation) shows features which are the hallmark of his earlier sermons:

> Peter, Peter, thou were oons bushop of Rome, the fyrst bushop of Rome, dyddest thou ever take this name upon the? *Summus, maximus universalis?* Noo, noo, noo. And why so? for the holy goost was in the.[36]

His use of the rhetorical question seems to differentiate Longland from other known court preachers,[37] and his allegorical interpretation of scripture separated him starkly from Colet, raising the question of why he was linked with the humanist scholars of his day at all.[38] He shows no signs of having mastered Greek, and his sermons on the psalms have been described as more 'thoroughly medieval' even than those of John Fisher.[39]

The clue to Longland's association with humanism seems to lie less in his sermons than in the practical expression of the Christian Man which he gave in his life; he gave personal and living testimony to the precepts which marked the leaders of the northern Renaissance. Moreover Longland, like Warham, Tunstall and supremely Fisher, could, as bishop, instigate a measure of reform. The abuses which Erasmus derided, Longland and his fellow bishops could, if they so willed, correct. Longland left little doubt, both in his own life and in his sharp criticism of the vices of his day, that he saw the church disfigured and attacked. Indeed in the sermon to the abbot and monks of Westminster he said as much:

> Today the church, whose former devotion (*pietas*) has cooled, is injured. And is she not injured by herself? Certainly by herself. Our true predecessors both monks and secular clergy led a holy and hard life, we a much easier and softer one, we who have stained her pristine beauty and devotion with worldly desires.[40]

The asceticism of Longland's moral theology and his personal life singled him out for the praise of the Catholic reformers like Erasmus, More and Fisher. It also fitted him for a diocese which had so many religious houses and parishes that it would not be too hard for him to find an area for his reforming zeal. Indeed, his contemporaries saw him as a bulwark against both Luther and the further demoralisation of the church. When three of Longland's early sermons were published he received a letter from Warham, to whom he had dedicated them. Admittedly the archbishop, who had been flattered himself, could easily pay Longland back in kind, but he indicates why in his view the church is in need of reform, and why Longland is just the man to do it. After explaining that the sermons have been read to him, Warham recounts that he:

> herd them with good deliberacion, and if my poor judgement and prayses might enything avaunce them which were soo universally approved and praysed by the consent of all the herers, I wold nott faile to wryte more att leghe [*sic*]. And more specially what manyfold causes of yo[r] commendations I finde in them bothe concernyng yo[r] fervente seale for reformation to be made as well of heretycell doctrynes, as of mysbehaviours in Maners, I assure you my lorde ye have therby a perpetuall memory if ye putt them furthe to be redde openly to the profecte of many. Whereunto I exhorte and hartely pray you. And I beseche you also, that when ye preche moo[re] such sermons (as ye doo many) that ye will continually putt them to prynte for the common prefecte. And of truthe I thynke veryly if all byshoppes hadde doon ther duetyes as ye have in settyng forthe christes doctryne and repressing of vice by preching and otherwise, the dignytyte of the church hadd nott ben hadde in such contempte as itt is nowe, And vertue hadd nott bene soo cold and almost extincte in mennes hertes, and iniquyte hadde nott hadde so

grette boldness and strenghe [*sic*] as itt hath, increasing day by day by the grete scismatyke and heretyque Luther whose malice I beseche almighty god shortely to emende or repress at his pleasure.[41]

The letter makes it clear that Longland was viewed as a reformer, and the question was where he would start: would it be by warming the hearts of the faithful by preaching, or by searching out heretics, or by careful visitation of parishes and monasteries? His fellow bishops had left a number of examples for him to follow. He could stay at court and delegate the care of his diocese as Wolsey and Campeggio had done. He could concentrate on visitation as did Geoffrey Blythe,[42] or he could put his courts and finances in order, as Sherburne of Chichester was doing, or, with West of Ely, he could commit himself to a heresy hunt.[43] Ambitiously, he might attempt all or some of these things. But Longland gave none of them his first priority. He saw the duty of a bishop as being 'To preache, to praye, to doo sacrifice and to offer'.[44] Central to the reform of the church was the life of the spirit, and only when a bishop got up from his knees was he to visit, correct and ordain. Scholar and ascetic as he was, it is not surprising that after his prayer and mass, Longland saw his role as a defender of the faith and visitor of the religious. He displayed little interest in the parishes of which he had no first hand experience, but a great deal in his cathedral church – once he had overcome an initial blunder.[45] He was apparently ignorant of the fact that he could not travel in Lincolnshire on the king's business without being formally installed as bishop in his cathedral church. He was told by the dean and chapter that this infringed the statutes and so he was personally installed as bishop on 13 September 1522 at 4.00 p.m. He had an uncomfortable time of it. He had to spend the night with the dean because his palace was not ready for him. It was not to be the last time, in his long tenure of the see, that royal duties which had called him to Lincolnshire conflicted with the expectations of his diocese[45].

This incident was symptomatic of the profound strain which Longland often found between his duties to the king and to the court and his responsibility to his diocese. In the first decade of his episcopate, which culminated in the first session of the Reformation Parliament, it is not always clear what his duties were. He was at court in 1522 and among those attending the king at Canterbury on the visit of Charles V.[46] He attended Parliament and convocation in 1523,[47] but it was not until 1524 that he was known to be the royal confessor and involved with the court in that capacity.[48] For all practical purposes this required that Longland be with the court at major church festivals, which in turn meant that his diocese lacked him at the very time when it might be hoped that he would preach. In 1525 he had to go to London for Christmas,[49] and he was much put out when because of illness he could not get to the king to hear his confession before Whitsun.[50] In 1525 or thereabouts he gave Wolsey, in whom he seems to have confided much, a graphic account of his adventures: he was at court for Trinity Sunday (7 June), Corpus Christi eve and Corpus Christi day (11 June). On the eve 'the king his Grace was shriven and on the morrow shriven and houselled'. He then goes on to tell the Cardinal that while in London 'I lay there this dangerous tyme of sweting, where many dyde on every side of me, and yett I taryed tyll itt came in to my house which forced me to flee.' Things were not better in Buckinghamshire or at Wooburn: plague broke out when he arrived and he was forced to go north to Buckden.[51] He seems to have been a member of the king's council by 1525,[52] and he gave Wolsey a great deal of help with the foundation of Cardinal College, Oxford. Not only did he solicit funds for the college[53] but he attempted to secure Richard Taverner as choir master for the chapel.[54]

The first stirrings of the royal conscience over the divorce greatly increased his burdens. George Cavendish, Wolsey's biographer, reported that the king first raised the matter with Longland.[55] Others were of the opinion that Wolsey prompted Longland to raise doubts about the marriage and to ask the king to suffer 'that the validity of the said matrimony might be well considered and examined according to right, justice and equity'.[56] Chapuys described Longland as 'one of the promoters of the affair'.[57] Certainly Longland would have been among the first to know if the king was having scruples, but there are no means of ascertaining what passed between himself and Henry in the confessional. What is clear, however, is that Longland supported the dissolution of the marriage at all stages. He was present at Blackfriars and presented the papal commission to the cardinals to enquire into the affair.[58] Longland, with the archbishop of Canterbury and the bishops of London, Rochester, Carlisle, Ely, St Asaph's and Bath and Wells, testified that he had been consulted by the king about the matter.[59] He was the obvious choice as theologian and *alumnus* for the king to send to the university of Oxford to solicit its view of the marriage.[60] Longland brought back the answer the king wanted, in spite of having been 'pelted with large stones' and confronted with considerable hostility.[61] It was perhaps his success in this affair which caused the king to select him as chancellor of the university in 1532.[62] He was either easy enough in his own conscience or enough of a casuist to accompany Henry and Anne Boleyn to France in the autumn of

1532.[63] It seems certain, therefore, that Longland was entirely in agreement with the king over the dissolution of the marriage, and he looked so much 'the king's man' in the winter of 1531 that there was a case for him, as there was for Stephen Gardiner, succeeding Warham in the see of Canterbury. In fact the royal choice alighted on another, less prominent, churchman, Thomas Cranmer, who had also supported the divorce but had been abroad in the second and third sessions of the Reformation Parliament. For Longland, though he took his stand with the king over the divorce, was not prepared to do so on every issue which was presented. In the first session Longland and his fellow bishops found John Fisher too extreme both in his attitude to the divorce and in his outburst against bills limiting non-residence, probate fees, and mortuary dues.[64] Where Longland was concerned it was very different in the subsequent sessions. The indictment of the clergy for breach of *praemunire* in January 1531 raised issues which Longland saw as critical for the church.[65] It was one thing to obtain pardon by buying the clergy out of immediate trouble, but it was quite another to probe the lengths and depths to which that terrifying statute could be employed. If *praemunire* would be objected against the clergy for the exercise of their spiritual jurisdiction, could it also extend further? A declaration of its precise meaning was needed.[66] Longland, therefore, emerged from the first three sessions of the Reformation Parliament not as a pliant royal servant, but as intransigent as the bishop of Rochester on some issues.

The strain of the conflicting claims of the diocese and the court, coupled with those presented by the divorce and the early sessions of Parliament, has left its trace in Longland's letters, particularly those to Wolsey to whom he was able to write with some frankness. Longland was not the relaxed man of affairs; he did not thrive on power and political involvement. Frequently his work at court left him tired, anxious, overstrained and in pain. In 1525 he wrote to Wolsey excusing himself from court attendance as he had been laid up for five weeks with a pain in his left hip from cold.[67] Also in 1525 Wolsey was concerned about Longland's health and dispensed him from abstaining from meat during Lent.[68] Gout, or arthritis, seems to have afflicted the bishop, who wrote of 'oone foote in payne'[69] and a little later that 'I am yet unwyldy.'[70]

Longland, therefore, between 1521 and 1530 faced a continual problem of divided loyalties: the court and the diocese. The problem was aggravated by the sheer size of his diocese, by his indifferent health and by the fact that in the eyes of his contemporaries he was a conscientious man with the will, if not the means, to reform the church, if only in the diocese of Lincoln. The conflicting claims upon him had to be placed in some sort of order: the court had to come first because he was under royal command, but what was he to do with his diocese? Should it be wholly delegated to a vicar general and suffragans, or could he get to it himself, as men like More and Warham clearly supposed he would?

This dilemma, so infelicitously resolved with the dean and chapter at Longland's unexpected installation, could actually be much more easily tackled in the diocese as a whole. Just because Lincoln was such a sprawling diocese and the work of administering it was always too much for any one individual, procedures of delegation, on a partial basis, were well established. In addition to suffragan bishops, who could help the diocesan with ordinations, consecrations and the receiving of vows from the religious, and any other duties which required episcopal orders, Atwater had appointed a *permanent* vicar general whose powers continued to be exercised even when the bishop himself was in the diocese. This was highly unusual at any time before the Council of Trent. The bishop and vicar general shared the episcopal load, and the vicar general bore it all if the bishop had to be in London.[71] This expedient was just the right solution to Longland's problems. It allowed him to appoint a team who could act together and fulfil all the episcopal functions when he was abroad or at court, but it allowed him to intervene whenever he wished. It recognised that Longland was likely to be away from his diocese more often than Atwater, but Longland could keep a careful check by means of letters and messengers, and he could intervene in any matter which particularly concerned him or which proved too difficult for his deputies. He prudently limited his interference to certain areas of activity; he intervened when a powerful layman or religious order was involved, thereby avoiding an appeal to the king to intervene in an issue which belonged to the diocesan. He watched over his rights with care and would act swiftly if a fellow bishop was encroaching on his territory – this was especially the case when the see of Ely went to Thomas Goodrich in the 1530s. He followed up any reports of ill living by the religious, by canons, or by priests in a secular college. He took a very active part in trying to rid his diocese of heresy, but he mainly left the care of parish churches and the orthodox laity to his vicar general. The only matter in which it was absolutely predictable that Longland would intervene, however trivial, was money. He could not abide being cheated, and even badgered the aging archbishop for the mortuary due to him on the death of the Warden of Higham Ferrars.[72] He wrote in the very first year of his episcopate to his commissary in Oxford where the rights, and therefore the fees, of the bishop were being challenged. Longland congratulated him for calling the 'heads before you in hearing, reading, counselling and debating, your bills, privileges and grants concerning your jurisdiction for the probation of testaments'.[73]

Longland was well aware that he was answerable to a higher power for his conduct in his diocese and out of it; he had himself stated quite plainly 'the hyer Dignitie he callis the unto, the Hyer and gretter accompt shalte thou make at that grette daye of examinacion'.[74] He could not know that he had scarcely ten years in which he might reform his diocese where he judged it appropriate. He could not foresee the day when the king and Parliament would direct him to reforms which he might not like. So how did he and his deputies conduct themselves in the early years, when confronted with the evils in the church which Longland as preacher had castigated and which others like Atwater before him had found too deep-rooted to cure?

II

1521–30: A TIME FOR REFORM?

1. THE MONASTERIES

John Longland was no stranger to monasticism. He had never, as far as we know, tested his vocation in the cloister as Sir Thomas More had done, but he had preached to a monastic congregation before he became bishop, and it is clear both from his sermon and from his later injunctions to religious in his own diocese that he was well read in the rule of St Benedict and could place in his preaching a severe and contemporary interpretation of it. He preached to the monks of Westminster on the ominous text, 'I will go down and see whether they have done altogether according to the outcry against them which has come down to me.' The speech is attributed to God when he tells Abraham that he will visit Sodom and Gomorrah, and, as Longland was to discover, the comparison of the religious orders with those ill-fated places was not altogether inappropriate.[1] He asked his congregation to consider

> whether you have struggled against the yoke of poverty and shaken it off; whether you have borne the yoke of obedience and chastity patiently or not. For to you Christ says, 'Take my yoke upon you and learn of me, for I am meek and lowly in heart.' Learn because I am pure, born of a virigin most pure. Learn because I am poor, not having where to lay my head; and I am obedient, made obedient unto the father even unto the shame of the cross. By these three precepts Christ's yoke (which is the same yoke as that of religion) is made perfect.[2]

Longland then turned the thoughts of the monks of Westminster to the question of their poverty, and he exhorted them:

> Let your frugal table, your hard bed, your mean clothing bear witness to your continual self-control. Let your shabby attire be the sign of a spotless mind, let food be simple and temperate and not fan the flames of lust; keep your cells arrayed with numbers of books to serve for Paradise, whence, as from the tree of life, you may pluck the ripe fruits of the scriptures. Never let a book be out of your hand or out of your sight. Let your prayer be without ceasing and let not your waking thoughts be open to vain imaginings nor let vain imaginings breed various passions.[3]

If poverty consisted of simple fare and clothing, so obedience consisted in the unhesitating performance of an order:

True, humble, dedicated and perfect obedience is that by which a man denying himself and following Christ through love of God, subjects his will in all things honourable, and not illicit, according to the rule of the church to the will of a superior or prelate.[4]

And chastity for the religious consists pre-eminently in shunning female company.

Why, therefore, O monk, servant of the Almighty God, especially chosen for the household of Christ, why do you seek the conversation of women? Why indoors, why in sacred and profane places, why in any place at all do you endure to stay with them?[5]

The diocese of Lincoln had 111 religious houses, by the time Longland became bishop, including some which were exempt from episcopal jurisdiction.[6] The order with the greatest number of houses was that of the Augustinians, who had twenty-three houses of canons and five of nuns. There were five male Benedictine communities and nine female ones. There were also five houses of Cistercian nuns, one of hospitallers and one of Bonshommes.[7] A comparison between the numbers within the houses of Lincolnshire in 1440 and the numbers in the same houses in 1536 suggests that they were falling: Crowland had thirty-six monks in 1440 and only twenty-nine in 1536. Numbers at Stainfield and dropped from twenty-one to sixteen. Humberston in 1536 had only four inmates whereas in 1440 it had had twelve, and Louth Park had declined even more dramatically from sixty-six in 1440 to eleven in 1536.[8]

If Longland wanted to improve the morale of the religious he would need to seek the cause of the decline in numbers. His sermons suggest he was interested in the religious life, and he certainly visited a number of the houses in his diocese – in contrast to the parish churches which were visited exclusively by his deputies. He normally left the primary visitation of a house to either his vicar general, Dr John Rayne, or his commissary principal, Henry Morgan.[9] Rayne had been ordained in the diocese of York and had behind him some years as an advocate at the court of Canterbury; he was a Cambridge lawyer whose rapid advance to some of the more lucrative prebends in the diocese came after Longland's translation. He was to die at the hands of the Lincoln insurgents in 1536 and clearly recognised that 'in the midst of life we are in death'. His will proved to be prophetic: it contained the unusual formula 'considering the frealte and unstableness of this world and that the fearful tyme of death ys uncertain "et nescitur qua hora"'.[10]

2. Remains of the Bishop's Palace at Lincoln

Longland normally only visited a house if his deputies were alarmed by the religious life led within it. As a result, it is all too easy to get a distorted picture of the religious by concentrating on the houses visited by Longland in person. It is also simplistic to treat the reports of one inmate as true. But where Longland did intervene in a visitation, it is highly probable that the house was in a state of severe disorder. In an attempt to keep in their proper proportion the lurid tales which the visitation accounts reveal, it is helpful to tabulate them; obviously where a house is in grave disorder more than one visitation took place, but of a total of forty-eight houses visited just one-sixth were in a sufficiently bad state to be visited by the bishop; only one house which he visited was in reasonably good order, and that was Burnham abbey which he visited only a few months after his translation to the see.[11] It is placed in brackets in the table.

Table 1. *Number of religious visited and nature of findings*[12]

Order	Visited	Visited by bishop	Reported in good order	Reported with serious faults	Records incom-plete
Augustinian					
canons	23	3	7	13	3
nuns	4	(1)	2	1	1
Benedictine					
monks	5	2	1	5	0
nuns	9	2	2	5	1
Cistercian					
nuns	5	1	0	5	0
Hospitallers	1	0	0	1	0
Bonshommes	1	0	0	1	0

Of the Augustinians, it can be seen that nearly a third reported '*omnia bene*'; Bushmead was observing the rule in spite of having only five canons;[13] and the eight canons at Canons' Ashby seem to have heeded the advice given them by the vicar general in 1520, since they were using their refectory, as ordered, and they had a grammar master – only the butler aroused comment from the visitor.[14] At Chacombe numbers had increased and the observance was above reproach,[15] and at Stonely, Newnham and Newstead, all was said to be well.[16] The reports made at a large number of other houses, however, suggest that the canons were taking liberties with the rule, and although only three houses were in a sufficiently bad state to require the intervention of the bishop there was clearly much requiring correction in their other houses. At Kirby Bellars one canon was accused of incontinence, greyhounds roamed the property and the canons did not bestir themselves for matins.[17] Enclosure seems rarely to have been kept in even a notional sense: canons not only left their houses at will during the day but they might even sleep out.[18] At Wellow, in June 1525, few rose for matins, as the habit of drinking after compline caused the brethren to sleep through the early hours of the morning. Hunting dogs were cared for, and the canons wandered into Grimsby when the mood took them.[19] Longland did not visit Wellow in person but he was sufficiently appraised of its state to take pains to secure Robert Whitgift as the new abbot in 1526.[20]

Reports of this sort were a common occurrence in the fifteenth-century visitation returns, and they occur in other dioceses beside that of Lincoln.[21] One of the explanations which perhaps accounts for the failings of the Augustinians is that they appear to have been still forcibly recruiting boys into the religious life. There is not a great deal of evidence of this, but enough to show that it was still happening. William Bell of Huntingdon appeared before the vicar general in 1529. He admitted that he had received the habit of the Austin canons of Leicester when he was only seven years old, and that he had been sent away to their house at Huntingdon; he alleged that he frequently ran away, and was captured and imprisoned and finally forced to make his profession at the age of twelve. He finally managed to escape when he was thirteen; he hid ten miles from Huntingdon and, eventually when he was twenty-two, contracted a marriage. His story was corroborated by one William Castell, with whom he lodged, and the evidence convinced the vicar general sufficiently for no further proceedings to have been taken against him.[22] If the case was not an isolated one, and boys were forced in youth or adolescence to enter a monastery, then clearly they would make the best of a bad job by using their time and the endowment of the house to sustain a life of pleasure which might well not have been theirs outside the convent doors.

The faults of the Augustinians which were left to the bishop to correct went for beyond the lapses in offices, in enclosure and in silence which were officially 'corrected' by his deputies. Three Augustinian houses were brought to his attention: Great Missenden, Dorchester and Leicester. His visitation of Dorchester revealed a state of affairs which was a far cry from the ideals held up for the monks of Westminster. We do not know whether Longland or his vicar general started the long series of visits to the abbey. The first initiative seems to have been the bishop's own, though it must have been prompted by a visitation of which we have no record. In 1528 a letter from the bishop to the abbot and convent announced that on account of the neglect of the religious life in the house, the bishop had appointed William Goldington of Newnham as prior.[23] This was followed by the bishop delivering injunctions to the house in June 1529.[24] The findings that prompted them exceed the imagination. Longland had to order the canons to observe a timetable which he describes in such detail that it must be inferred that the normal sequence of offices and observances had fallen into total disuse.[25] In addition the bishop gave explicit instructions about locking the doors, and while some could be opened, women were never to be allowed into the cloister. The canons were to wear sandals 'communiter Voyde Shoys'.[26]

Though thoroughly basic and clearly unnecessary in a house familiar with the rule, these injunctions had little effect. When the bishop visited the house on 19 September 1530, he found that the new prior whom he had installed had been carried away by the spirit of the place: neither he nor the other canons got up for matins, and it was rare for anyone to do so for the simple reason that the bell was not rung. Instead of the daily reading of the rule which Longland had ordered, the prior never read it at all, and the consensus among the canons was that it was read about once a year. The prior's negligence was perhaps due to the other things which he had on his mind. He had a lady friend whom he had even brought to his cell, and after having his way with her he proceeded to celebrate mass (which horrified even his worldly brethren). The abbot had tried to correct him, but he had denied the charge, and certainly the opportunities for female company for the rest of the canons were many, since the bishop's efforts to keep the laity out of the cloister were unavailing: a public footpath ran through the cloister to the mill! Some of the canons went into Dorchester, one of them to hunt and fish, and there were rumours of a book on fishing which was doing the rounds in place of devotional reading. The bishop was at a loss to know why his injunctions had been so flagrantly disregarded. The canons said they had never seen or heard of them; the abbot had hidden the lot.[27]

Dorchester must have raised the question in the bishop's mind whether it was possible to reform certain religious houses. It would surely have shown him how feeble were his censures in contrast to the enormity of the problem which faced him: the abbot whom he suspended was on his knees begging for pardon, which was duly given, and others of the brethren were given penances, but a community so thoroughly lax as this one appears to have been was unlikely to be worried by episcopal censure. There seems to have been no way to deal with Dorchester except by closing it. It was precisely the kind of house which caused scandal and which resisted all attempts at reform. It was also the kind of house which lent a ring of truth to the reports of Cromwell's monastic visitors in 1535.

Equally intransigent was the Augustinian house of Great Missenden. A visitation by a commissary in 1530 had revealed a picture of debt, delapidation and disregard for the enclosure. One canon, Slythurste, was guilty of sodomy.[28] A year later the bishop made a special visitation (*specialiter visitans*). He found that the rule was far from the canons' minds: one of them, Roger Palmer, slipped out at night 'in his doblett and jerkyn with a sworde by his side' to his paramour, Margaret Bishop, who was also visited by the abbot from time to time.[29] That the bishop found his patience and the usual formalities of injunction strained, emerges from his injunction in June 1531. He said 'we will and strayetely commande you undre the peynes ensewing to kepe [these orders]. And for that ye be ignorant and have small understandying of Latin we have drawn our said injunctions in our vulgar englishe tong'.[30] He ordered the daily reading of the rule and reading at meals, and made particular provision for a man learned in grammar 'to instruct and teche the chanons in ther gramer'. Doors were to be kept locked and a reliable porter appointed; accounts must be better kept and repairs carried out. The influence of the laity on the affairs of the house was to cease and the canons were to avoid lay clothing. Slythurste was to be imprisoned.[31]

If Great Missenden and Dorchester shocked the bishop and raised questions in his mind about the feasibility of reform, then his efforts at correcting the canons of de la Pré, Leicester, showed him how powerful and insidious was the vested interest of influential members of the laity in the affairs of the religious. A showdown with an erring abbot could result in unwarranted intervention into his episcopal jurisdiction by members of the court. The observance of the rule at Leicester was at best notional: the canons ate and drank when they wished, and one brother celebrated mass only once in a week and scarcely went to confession once in a month. Others had licences to choose their own confessors. Servants had brought hunting dogs into the monastery and there were rumours of bad husbandry. Faced with this in 1518, Atwater had ordered obedience, the proper commemoration of benefactors and the keeping of enclosure.[32] This had been ineffective. When John Rayne visited the monastery he learned that the novice master was disliked; some claimed he was idle, others that he had favourites. The abbot kept his own table in the refectory and to this he invited seculars but rarely his brethren. One monk had a dispensation to live in the house without doing the work of a canon; his servants, horses, dogs and fowls were a nuisance and a liability. Other canons too had greyhounds who fouled church and cloister alike. The seniors were ignorant of the financial state of the house, and an excess of servants and the usual disregard for enclosure did not augur well for the monastery. The cause of the trouble was the abbot, Richard Pexsall, who was the prime offender; he had ordered his brethren to keep quiet about the faults of the monastery, rarely celebrated mass, and inconvenienced the house with his dinner parties. His horses grazed in the monastery meadow. Rayne also tried to give some suitable injunctions, and, in language which defeated the scribe, he tried to sort out the problems caused by the dogs; he ordered the abbot and canons to keep in future only 'iii brase de lez greyhoundes, and ii and iii cowple off spanyells pro le haris'. He also told the abbot to take the advice of the seniors, but Rayne probably knew that the only advice which the abbot would take came from his court friends who no doubt enjoyed feasting at his table. This was a case for Longland himself to deal with; his injunctions are not dated in his register but they would appear from the surrounding material to have been given in 1531.[33] Longland saw at once that the abbot was the cause of much of the trouble and besides finding him negligent also described him as *prevaricator tui ordinis*. He even suggested that the abbot was endangering his own soul (*in anime tue periculum*) and this may have been true; at any rate his cynical view of the religious life may be judged by the fact that when he made an appearance in choir he had with him his own fool who reduced the canons to helpless laughter and brought the offices to a standstill. The bishop also ordered that in future canons were not to be received whose morals, learning and age were unsuitable, and the reception of any must have the vote of the whole chapter behind it – perhaps another indication of boys being forced into the monastic life. His other injunctions deal with the enclosure and other breaches of the rule, but what could Longland do to correct a house which had already defeated his predecessor and his vicar general? He had learned enough from Dorchester to see at least that his injunctions were read 'lest in the course of time they be forgotten or any of you in future try to pretend to be ignorant of them',[34] but that was unlikely to worry the abbot. Longland seems to have threatened to deprive the abbot, but this took time as Pexsall mobilised his political connections and wrote to

Cromwell with a gift of £40 'beseeching your mastership to use it as you shall think best for my quietnes in Crist, and that I may have of the Kinges grace or of your mastership a proteccion that myn ordinary have no such stroke in my house as he hathe had, to the disordre of me and myn'.[35] Longland was then confronted with having to deal with the abbot and Cromwell, and he explained to Cromwell that 'The place is almost undone by hym, and the longer he tarrieth therein, the more it shall decay'.[36] It was not until 1534 that Longland ousted Pexsall from his post as abbot, and installed in his place John Bourchier whose onerous duty it was to comfort his predecessor in his retirement, and to help him find the money to pay his taxes.[37] It was as well for the bishop that he did not have to deal with any Augustinian nuns, who were not as errant as their male brethren; the only problem which his vicar general found was that Goring was threatened by debt and delapidation.[38]

The Benedictines, like the Augustinians, had a rule which was not intended to produce ascetic feats or mystical devotion. Both rules were designed for the ordinary man or woman and not the high flyers who wished to serve God in a different and severer form of monastic life. It is not therefore a matter of surprise that, like the Augustinians, the Benedictines had some communities where the religious life had sunk to the level of that of the most lukewarm of the brethren. This had happened before and would, if allowed to do so, happen again.[39] Some Benedictine houses seem to have been in a healthy state: St Neots had increased in numbers between 1520 and 1530,[40] and a previously disorderly house, Ramsey, had done the same. Observance had improved: few in 1518 had got up for matins, and the prior, whose election had been rigged, revealed the secrets of the house in a drunken stupor. There were tales of a secret door giving access to the dormitory, and while the young monks had sought to avoid the rain which poured through the roof onto their beds by going to matins, their older brethren played at dice. But the situation was not beyond correction, and twelve years later, though repairs were still needed and the prior's addiction to the bottle had not abated, offices seem to have been said and enclosure kept.[41] In contrast, at Humberston things had taken a turn for the worse: there was only an abbot and three monks. The monks played tennis when they could, but the abbot had no gift for the game and tried to work off their energy by making them farm and as the scribe graphically put it 'To [go] in the water to the calff of the leg [or] to the knee to fetche the hay owt of the water'.[42] The Benedictine houses for women were depleted in numbers.

There were four nuns at Ivinghoe and the vicar general wished to bring the numbers up to six.[43] At Godstow, age was the problem: in 1518 the prioress was too old to join the offices; in 1535 a new prioress, Katherine Buckley, was elected, but she was described three years later as 'a woman of over eighty years and not likely to live half a year'.[44] Clearly there was a shortage of vocations for the Benedictine nunneries, and the decline in some houses from the standards of the rule required the personal intervention of the bishop.

We know from injunctions in his register, which are cross-referenced in Longland's own hand, that the bishop knew the Benedictine rule well; and with that knowledge behind him, and with his high ideals of monastic reform, it is not wholly fanciful to suggest that Longland was shocked by some of the houses he visited and genuinely at a loss to know how to discharge his duty of correction.[45] The gulf between the theory and the practice must have struck him forcefully at Little Marlow. In September 1527, Longland was at the house to receive the profession of a sister which is given us in English in his register:

> I here renounce for ever and utterly forsake the world, and property of temporall substaunce and goodes of the same And all other worldly delightes and plaisures, taking me wilful poverty, vowing also and promysing ever to live in pure chastite duryng my lyffe ... And utterly from hensforth I forsake myne own propre will And nott to folowe the same but to folowe the will of my superior in all lawful and canonycke commandmentes And to observe this holy ordre and religion accordyng to the holy rule of Seinte Benedicte And all the laudable constitutions of this monastery by the graciouse assistence of our lord Jesu Christe.[46]

It was in contrast to a vow as demanding as this that the bishop had to deal with nuns who had taken that vow and were totally ignoring it. At Little Marlow in 1530 he found only six nuns, but the ladies would not be content with a plain headress; 'We Inigon [sic] unto you lady priores [he told them] that ye cause everych of your suster to were the lynnen of there heddes lower then they have used to do ... playn without rolle.'[47] The wearing of fancy head-dresses would have seemed to the bishop to manifest something less than 'pure chastity'. The two other Benedictine communities with which he had to deal were also nunneries. At one the problem was debt, which the life-style of the prioress was not helping to diminish. He found Studley without an ordinal or infirmary and with its valuable woods cut down for the benefit of Cardinal College.[48] In his injunctions Longland suggested that the sisters should live 'in a scarcer manner' and should avoid having 'too many servants'. They too were to wear plain veils.[49] Both Little Marlow and Studley could probably have been reformed, particularly if amalgamated, but the problems of root and branch reformation by the ordinary are dramatically seen at the Benedictine community of Elstow.

The bishop visited Elstow in August 1530. He found that an awkward bailiff was causing trouble, that the abbess' chaplain did not go to matins and had not done so for six years, and that the abbess and her chaplain kept a private table at which the favoured few were entertained.[50] In October Longland issued his injunctions and asked that the sisters eat together, that the abbess should have four sisters with her when eating with the chaplain, and that these sisters should be changed. No nun was to wear a low cut dress or veil which did not distinguish her from secular women, and the offices were to be observed and the enclosure improved.[51] Two months later the bishop's special commissary, Robert Gostwick, was sent to the house. He was met with a chorus of '*omnia bene*' and a desire to eat, not in the refectory, but in households.[52] In June 1531 the bishop was back and he removed the abbess and others from office on the grounds of their flagrant disobedience. He installed Eleanor Snow as prioress.[53] A month later the vicar general arrived to be met with open rebellion. Rather than accept the new prioress, certain of the nuns had walked out of chapter. One nun, asked why she had done such a thing, replied:

> [My lord bishop] ded commaunde my lady Snawe to be prioress, she sais she cannot fynde in his hert to obbey hir as priores, and wyll rather goo out of the howse (by my lordes licence) or she wyll obbey her. She sais ... that she wyll never obbey hir as priores ... she will shewe noo cause at thys tyme wherfor she cannot love hir saying that the priores makes every faute a dedly syne.

Another nun went further, and quoted the rule at the bishop's visitor: 'They war wont to have the priores chosyn by the abbes and the convent not by my lord, after seynte Bennetes rule, and that she wyll take my lady Snawe as priores as other wyll doo and noo otherways.'[54] At the end of the month the bishop deprived the old prioress, re-instated his nominee, the Lady Snow, and removed from all conventual offices those who had taken part in the walk-out. But it took a diet of bread and water to bring at least one of these nuns to heel. The nuns certainly showed spirit, but they were a long way from that promise 'to forsake myne own propre will'.[55]

The nuns of Elstow showed just how far a community might go in avoiding the bishop's injunctions either by ignoring them or by openly defying them. It raised questions about the proper means of reforming the religious which had been apparent throughout the middle ages. It was not that all communities were like Dorchester or Elstow: it is clear from the visitation records that they were not. The problem was how to deal with the few who thought nothing of disobedience and who were not above taking their fight with the bishop to the court. In these circumstances the dissolution of a house was probably the only way to prevent its disobedience spreading, and certainly the dissolution of the Benedictine community of Littlemore (which had resisted Atwater's attempts at reform) to endow Cardinal College took away the scandal of a community which violated their own rule and the wishes of their benefactors.[56]

The problem of reform was not made any easier if a house was exempt from the jurisdiction of the bishop. Longland was not the ordinary or visitor for the house of Thame, but he was said to be the founder and therefore allowed to know what was going on. Longland submitted to the visitor, who was the superior of another house in the same order, a list of complaints against the abbot; they included embezzlement, incontinence, sodomy and the neglect of his charge. He submitted that abbot and brethren alike were ignorant of the rule of St Benedict and that the monks were to be seen shooting bows and arrows on the fields of Thame alongside the local yokels.[57] To these allegations the abbot made specious replies before the visitor issued his injunctions, and to those also the bishop made answer. This time it was the bishop's turn to seek help at court, and he wrote to Wolsey about the possibility of removing the abbot: 'unless they mought have a gud wisse, pollitique and realigouse man in that rome', he suggested that all would be lost. He put forward the name of Robert King of Bruern, later to be his suffragan and bishop of Oxford, as an alternative.[58] He eventually won, but as King left Bruerne and knocked Thame into order, so Bruerne suffered. There just do not seem to have been sufficient numbers of dedicated religious outside the Charterhouses and Syon to sustain the monastic life at a competent level in so many houses. A reformer faced with the problem of the religious orders in the diocese of Lincoln could certainly reform some, as St Neots and Ramsey indicate, but he would need to close some of the smaller houses, particularly the nunneries; furthermore he would need to be immune from court blackmail, that is from religious going behind his back to the king and soliciting royal interference. Admittedly the houses which Longland visited were the worst in the diocese but it was for just that reason that they pose the question of reform so sharply.

2. THE SECULAR COLLEGES

The colleges which were governed by the members of the foundation – usually about half a dozen priests – also attracted Longland's attention, and while they too raised the problem of long-term reform, it would seem that Longland made some headway with two of them. Most of the colleges were in reality large chantries; their duties were those of intercession for the departed and nothing else.[1] Others, like the Newarke college in Leicester, combined chantry duties with the management of a hospital for poor folk. By far the largest collegiate foundation in the diocese was that of the cathedral church of St Mary of Lincoln, which had, in addition to fifty-eight canons (few of whom actually resided in the close), vicars choral who deputised for the absentees, and poor clerks who had the duty of keeping the altars and assisting at mass and the offices. In addition, within the close there were a large number of chantries which might be served by a vicar choral; and stipends for a chantry priest to sing at one of the altars within the cathedral had been endowed by a number of wealthy benefactors. Longland himself sought permission from the dean and chapter in 1528 to erect a chapel for his burial, where priests would sing for his soul. It survives to this day at the south side of the cathedral.[2]

The relationship between the bishop and these colleges could be strained; statutes hemmed the bishop in on every side, yet two collegiate foundations claimed his special attention: the cathedral church at St Mary of Lincoln, and the college of St Mary in the Newarke, Leicester. He took considerable interest in the former because he saw it as a small enough unit to reform – and a very important one, because only the intervention of the diocesan could save it from active royal intervention.[3]

In spite of his initial difficulties, Longland retained close ties with his cathedral church. The patronage of its canonries lay with him, and there were to be many moments, later in his episcopate, when it seems as though he felt that the fate of the bishopric and the cathedral were inextricably bound up together.[4] On 4 August 1524, Longland began a personal visitation of his cathedral church.[5] The complete book of the *detecta* of the visitation has, unfortunately, not survived, but some idea of his main findings can be gleaned from his register and from some miscellaneous material found among the archives of the dean and chapter of Lincoln.[6] It seems that the poor clerks caused the bishop some concern and that he was anxious to amend their statutes. They had a long history of trouble behind them; all too often they were out at night drinking or playing at dice, and, on one occasion at least, they had nearly burned down the cathedral in their attempts at catching pigeons.[7] They were supposed to go to school, and there is a note in the accounts of the common fund that a certain John Plumtre was paid £13.6s.8d. for teaching them grammar; he had a deputy who received £6.13s.4d. for the same purpose.[8] But the repetition of orders for poor clerks to go to school suggests that they were adept at playing truant.[9] The new statutes which were drawn up for them, and which contain insertions and amendments in Longland's own hand, indicate not only his personal aspirations for their future conduct, but his knowledge of their past misdemeanours. He ordered the clerks not to keep 'dog, hauke nor furete except one common dog among them all'. They are not to play cards or dice, or hunt, nor may they 'use any other unlawful or unhonest games or play'. To do so would cost them a fine of $\frac{3}{4}$d. Any clerk who was a common 'childer or railer or a raser or begynner of eny striffe or slaunder emengest his fellows shall pay in the name of a payne for every tyme so saying vi d'. Anyone drawing a sword or knife on his fellow was fined 12d., and if 'which god forbid ... he draw blode of any of his fellows', he was to pay 6s.8d., in addition to any punishment imposed by the chapter. To haunt houses where 'eny women of evell or suspect conversacion' resided brought the fine of one shilling, and to stay the night at such a place incurred the fine of 6s.8d. – which was nearly one third of their annual stipend. Further fines were imposed for leaving gates open and using the paths between various buildings as privies; and all clerks were to know the statutes.[10] On 10 November 1526, the poor clerks appeared before the chapter and were sworn to obey the new statues. It is doubtful whether they were any more effective than the old ones. Three years later John Walkewood, a poor clerk, was not merely accused of wandering around the close at night and receiving money acquired by false means, but of playing at dice – and loaded dice at that.[11]

The clerks were not the only inhabitants of the close to gain the bishop's attention. Certain canons were neglecting their obligations to repair their prebendal churches and to exercise their duties of correction within their prebendal boundaries.[12] In February 1525, the bishop ordered the dean and chapter to implement the injunctions given at the visitation and particularly to see to the repair and discipline of the prebendal churches, and he went on:

> If you so not [repair] I must and will supply your duty. I assure you there is more misliving commited within jurisdictions of my prebends than in much part of my diocese beside.[13]

At his visitation Longland had found six canons in residence of whom three were office holders: John Constable was the dean, Simon Grene alias Fotherby was the precentor and Nicholas Bradbridge was the chancellor. The other residents were Edward Darby, the archdeacon of Stow, Christopher Massingberd and John Talbot. In the bishop's view the number of residents was too small and it detracted from the dignity of the cathedral to have so few canons in residence there, as well as placing a heavy burden on the residentiaries:

For as much as my cathedral church hath not so many residenciaries as of old time hath been accustomed, to the maintenance of the honour of God there and of that church, whereby households there are fewer in number and houses within the same close decayeth and falleth into ruin with many other inconvenience that ensueth of the same ... the four dignitaries of my said church ought to be resident [and] there make their abode and further the treasurer (next unto the dean) hath cure and charge and ought specially there to be, and hath of long season been absent from the said church whereby many things are more out of order in the same.

His remedy for this situation was to appoint Richard Parker as treasurer in the expectation that he would reside.[14] In fact, in just the cunning way in which the religious foiled the bishop's attempts at modest reform, so did the dean and chapter. After the appointment of Parker, all went well for a while and Longland's views on residence prevailed. But in July 1528 the dean died.[15] Wolsey wanted to fill the post with a candidate who would certainly *not* be resident, but Longland had his eye on George Henneage, a lawyer of some distinction who had been to study at both Cambridge and Bologna.[16] The bishop, therefore, wrote to the cardinal to secure the deanery for Henneage:

... for in consideracion to have a dean ther resident and presente of the weal and gud ordre of the chirche, as I am to my pouor bounden to provide for that purpose, I was desirous according to my bond and dewty to move your grace for master henneage.[17]

On 22 August Henneage was elected and within six weeks he was installed by proxy,[18] but by September, just as Longland hoped, he went into residence.[19] In the meantime, there had arisen among the residents a problem which would, if successful, foil Longland's desire for his residentiaries to reside and might well have spelt the end of canonical residence.

The problem was one of income. The stipend of a residentiary was derived from the common fund. When all the cathedral expenses had been paid (except for those relating to the fabric) the residentiaries divided the remaining sum between them. It followed that the bishop and his residentiaries were likely to disagree on the number of canons in residence, since the more residents there were, the smaller the dividend each would receive. If the bishop were to introduce more and more residentiaries into the close, an unscrupulous residentiary might find means of securing for himself, under the guise of a pension, a *fixed* sum which would not be tied to the surplus in the common fund. It was precisely this issue which concerned the canons after the election of their new dean, and which Longland moved swiftly to prevent.

The affair began quite innocently. Edward Darby, the archdeacon of Stow, was a familiar figure in the close; he was probably older than the bishop and had passed his days in the service of the cathedral and his archdeaconry. He had first come into residence in 1508 at much the same time as the former dean, John Constable,[20] and he was clearly a loyal member of the chapter but an infirm one. Christopher Massingberd was away and the dean was not yet in residence, so there were even fewer canons than usual for chapter meetings. The archdeacon was ill, and he too was unable to get to chapter. The three remaining residentiaries decided that 'on account of the constant and continual infirmity under which he [the archdeacon of Stow] is known to labour, [and that] he had not been able, and is not able, to serve the church in his course nor to keep major or minor residence as he would have wished if this infirmity had not hindered him' in lieu of residence the old archdeacon should be granted an annuity from the common fund of £16.[21] Clearly he was not expected to live, and his fellow residentiaries wanted to free him from the anxieties of residence in his last days. This seemed like an act of compassion, but it also had dangerous implications as a precedent: not only would it reduce the dividend from the common fund payable to all (until the old man died) but it might be claimed by others who would also be a drain on the common fund.

When Christopher Massingberd returned to the close on 15 December, he was in buoyant mood; he had been appointed precentor. But he then learned what had taken place in his absence, and on 5 February he formally protested:

> whereas of [their] great benevolence and favour [the residentiaries had granted the archdeacon £16 per annum] I protest that, owing to my absence, and the contravention of the said statutes and customs, I do not intend to consent to this your gift and grant to the prejudice of myself and the church and ... do not intend to consent to the said grant of an annual pension of £16.[22]

The fat was in the fire. But quite suddenly Massingberd withdrew his protest,[23] and one can only suppose that he had been alerted to the much wider implication of the apparent generosity to the old man. On 22 April (three days after Massingberd's withdrawal) the dean and chapter unanimously agreed to extend the privilege of an annuity to *all residentiaries* irrespective of seniority, age, or state of health. They granted the archdeacon his annuity '*on condition that a like grant* have force and effect in the case of George Henneage now dean, and of *every other residentiary then present in chapter*, if and in case, he should wish to give up residence after due protestation'.[24] Thus, the expedients devised to meet the illness of a long-serving and faithful member of the close were to be made a right of any canon residentiary in the cathedral in 1529. The residence of all canons and office holders was in the balance, particularly if the decision was extended to new recruits as well as to old ones.

The annuity for the old archdeacon was once again confirmed,[25] and it remained to be seen whether any residentiary would try to obtain a comparable annuity at the expense of the common fund and at the risk of depriving his cathedral of a residentiary and his colleagues of yet more of the final sum from which their dividend would be drawn. Ironically, the first to try was the treasurer whom Longland had supposed would be so loyal and resident a member of the chapter. In June 1529, Richard Parker protested minor residence, which meant that he need reside in the close for seventeen weeks. In September of the same year he asked for an annuity of £16.[26] The grant was duly made, but that was not to be the end of the story. Two weeks later John Pryn, the newly appointed canon and prebendary of Ketton, came into residence and made a spirited attack on his fellow members of chapter for changing the intention of the statutes with regard to residence and of depleting the common fund of monies which would otherwise have been shared between the residentiaries. New though Pryn was to chapter business, he saw the implications of the grant to Parker:

> by your common counsel and consent you have granted as well to the dean as to all and singular the members of chapter then being in greater residence free power of claiming and obtaining a like annuity of £16 whensoever it shall please them, and have caused this to be recorded in your register to the no slight prejudice and grievance of me, John Pryn, and to the manifest dilapidation of the goods and property of the cathedral, and to the inevitable diminution of divine service and of hospitality therein.

He also accused the canons of pocketing a fee for extending a lease, to the loss of the common fund, and of allowing sums from the common fund to be applied to repairs which by the terms of the lease should have been undertaken by the tenant. Pryn clearly saw that his colleagues were out for all they could get, and were not interested in keeping the common fund with a steady level of income in order to meet the dividends which residentiaries had a right to expect. Accordingly he called their bluff; he said, 'I appeal to the reverend father and lord, the lord bishop of Lincoln ... and I appeal to the Apostolic See. And ... in all and singular the[se] premises I submit myself to the reformation ruling and sentence of the said reverend father.'

The chapter was thunderstruck, and hastily met to consider the appeal. They neither allowed nor refused his appeal but left the whole affair to be considered by men learned in the law.[27] By late October, the canons had clearly considered the position in detail and were anxious in future to leave the Holy See and the bishop of Lincoln out of their affairs. But Richard Parker still asked for his annuity. He was told:

> This grant greatly affected the state of the church and notoriously tended to the dimunition of divine service and the bishop opposed and still opposes its payment because it was issued without his consent, and has wished and commanded the chapter so to oppose it.

The bishop had intervened. And the most the chapter would do was to give £16 to the aged archdeacon and a nominal £10 to Parker which would be decreased if the archdeacon also agreed to a deduction.[28] Parker was satisfied and so was the bishop. The accounts of the common fund record payment of £16 to the archdeacon – who did not die quite as quickly as his fellow residentiaries anticipated. It was not until 1543 that he finally took his leave of them.[29]

Longland had obviously had to work hard to save the common fund from being a milch cow, and (perhaps more important) to save the daily worship of his cathedral church from being a token affair, performed by vicars choral and poor clerks. Pryn was appointed by him, and the speed with which the chapter changed its tune suggests that Longland used Pryn to keep the canons in order and to defeat the money-grabbing activities of the treasurer. He recognised that he had made a bad choice in Parker. It was a lesson learned well. If Longland had not achieved a measure of reform, he had at least stopped a move which, if allowed, would have left the cathedral as a mere shell. Longland recognised that in the coming years the cathedral could be used either by himself or by others sympathetic to Protestant convictions which were at war with his own. Which it was to be, depended on him.

The other collegiate church to which Longland gave his personal attention was the college of St Mary in the Newarke, and as with the cathedral the limitation of a reformation from within is seen all too clearly. A diocesan bishop in person could not risk a root and branch reforming policy, and that was what was needed at Newarke.

The college at Newarke comprised twelve canons, of whom the dean was one, and of which the patronage lay, not with the diocesan, but with the king.[30] The canons were normally men of local standing whose rank and education were not usually exalted enough for them to aspire to a cathedral canonry, but who would have found all but the largest and most prestigious churches beneath their social standing. The college also had thirteen vicars who assisted the canons to fulfil the liturgical wishes of the founder, namely, to intercede for the soul of the earl of Lancaster. In this sense Newarke was just another chantry, but a very big one. But the canons of Newarke also had an additional responsibility, namely, that of administering a hospital for poor folk.[31] When Atwater visited the college in 1518, a new dean had just been appointed: George Gray, an aristocrat among the clergy, whose mother was the marchioness of Dorset, had accepted the deanery, which he clearly considered suitable for one of his birth. Atwater had found that resident canons and vicars alike neglected the offices, women came into the college and were entertained by the canons and vicars. If there was no other sport available, the clergy took to the local taverns. The dean disliked yielding pride of place to anyone, and claimed for himself alone the patronage of all the livings in the gift of the college; and there were unmistakeable signs that he would conduct the affairs of the college in a high-handed way.[32]

Serious trouble did not arise until Mary, Lady Hungerford, and her second husband, Sir Richard Sacheverell, took up residence. The dean, conscious of his aristocratic forbears, was embarrassed to have another person of consequence in the precincts, and, moreover, one to whom he was distantly related. It did not take long for factions to develop and pitched battles to occur between the servants of Sacheverell, egged on from time to time by discontented canons, and the vicars and servants of the college. Unlike the case of the cathedral church of Lincoln, these disputes could not be settled in the chapter, of which Sir Richard was not a member. Quarrels were therefore sustained by such expedients as throwing holy water about in sufficient quantity to douse the opponent, or tricking the porter into opening the gates only to assault him and abuse his wife. More unnerving still was the fact that on at least one occasion Sir Richard's men had stood in front of the dean's stall with their hands on their daggers, allegedly deep in prayer, but probably to discomfort the dean by their studied insolence. The dogs, hawks and hounds of the eminent guests came into the church and not only fouled it, but apparently made the offices inaudible as well. If the vicars of Sir Richard's servants were out of the college precincts and thereby beyond the jurisdiction of the dean, anything might happen: it was alleged that a servant of Sir Richard's had struck one of the dean's servants on the head and another had been taunted and chased.

The matter was serious: the dean appealed to the council, and Longland was asked to preside over a wrangle between the dean and Sir Richard. Longland's injunctions show precisely the limits of episcopal power even in the hands of one who had the ear of the king. Longland should, and possibly could, have ordered Sir Richard and his wife from the college. Instead, he gave mild rebukes to the dean for being autocratic and to the canons about attendance at offices and dogs:

> Since holiness becometh the house of God, and it is fitting that the place should be clean where prayer is made to God, pardon of sin is besought, Christ's Body is sacrificed and the sacraments administered, we enjoin ... that [dean, precentor and provost] shut dogs and hawks out of the church and that they cause the church to be repaired.

He ended by leaving the college in a state little different from that in which he found it, but with the fond hope that the dean and chapter would conduct their business 'honestly, lovingly and in quiet, without strife and wrangling'.[33]

When Rayne visited the college in 1528, the brawling had ceased, and in the subsequent years the worst that could objected against the canons was their delight in female company and their tendency to put the wealthy and not the poor in the hospital. Whether this comparative peace was due to the bishop or the death of Sacheverell is a moot point.

The remaining seven collegiate foundations in the diocese were not visited in person by Longland but by his deputy, John Rayne, with varying success. At Irthlingburgh, the vicar general's visistation and the activities of the clergy were brought to an abrupt conclusion by plague and the college was not visited again until 1538.[34] At Fotheringhay, where Atwater had found the fellows neglecting the divine office, squandering the endowment, and, in one case, enjoying the warmth of a woman's bed, Rayne had found little improvement. The master of the college rode to London on dubious business more often than on the affairs of the college, and he was reputed to listen to the complaints of 'oon of the plough men rather than the complaynt of oon of the clerkes'.

The fellows took books into the chapel to read while the offices were in progress, and the clerks were said to sing them badly, partly at least because they whispered their way through them, and showed neither respect for the fellows nor for the statutes. No one seemed to know where they spent the night, and it was claimed by one clerk that they did not know whether they were supposed to sleep in or not (*clerici ignorant an pernoctarent infra collegium necne*). The clerks were lucky if they got breakfast, and the business affairs of the house were in disarray: grazing land had been leased out and the college had no livestock; they did not store food but bought it at need when it was at its most expensive, and not surprisingly the college was in debt. The report of one fellow echoes through the rest and seems to toll the bell for this chantry foundation: he told the chancellor, 'The place goothe not forward'.[35] The injunction to the master and fellows to attend to the offices and not to read or talk in them, to improve the husbandry and to cut down on the number of servants, could have had little effect in a college where the service of God had been neglected for at least twelve years. Such reports raised questions about the motivation of chantry priests, who may have known little of their benefactors and found the work of praying for them tedious and mechanical.[36] Longland and his deputies must surely have found the large chantry foundations as impervious to reformation as some of the religious houses. Longland's personal conviction of the worthwhile nature of their purpose will be apparent in his benefactions, but he can have had few illusions about the difficulty of reform.

3. THE CLERGY

In contrast to Longland's measured but regular intervention in the affairs of the religious houses and secular colleges of his diocese, he left the welfare of the secular clergy and the oversight of the worship of their parishes almost exclusively in the hands of others. An obvious reason for this was his limited time, but he may also have recognised that his predecessor had visited a large number of deaneries, certainly well over half of the diocese, and that his own priority in terms of time was the religious orders. He was in a sense confirmed in his choice by the fact that few cases arose which were so important or which involved such influential people that they required the active intervention of the diocesan. Longland's deputies seemed to have spotted faults elsewhere well enough, and it is unlikely that they missed them in the parishes. It may well be that Atwater's own intervention had done something to correct the more glaring abuses among the clergy, and Longland was, for the time being, right to intervene in their affairs so little.

The secular clergy, however, were far from being perfect, though their individual imperfections, while they might inconvenience a parish, were unlikely to have more grave repercussions. A scandalous Augustinian house might infect the whole religious congregation and continue in its negligence for a long period of time; religious communities were, in law, undying corporations. But a parish priest would usually submit to correction by the vicar general, and, if the priest was obstinate, he was also mortal. Death might claim him before an episcopal visitation did so. But if Longland had enlarged his vision he would have seen how extensively the heretic Luther had changed the religious scene. It would no longer suffice for a parish priest to be able to administer the sacraments. Knowledge was needed to support one idea of the sacrament rather than another. The battle of the Catholic and Protestant reformation would be fought in the parishes of England.

In the first decade of Longland's episcopate, however, Luther's influence seemed confined to the universities and the London booksellers, and while there were Lollards in Buckinghamshire, they were mainly poor folk who would abjure in many cases rather than accept martyrdom.[1] There was nothing at all to suggest, even in 1529, that England would not remain in the papal fold. It is all too easy to pick out signs of *later* developments just because these proved to be the seeds from which the church in the future would grow. But this distorts the picture as men at the time saw it. For them a break with Rome, the dissolution of the monasteries and chantries, and the attempts to bring the vernacular into religious life were highly unlikely to happen, particularly under a king who had written in defence of the faith against Martin Luther. Even in London, as Dr Brigden has found, no real anticlericalism existed, and she suggests that Hunne's case 'was remembered precisely because it was singular'.[2] The king, because of his marriage, was admittedly involved in extensive diplomacy and the niceties of canon law,[3] but there was no reason to suppose that Henry would go back on his defence of the sacraments; and Longland, as his confessor, had some justification in thinking he knew the royal mind better than most. It was not, therefore, irresponsible on Longland's part to leave the affairs of the clergy and their parishes in the hands of his deputies and to intervene very rarely if at all.

Ordinations could be conducted as well by one bishop as another, and Longland had several suffragans. He appointed John, bishop of Mayo in

Ireland, as suffragan with particular responsibilities for the archdeaconries of Northampton, Huntingdon and Leicester; and he was assisted from time to time by at least four other suffragans who helped not only the bishop of Lincoln but other diocesan bishops as well.[4] Though each suffragan was given an area of the diocese in which to work, in effect this division was ignored – not least because many more ordinations took place at Lincoln than elsewhere, and these would have placed too great a burden on any one individual. The suffragan bishop was but a figurehead, which may account for the presence of the erring abbot of Dorchester among their number; as he could not control his house, he was unlikely to be trustworthy with anything more onerous than faithfully following the ordinal.[5] On one occasion Longland conducted an ordination himself,[6] but it was not until his episcopal authority was threatened in 1534 that he took this part of his work sufficiently seriously that it could not always be delegated. Equally, it was rare for him personally to admit a candidate to a benefice, though there were occasions when the scribe noted that admission was *coram domino* or *coram episcopo*.[7] Unlike his predecessor, he rarely presided over his court of audience,[8] but he made an exception in a marriage case involving the gentry, and, in a heresy case, penance was reserved to him.[9]

The canons dealing with ordination presupposed examination before a candidate be admitted to any order, minor or major, but there is scant evidence to suggest that these examinations were conducted or were taken very seriously under Atwater; no trace of them survives in his register.[10] There is, however, some evidence to suggest that these examinations were taking place, perhaps spasmodically, in the early years under Longland, and that they were rigorously administered after 1532. One examination of ordinands is recorded in the register for March 1525,[11] and examinations were regularly recorded after December 1532.[12] It is possible that the new canons which passed convocation in the third session of the Reformation Parliament caused the scribe to record more precisely what had been in practice before, or it may be that the examinations after 1532 were new in their form and stringency. The canons of 1532 required that a candidate for the subdiaconate should understand the epistles and gospels contained in the missal, and that he should be able to construe them grammatically, and thereafter that he should be well instructed in the duties of each of the orders which he was to receive, whether priest or deacon, and that he must be conversant with the offices of the church, (*promptus et expertus*).[13]

Bishop Atwater in the six-year period of his episcopate held in person or by deputy thirty-five ordinations; Longland over a similar period (1522–7) held in person or by deputy thirty-three ordinations. The number seeking ordination to the priesthood was greater under Atwater than under Longland, but priests came in similar proportions from the monasteries, the universities and the diaconate. Later in his episcopate, Longland would be confronted with a dramatic drop in the numbers presenting themselves for the priesthood, but the average number ordained priest per annum between 1522 and 1535 was just over 126 whereas under Atwater it had been just over 172 (see Graph 1).

Table 2. *Ordinations 1515–20 compared with 1522–27*[14]

Year	Total	% religious	% beneficed	% unbeneficed	Bishop
1515–20	1036	25.9	3.2	70.9	Atwater
1522–27	844	26.3	4.5	69.1	Longland

The drop in numbers did not occur steadily under Longland. The numbers ordained priest in 1522 were higher than in any subsequent year, but this was probably because a backlog had built up during the vacancy in the see. In the diocese of London there is a steady decline in ordinations between 1524 and 1527, and thereafter, though numbers picked up, there were some very lean years between 1531 and 1535.[15] In Lincoln, numbers declined between 1523 and 1525 but they rallied again by 1526 and were not to drop dramatically until the 1530s. Nevertheless, they were always lower than they were under Atwater.

Various explanations may be given for the gradual decline in numbers and the disenchantment with the ministry. It is possible that the examination of March 1525 was part of a more testing attitude to ordination which had long been urged and of which the canons of 1532 were an expression;[16] this would account for the fact that the numbers progressing from the subdiaconate to the diaconate and ultimately to the priesthood are relatively constant. If the subdeacons were carefully examined there should be little wastage in the numbers going up the scale to the priesthood. Thus in 1522 a total of 148 deacons were ordained, and 154 subdeacons. In the following year 147 were ordained priest – just one fewer than the previous number of deacons.[17] Some candidates had a dispensation to receive all orders together, but the majority took a year to move from one to the other, and few casualties seem to have occurred on the way. It is just possible, therefore, that examination weeded out some aspiring clergy under Longland.

The priesthood may also have offered fewer opportunities in terms of either a benefice or a curacy after 1520 than before. The opportunities of a benefice were not high in 1521 and this may have deterred the worldly wise from going into the church. Just how desperate some priests had become is seen over a short period in which Longland's registrar recorded how long it took for a presentation to be made to a benefice after the death or resignation of the previous incumbent. Suitable authentication in terms of a resignation deed or evidence of death was required in addition to the presentation deed duly attested by the patron of the living. But in spite of these administrative complications, a vacancy at Beelsby was filled in two hours.[18] Beelsby was in Lincolnshire, and the patrons, the dean and chapter of Southwell, were in London, while the vicar general who could admit the aspirant was at Buckden. The journeys involved would not be possible in two hours; it looks as though the previous incumbent, who had resigned, gave the aspiring incumbent his resignation deed so that he could take it to the patrons and press his own claims to the benefice before anyone else knew that it was vacant.

These were exceptional cases, and most vacancies took two months to fill; but Brafield on the Green in Northamptonshire was vacant for only three days. There the patrons were in Northampton and the vicar general was luckily at King's Langley. The living, a vicarage, was hardly a prize. It was worth £6.13s.4d. in 1526[19] and was one of the poorer livings in the diocese. Beelsby was a rectory and worth £8.[20] It looks as though competition was fierce, and rumours of an incumbent's death could be greeted with unseemly elation: one man was in such a hurry to succeed to Ashby de la Zouche that he asked to be admitted before the previous incumbent had died![21] The ambitious were like vultures on the field of battle and the evidence suggests that they needed to be. Ordinations to the priesthood of men who had not already got a benefice but only a putative title[22] averaged eighty-two per annum[23] but vacancies averaged sixty-two per annum (see Graphs 1 and 3), and so there were always likely to be more priests than benefices. There was, therefore, nothing new in the intense competition for them which was so well documented in the first decade of Longland's episcopate, and which would partially account for the drop in ordination numbers. But most ordinands did not immediately get a benefice, so, we must ask, was something happening to the vacancies or to remuneration of the unbeneficed which additionally explains the decline?

As Dr Zell has noted, we know very little indeed about the unbeneficed clergy. They rarely seem to have stayed in one post for any length of time and they are very difficult to trace as they are apt to change dioceses.[24] But if the number of posts for the unbeneficed declined, we would expect to see this reflected in the ordination lists.

There is in fact *no* indication that vacancies for the lower clergy were fewer in the 1520s, or that lack of job opportunity caused a decline in ordinations. Obviously before the dissolution of the monasteries and chantries, the most dramatic way in which this could happen was by a sharp decrease in pluralism and non-residence and, therefore, a decrease in the number of curates required to fill the post of the absentee. In non-residence, pluralism and absenteeism, the aspirations of the successful and those of the lowly clerks meet: the successful clerk could almost measure his stature by the number of benefices he held; the unbeneficed could be sure of a job if non-residence and pluralism increased.

It is very hard to assess whether the rate of pluralism and non-residence was increasing in the diocese of Lincoln. The visitation returns are stark and mainly cover the 1530s, but we may be able to reach an approximate figure by using the subsidy returns of 1526 as a guide to the level of non-residence and pluralism in the diocese in the first decade of Longland's episcopate. When, in the subsidy returns, a rector or vicar claimed a deduction against taxation for his curate's stipend, it may be assumed that he is likely to have been non-resident. Obviously there were many curates who were paid for by the parish, and the fact that their stipends are not allowed for in the incumbent's return masks the possible absenteeism of the rector or vicar. Similarly there would be priests who chose to pay a curate for the help he would be to priest and parish alike, and such payments would seem to distort the picture of non-residence derived from the subsidy in the opposite way. But there is an indication that the latter group may not have been allowed to claim their curates' stipends against tax. In any event, if we compare our estimates for non-residence from the subsidy with the only available visitation returns of a comparable date, those from the archdeaconry of Leicester, the subsidy returns do appear to be a reasonable guide.

Of the fourteen livings to which the house of de la Pré, Leicester, had the patronage,[25] the subsidy returns suggest two or possibly three cases of non-residence: William Gillot, the vicar of Barrow on Soar, Richard Rolleston, rector of Blaby, and possibly Robert Pachet, vicar of Theddingworth.[26] The vicar of Barrow on Soar had other livings in plenty and was certainly not resident,[27] and visitation evidence confirms that Rolleston was not residing in 1524.[28] It is less easy to determine the whereabouts of Robert Pachet of Theddingworth. Pachet is listed in the subsidy as having a taxable revenue from the parish of £7[29] but this is said to be net (*de claro*) and we are not told whether he was allowed the stipend of the curate. Since he was the bishop's commissary in the archdeaconry of Leicester as well as the archdeacon's official, he was unlikely to have resided continuously.[30] The subsidy does appear to a be a limited guide to non-residence and it tallies quite well with the findings in other dioceses.

From the subsidy in the Lincoln diocese it would seem that 28.6 per cent of incumbents were non-resident, and that there would be a need for some 496 curates to serve their parishes. In Buckinghamshire, by using the Muster Roll, Professor Chibnall suggested a figure of 34 per cent who were non-resident, and the subsidy for the same area suggests 30.2 per cent.[31] Outside the diocese of Lincoln, different estimates have been adduced. The sources in London are difficult to handle, not least because the diocese attracted pluralists who were likely to be resident in one of their livings but not in all. Dr Brigden has suggested that between 1521 and 1547, 34.4 per cent of the clergy were pluralists.[32] In Kent the incidence of non-residence is considerably lower: the see of Rochester had only 22 per cent pluralist incumbents and that of Canterbury 15 per cent.[33] In the diocese of Ely, at a slightly earlier date, Dr Heal has suggested that 25 per cent of incumbents were not resident.[34] In any diocese a great number of non-residents were graduates who were in royal or episcopal service. In the first decade of Longland's episcopate 38 per cent of non-residents were graduates, a much lower figure than in Lancashire, where the number of graduates not in residence never fell below 63 per cent of the total number of non-residents.[35] It looks, therefore, as though the prospects for ordinands were considerable if they would take a curacy and act as the deputy of an absentee incumbent. In the diocese of Lincoln, at least, those prospects look as though they were *better* between 1520 and 1530 than they had been in the previous decade when only about 24 per cent of incumbents were not resident.[36] Whatever the reasons for the drop in ordinations were, they could not have been that of the shortage of suitable curacies.

Only one suggestion remains to account for the falling off in numbers of men offering themselves for the priesthood: taxation. The lower clergy were taxed alongside their beneficed brethren in 1523 and 1526.[37] The grant by convocation to the king in 1523 was of a half of one year's revenue of all benefices in England, to be levied over a five-year period. For this subsidy, a new valuation was made; not only was the incumbent taxed, but curates, chantry priests and stipendaries were taxed as well.

Those who had less than £8 paid only a third of their stipend. Unlike the assessment of the tenth for the *Valor Ecclesiasticus* in 1535, an incumbent who was not resident was exempted from taxation on the sum payable to the curate, and the subsidy instead of taxing the benefice or just the incumbent taxed the lower clergy as well. The subsidy was the precursor of many heavy clerical taxes under Henry VIII, but after 1535 the non-resident was not treated so leniently.[38]

Whether a curate became a rector, or spent all his life going from one unbeneficed post to another, depended to a great extent on those who controlled patronage either in his area or in the diocese. Patrons always faced a dilemma about the particular interest which should be advanced by the gift of a living. Was residence to be an important consideration, or was the benefice to be used to advance the education of a poor scholar at university, or should it be deployed as a means of flattering the great and getting the ear of the court or achieving a benefit within the shire? Obviously needy younger sons were claimants for a family living, and graduates of the universities might look to a former college for support. The interest of the parish was, therefore, only one among many considerations. The bishop himself in his patronage displays the problem of priority all too clearly. He was torn in his early years between the claims of relatives, of scholars and of diocesan officials – and all before he could consider the needs of the parish. Of the twenty-six parishes in his gift before 1526, when we can actually measure residence and academic qualification, we find that he bestowed exactly half of his livings on priests whom we know, and he probably also knew, could not be resident.[39] This was common practice amongst all patrons, but to confer vicarages on non-residents was to show more obvious indifference to the needs of the parish. For the most part, the greater tithe from these parishes went to the non-resident rector, and if the lesser tithe went to a non-resident vicar, the parish might feel with some justification that it was being used as a milch cow. Waterperry, Marsworth and Mumby were conferred by Longland on vicars who were unlikely to reside. His reasons for doing so were no doubt the result of his interest in scholarship and his close involvement with the university of Oxford; he collated sixteen Oxford graduates or intending graduates to livings before 1526. His nephew Richard Pate received the most valuable living in his gift, that of Wheathampstead, valued at £33 in 1526.[40] Pate was a courtier and diplomat and, at this time, was busy on the king's business.[41] These clergy were perhaps better exercising their talents outside the narrow confines of the parish, but whether they should have been financed by the parish was a question which, as yet, was not seriously raised.

Like Longland, other prominent and reforming churchmen used their patronage to promote graduates and royal servants: Thomas More presented three priests to livings in the Lincoln diocese, and only one was a resident.[42] The three vacancies in the Lincoln diocese which John Fisher, bishop of Rochester, bestowed went to scholars or courtiers who did not reside.[43] There was nothing remarkable in this use of patronage even among those whose names are associated with reform. The Catholic reformers had not yet extended their horizons to the parishes, and were too involved in the other claims which might forward reform, those of the university undergraduate, or of men who would reach positions of power in royal or episcopal service. The resident graduate in the parish would only become a first priority when the faith had to be actively defended in the parishes. That moment was not far away, but it had not quite come.

The patrons with the greatest number of livings at their disposal were religious houses, most of whom were concerned to promote clerks who would serve them at court or who were in the entourage of others who could be persuaded to do so. Sixty-three houses of Augustinian canons made 234 presentations between 1521 and their dissolution; the Benedictine houses made 137; the Carthusians fifteen, and the Cistercians nineteen.[44] The houses which were best known for the meticulous nature of their observance of the monastic rule, like the London Charterhouse,[45] made two presentations only, one of which, Edlesborough, was certainly given to a non-resident.[46] In their other parish of North Mymms, though the vicar may have resided, the Charterhouse was withholding the grazing of the cemetery from his use.[47] To be 'reformed' in one sense was not to be reformed in all. The Charterhouse at Axholme presented friar William Pettows to Sharnford in 1524: he was to stand by Katherine and be hunted as a dissident, but he was noted in his parish for not repairing his church.[48]

The livings of the Cistercians were few and they were mainly poor. Of the nineteen presentations made by ten houses of the order, eight were to graduates.[49] Two vicars did not reside: Robert Palmer, vicar of Whitchurch, and Robert Marlar of Soulbury.[50] Nicholas Bonner had a benefice in the presentation of the Cistercian house of Revesby. He also had a living in Nottinghamshire, but he seems to have preferred Lincolnshire.[51] No religious order and no single house, with the possible exception of the Benedictine nuns of Godstow, appears to have operated one single discernible policy in their gift of livings: Godstow presented Oxford graduates to all its parishes.[52] The opportunity – which all patrons, but particularly the bishop himself and the religious orders, had

– to use patronage in a programme of church reform at the grass roots went unnoticed. The day was yet to dawn when the defence of the church would depend on the quality of teaching in the parish and not just at the universities.

Though Longland did not himself visit the parish clergy and left their supervision to his deputies, he had very clear ideas of what should be expected of the parochial clergy. He preached that priests ought:

> daily, nightly, hourly, yea continually either to pray or to study or to preach or to give good counsel or to offer up the most holy sacrifice ... or to be ever ready to minister the sacraments at all times of the day and night as necessity shall require ... Now to christen and confirm [*sic*], and now to minister the sacraments of penance and order, now the sacraments of the altar and extreme unction.[53]

Despite his words, he did little to see that these things were done unless the delinquent was a man of stature. He wrote to the archbishop, William Warham, when the prelate's nephew was trying to avoid the payment of a stipend for a priest, saying,

> And that it may please you in the way of charity for the honour of God, for your discharge and mine and for the spiritual comfort of men's souls that your kinsman Mr. Wareham, parson of Tring, may do as other of his predecessors there parsons have done, find a priest at Wigginton which hath in old time been a parish church as by records doth openly appear.[54]

If an incumbent or curate seemed to have slipped through ordination without sufficient scrutiny and to be showing signs of inadequacy, once again the bishop could intervene. Robert Draycote, on being admitted by the vicar general to the vicarage of Waterperry, promised diligently to study and to appear before the bishop for examination. He failed and was deprived.[55] The only time when the bishop could be guaranteed to interfere in the affairs of the parish was if there was a suspicion of heresy among the parishioners or in the person of their priest.

4. THE LAITY AND THE CHURCH

Longland was quite clear about the role of the layman in the church. He was to obtain the grace of the sacraments from which alone he would be able to do good works. Longland recognised that God could call men to his service in other ways than by the sacraments. The 'thief on the cross inwardely was called by god, by a secret maner, by an inwarde workynge'. But for most laymen their call was to acknowledge their sins, and then, as man havinge grace, doth proffet and prospere inwardely in his soule, and that all his warkes and deades by this grace ar meritoryous, profytable invaylable in that he soo beinge in grace, standes in the hyghe favour of God, lykewyse man lakynge grace decayes in his soul, goys bakewarde in good livinge, standes not in the favour of God, his deades ar not merytorious, his warkes ar nott afore God acceptable butt liyth as in maner dede.[1]

Grace was pre-eminently the result of frequenting the sacraments, and in this Longland recognised in a sophisticated way a fact which would have been commonplace to most of the laity in his diocese: their views of the church were primarily formed less by the scandals of London or the court (whether those arising from Hunne's case, from Wolsey's pomp or from Anne Boleyn's ill-fated flirtations) than by the encounter of the individual with God in the parish church. It was there that religion was judged, and this applied with equal gravity to parishes managed by curates for non-resident rectors as to those in which the incumbent resided. Obviously most villagers would travel on occasions through and into other parishes, perhaps on their way to market, or as an act of piety they would visit a great shrine like that of St Hugh in the cathedral church at Lincoln; or they might go further afield to Walsingham, or Canterbury and even in some instances to Santiago, or to Rome. We know from the well-documented lives of men like Martin Luther that such travel could change or modify their opinions about the church and detract from or augment the spirituality which (however badly) it existed to foster. But the working of grace in them and the good works which it produced or failed to produce have largely gone with them to their graves and to a different Judge. To study lay piety before the Reformation can very easily become the study of the outside of the parish church, while remaining ignorant of what went on within it.

Some glimpses of individual aspirations can be retrieved from wills. Formularies or introductions to wills can, in the 1540s, sometimes be used to suggest whether the deceased believed in the intercession of the saints, but the wills themselves may tell us far more. They show what the deceased wished to perpetuate by the application of his earnings in the form of a bequest, and they reveal enormous differences between archdeaconry and archdeaconry. Different areas show different emphases on the faith: how great these could be would be shown in the Pilgrimage of Grace, but even before that, it becomes clear that what was true of Lincolnshire was not necessarily true of Leicestershire.[2] Obviously wills are not wholly reliable as indications of the state of mind of the testator when he was alive. Most of them were made at the sick-bed where the parish priest, whose duty it was to hear the confessions of the dying and administer extreme unction, would have exerted a powerful influence. Very frequently a priest or clerk is noted as being present as a witness to the will, and one Buckinghamshire testator made clear that while he was 'in good and hole mind', he was, nevertheless, 'seke in body dredying the peryll of death'.[3] In situations of this kind the testator might be unduly influenced to bequeath money for religious purposes: to his parish church, to religious orders and to causes which would serve to assist his soul in its ultimate ascent to heaven. Professor Jordan has put the bequests from certain areas into the perspective of the sixteenth century, and it is clear that most of our wills for the reign of Henry VIII belong to the 'pre-Reformation' pattern of giving; but it is also clear that, in the three archdeaconries selected here for comparison before 1530, in the mid-1530s and in the mid-1540s there were large and significant patterns of giving and that these patterns shift even within a ten-year period.[4]

Table 3. *Bequests for specific purposes made in three archdeaconries, 1521–30, rendered as a percentage in a sample of 50 wills in each archdeaconry which included bequests to that purpose*[5]

	Arch. of Lincoln	Arch. of Huntingdon	Arch. of Buckingham
	1530	1529/30	1521–23
Works of the cathedral	93%	92%	98%
Other bequests to cathedral	25%	0%	2%
Own parish church	76%	92%	86%
Other parishes	29%	24%	16%
Religious orders	11%	8%	0%
Friars	22%	16%	0%
Guilds	14%	10%	2%
Intercession for departed	22%	60%	26%
Bridges and roads	0%	16%	10%
Poor	0%	2%	0%
Orphans and sick	0%	0%	0%

The fabric of the cathedral church commanded 1d. or 2d. from most testators, but it is interesting that Buckinghamshire, which was not conspicuous at this date for religious philanthropy, should have given more than either Lincolnshire or Huntingdonshire, though Lincolnshire gave more to other causes in the cathedral. Huntingdonshire showed more interest in the fate of parish churches, be it that of the deceased's parish or that at which he was baptised or married. Buckinghamshire gave nothing to religious orders and not a great deal to intercession for the departed. Again Huntingdonshire is very conspicuous in giving twice as much to intercession for the departed as either of the other two archdeaconries, and this was often linked (as was not the case in Lincolnshire) with a bequest to a religious order; St Neots and the friars of Huntingdon and Bedford were left money to say a trentall, or more masses for the deceased, in contrast to both other shires where money might be left for these things, but not to a religious order to perform them.[6] It is possible that in Buckinghamshire the poor quality of the local religious houses, especially Missenden, Thame and Dorchester, deflected bequests from the religious, and that the Lollards of the region had cast so much doubt on the existence of purgatory that prayers for the deceased were thought largely unnecessary.[7] The discrepancy in the amount bequeathed to guilds may not be as dramatic as it appears, though again it is Buckinghamshire which is conspicuous for the paucity of bequests. In Lincolnshire and in Huntingdonshire, guilds frequently took upon them the obligation to pray for the deceased. A few guilds seem to have performed other functions besides those of intercession for the departed, but only that of Our Lady at Boston, to which one bequest was made,[8] appears to have included schooling and the care of the poor among its functions.[9] In Huntingdonshire the proximity of the Great North Road and the route east to Cambridge was clearly a source of profit and concern. Testators specified that they left money for 'Botlebridge', 'the brook at Bawons gap', and the highway between 'Mawdelyn cross and Hyve crosse'.[10] The proximity of Cambridge was important, and bequests were made to confessors in the city or to orders of friars who may well have fulfilled the same function.[11] Lights to burn in front of saints, and torches as well as bells, were frequently specified in wills. All were in a sense bequests for an essential item for the parish. The church was only lit, particularly in winter, by its lights and torches, and the bells did not merely summon to church. They served to remind those within earshot, not only of the Angelus and a call to prayer, but also of the approximate time of day.[12]

It was one thing to provide for the parish in face of death. It was another to live there and fulfil obligations within it day by day. Everyone was obliged to attend the parish mass at least on Sundays and saints' days, and they did so not only for devotional reasons but also for the social purposes that such a gathering provided. The village was the parish, and the church its meeting place. The noise of talking in church (frequently throughout the whole service) which interfered so much with the prayers of the devout of Kirby Bellars[13] was symptomatic of the social service that, quite apart from the devotional one, Sunday mass served in the community. There the village talked and frequently brawled, and while inns provided the same sort of centre, they did so on a much smaller scale. The possibilities of settling a village row at Sunday mass were real enough, and there is evidence to suggest that this happened from time to time. On one occasion, at Godmanchester, such a quarrel interfered with the giving of the kiss of peace, and the argument got so heated that the curate could not hear himself think.[14] Since much village business tended to take place either during or after mass, it is hardly surprising that few were to be found not attending it, even in the Lollard area of Buckinghamshire. Only seven cases of a failure to attend mass occur in the *acta* of the archdeaconry of Buckingham between 1483 and 1523.[15]

The obligations of the laity to the church did not end with attendance. Parishioners were bound to keep certain parts of the church in good repair, and both the nave and the cemetery were apt to be their responsibility. Faults in the fabric might go uncorrected for many years.[16] In Buckinghamshire the faults which were reported in 1492–5 can be compared with the faults presented at the visitation of the bishop in 1519–20. Eighteen parishes reported between 1492 and 1495 some twenty faults which were uncorrected in 1520. Of these, eight should have been corrected by the parishioners themselves, and the remaining ten by individual or corporate rectors. Parishes had difficulties in looking after their cemeteries, which all too often became a useful grazing area, but the financial commitment involved in large repairs of either the nave, which was the parish's responsibility, or the chancel, which was the rector's, were sometimes very great, and time was needed to find the requisite amount even to start the work.[17] In Lincolnshire it was extremely rare between 1500 and 1538 for any fault to go uncorrected for long. Of just over fifty parishes reporting defects in 1500, only two reported the identical fault again, and in these cases there is some doubt whether repairs had been carried out in the meantime.[18] In 1538, when they were again visited, only two made a report identical to the original one: the Augustinians of Wellow neglected to repair the chancel at Tetney, which seems to have been unrepaired right up to the dissolution of the house.[19] Similarly the Carthusians at Coventry had difficulty with the chancel at Haugham: the parish alleged it was left unrepaired, but the vicar said that repairs were complete by 1538.[20] The difference in the progress of repairs in Lincolnshire and Buckinghamshire seems at first glance to suggest that the laity of Buckinghamshire extended their lack of devotion well beyond their wills. But this would be an unjust inference: the visitation material for Lincolnshire is much more complete than that surviving for Buckinghamshire, and the silence on matters of fabric repair which sometimes marks the Buckinghamshire records may well be the result of a tired or lazy scribe in one year and not in another.[21]

On certain occasions the laity encountered the church under a different guise from that of the parish. The jurisdiction of the ecclesiastical courts was wide and some laymen would fall into their clutches in life as well as in death. They would, however, rarely meet the bishop in his courts. While Atwater had presided over his court of audience in person for much of the time, Longland delegated this duty as he did many others.[22] Longland presided as judge in only two cases: one concerned marriage, when influential parties were involved, and the other concerned a matter in which he was particularly interested: heresy.[23] The church's jurisdiction over probate meant that relatives of the departed were obliged to appear before the courts in cases of intestacy; the goods of the deceased were listed in an inventory and the court appointed administrators answerable to itself. It was, therefore, of national interest that the probate business of the courts be handled fairly and quickly and that the court be easily accessible to every kind of person. It was precisely because of the importance of the ecclesiastical courts that Parliament passed a statute limiting fees payable to the courts for probate in 1529.[24] In the preamble to the statute, the Commons claimed that fees were oppressive and that unlawful exactions had been made in probate cases. This would appear to be strong criticism of the church in its contact with the laity at the most vulnerable moment in many lives, the point at which grief could be exploited much more easily than it could be in other less traumatic experiences. But were the Commons correct in alleging that such exploitation had, in fact, taken place?

There is little to substantiate the Commons complaints (which were to find expression in the Reformation Parliament) about delays in probate business, as Table 4 (p. 52) indicates.[25]

This prompt dispatch of business in the ecclesiastical courts, where probate was concerned, does not appear to have been confined to the diocese of Lincoln. It was normal in the diocese of Chichester, and it has been shown to have been similar in Norfolk and Winchester.[26]

A further grievance alleged by the Commons was the matter of fees. Here, it is less easy to test the accuracy of the complaint. Evidence about the fees for probate of wills does exist, but it is very rare indeed to have a valuation of the goods of the deceased as well, both in the diocese of Lincoln and elsewhere.[27] Equally, to try to assess the value of the deceased's goods by using the subsidy rolls has proved an onerous and

Table 4. *Times taken in granting probate, 1520–30*

1520–3 Bucks.	
Probate in under one month	11
Probate in over one month and up to two months	25
Probate in over two months and up to three months	7
Probate in over three months and up to four months	1
Probate in over four months and up to five months	2
Probate in over five months	4
1530 Lincs.	
Probate in under one month	12
Probate in over one month and up to two months	8
Probate in over two months and up to three months	9
Probate in over three months and up to four months	5
Probate in over four months and up to five months	1
Probate in over five months and up to six months	8
Probate in over six months and up to one year	6
Probate in over one year and up to five years	1
Probate in over five years	0

unrewarding task. Evidence from the archdeaconry of Lincoln suggests that the fees charged for the probate of wills was to the Stratford scale which had been used throughout the fifteenth century, but in the archdeaconries of Bedford and Huntingdon it would seem that the scribes were charging high fees of anything from 8d. to 2s. for writing out wills.[28] What is very clear, however, is that the Commons in their legislation in 1529 were enacting not only a different scale of fees in which the fees of scribes and officers of the court were included, but also a scale which benefited certain sections of the laity, notably the wealthy, very significantly indeed. A comparison of the fees for probate charged in the archdeaconry of Leicester in 1525 from the Stratford scale, and fees charged in 1536 from the Parliamentary scale, not only suggests that the vicegerent's probate court sitting under William Petre was creaming off the probate business arising from the death of the wealthy,[29] but also that within the archdeaconry certain sections of the community got off very lightly indeed, as Table 5 suggests.[30]

Under the Stratford scale fees for the scribe and other officers of the court are excluded from the fee. Under the Parliamentary scale they are included in it. Yet this was not sufficient to deter exploitation. In the decade following the statute certain 'incidental' fees came to be included in the charges which were *additional* to that allowed by the statute. Even in the case of the very poor, after 1529, those whose wills were *in forma pauperis* (that is, ineligible for a formal fee) paid scribal fees. These costs seem to have obtained in the archdeaconry of Norwich,[31] though not in

Table 5. *Stratford testamentary fee scale compared with that of 21 Henry VIII c.5*

Stratford scale Value of goods	Fee	% of wills charged in 1525	Parliamentary scale	Fee	% of wills charged in 1535
0 to £1.10s.	nil	2.9%	0–£5	nil	18.0%
£1.10s.–£5	1s.	12.5%			
£5–£20	3s.	37.5%	£5–£40	3s.6d.	72.7%
£20–£40	5s.	8.3%			
£40–£100	10s.	2.9%	£40 or over	5s.	9.0%
£100–£150	£1	36.2%			

the archdeaconry of Leicester as far as we know. Aside from scribal fees, Parliament obviously released from payment the very poor, as had been common practice, and the scale was altered to the advantage of the rich, particularly as a graduated scale was not provided for those with goods in the £5–£20 band, or for those above it. Curious anomalies arose: effectively those at the lower end of the scale £5–£20 would pay *more* than they would have done under the Stratford scale, while those having goods of more than £40 paid considerably less.

The percentage of wills falling in each part of the scale differs between 1526 and 1536; by 1536 more people were exempt from payment and, therefore, more are predictably found in that category (18% instead of 2.9%). Most testators were in the £5–£40 band, and particularly in 1526 they were concentrated in the £5–£20 sector – which highlights the injustice in the Parliamentary scale of a flat rate comprising large differences of wealth.

There is no evidence at all of either hostility to, or disregard of, the courts' right of probate, and the ecclesiastical courts of the diocese seem to have been a cause of difficulty in only certain sorts of business. The consistory books of the bishops of Lincoln have not survived for the early sixteenth century so that we do not know in this period how much litigation arose because of a failure to pay church fees, whether those of tithe or mortuary. There is a strong suggestion from a fragment of the commissary of the archdeaconry of Leicester's court book that mortuary was a source of grievance. In the 1520s, at one sitting of the court in Leicester, of twenty cases heard seven concerned mortuaries. The book in which this record is preserved is scrappy and difficult but there is enough cryptic material extant to suggest that this was not unusual.[32] Tithe cases are sometimes mentioned but the loss of the consistory material leaves us only with references to them, and little more.

Most instance cases (that is to say, litigation brought to the court by one or other party and not instigated through the procedure of visitation and detection) seem to have satisfied one party, otherwise litigation of that kind would not have continued; but the loss of consistory evidence makes only guesswork possible about the number and kind of cases usually brought.[33] The most unpopular of the cases likely to be heard either by the bishop himself or by his deputies were the *office* cases in which an individual, clerical or lay, was accused of an offence which violated the order of the church: cases of adultery, fornication, violence in church, withholding dues from the church, or failure to attend to its teaching were the most usual. These were likely to be irksome because they might be made frivolously and would then involve the accused in unnecessary travel and expense; and if proven, they could involve him in the humiliation of public penance. At the level of the archdeacon's court about one third of all cases were admitted, but the figure is necessarily tentative because some cases seemed to go on for a very long time and to change their shape as they did so. Nicholas Barton, for instance, rector of part of Waddesdon, was accused of conjuring up the devil with the psalter. He was also accused of adultery. He denied the adultery, only to be accused again of magic, though he had neither admitted nor denied the first charge of magic. He was then accused of calling a parishioner a 'churl and bondman', and thereafter of keeping money from the church. The charge of withholding money was admitted and amicably settled, but the charges of magic and adultery seem simply to have been dropped.[34] We do not, therefore, know whether he had been maliciously cited or whether the charges against him had some truth in them. A malicious citation, if this was one, was at the very least inconvenient. But in spite of the possibility of malice which the jurisdiction of the church over morality almost invited, there is very little evidence of any resentment about the jurisdiction of the ecclesiastical courts.

Only one case survives from the records to suggest that there was any contempt of court and open defiance of the church's orders. One William Bankes was charged by the churchwardens of Loughborough for his alleged 'misliving' and for having fathered two illegitimate children; the mother was named Elizabeth and was 'his wiffes brother's daughter' – that is his niece; his wife was also godmother to the child.[35] Bankes appeared and answered and admitted the charge, and was given a penance. Unusually, he was to go in front of the procession barefooted and bareheaded and clad only in his shirt and receive the discipline at the four corners of the churchyard, and thereafter he was to offer a candle in the mass. It was obvious that the judge sought to make an example of Bankes and to see that his offence was not repeated. Bankes was to repeat the whole procedure, but without the whipping, on two further Sundays and to say certain psalms on feast days and Sundays. This was a stiff penance, and Bankes alleged he had done penance already and would do no more; he told the court 'I will nott sweer nor doo no pennaunce for you nor ye shall not by my Judge for I doo intend to go to a superior judge.'[36] A long altercation followed during which Bankes was excommunicated and proved so obdurate that he was handed over to the secular arm and taken by the sheriff of Leicester to prison.[37] Six days later he acknowledged his fault, and this time not only was the same penance to be performed, but additionally he was to be paraded in Loughborough on market day with the apparitor proclaiming to all and sundry that he had lived badly and disobeyed the church, and between each penance he was returned to prison.[38] Bankes was perhaps a little unlucky; the discipline was rarely imposed either in the diocese of Lincoln or in other dioceses,[39] and there are only four cases where it was imposed in the archdeaconry of Buckingham between 1483 and 1523,[40] and none in that of Leicester.[41] The aim of the judge was to see that the jurisdiction of the ecclesiastical courts was not flouted, and that citations to appear were given to apparitors who could thereby secure willing attendance.

The archdeacon's or the commissary's courts were likely to have the greatest problems in securing attendance, because, though they were close and did not involve long journeys, they were also familiar. In contrast, a summons to the bishop's court of audience could involve a long journey and an encounter at the end of it with an unfamiliar judge whose knowledge of canon law was likely to be greater than that of the accused. We have no real guide as to why certain cases arrived at the audience court, but it is absolutely clear that in those which did so the accused were normally guilty of the offence with which they were charged (see Table 6). Only one man in the first three decades of the sixteenth century is known to have ignored a citation to the audience court (by tearing up the citation) though there were those who did their best not to receive it.[42] Equally, there is some evidence that the court recognised that in its desire to avoid contempt it should spare the rod: it particularly recognised that humiliation, if it took the form of making a spectacle of a landlord before his tenants or of a priest before his people, might be too severe and too divisive a penance. Robert Amys, rector of Wymondham, had had intercourse with a local girl; at first he was ordered to do the usual public penance, but the chancellor then said that because his crime

Table 6. *Cases in the court of audience 1525–28*

Type of Case	Number accused	Admitted guilt	Denied guilt
Marriage	11	11	0
Morality / Fornication / Adultery	43	39	4
Magic / Treasure trove	2	2	
Tithe	2	2	
Provision of chaplain	1	1	
Testamentary	5	5	
Assault on clergy	1	1	
Non-residence	2	2	
Apostasy	2	2	
Defamation	6	5	1
Fees	1	1	
Debt	4	4	
Repair on church	2	2	
Neglect of church	1	1	
**Total:*	83	78	5

*L.A.O., Cj. 3 and 4.

was not notorious, his penance could be commuted to the payment of 10d. to the poor and to saying the psalter straight through three times.[43] William Persy of Spalding could not face the humiliation of public penance for adultery; this is hardly surprising since he was a married man and a gentleman of some consequence in Spalding.[44]

Longland would have seemed to the ordinary parishioner to be a bishop who reformed and reproved but did not comfort and console. The fact that he delegated the visitation of parish churches meant that the laity would encounter him only as a name, as the authority which made possible visitation and court process. That the bishop saw his work in terms of preaching and prayer and sacrifice[45] was something they probably did not know; certainly they could not until he gave his views on the duties of the bishop, after eighteen years of being one. Some would have heard him preach, but that seems to have been about the only personal contact that the bishop had with the laity of his diocese before the Reformation Parliament. His predecessor had been different and had often been seen on the road and at visitation. By the time of Longland's death the parish had become the battlefield for the consciences of England. The terrain was quite strange to him, and those who fought on it were unlikely in any number to know their spiritual father in Christ. The next decade would raise the question of whether the bishop

Table 7. *Distances travelled to the audience court*

1–5 miles	18.0%
6–10 miles	12.0%
11–20 miles	39.3%
21–30 miles	24.2%
Over 30 miles	6.0%

(Source: L.A.O., Cj. 3.)

had his priorities right – but before it came, a small minority of persons saw far too much of Longland; and, as we shall now see, the contact brought them shame and death.

5. THE CHALLENGE OF HERESY

The group of laymen who most concerned Longland were the Lollards, a heretical sect whose tenets were idiosyncratic, but who were distinguished mainly by their denial of transubstantiation and of the need for auricular confession. They also emphasised the teaching of scripture and the folly of the quest for God in certain works, especially if they were pilgrimages and were in honour of the Virgin and the saints rather than of God and his Son. This group did not have the sophisticated theology of their so-called spiritual father, John Wycliffe, and they were mainly weavers and threshers of comparatively low social status; they had little access to printing presses and had to use primitive translations of the Bible to sustain their interpretation of the faith. On their own they were comparatively harmless, but if their views, or similar ones, were ever embraced by theologians and printers, or by preachers and politicians, their threat to the Catholic church would take on a more serious potential. As Professor Dickens has suggested, they would provide 'a springboard of critical dissent from which the Protestant Reformation could overleap the walls of orthodoxy'.[1] Luther made possible just such a development, not least because of the interest taken in his theology by the students of Oxford and Cambridge. If graduates of the universities chose to make vernacular scriptures and heretical theological books available to the laity, the Lollards had both the will and the mobility to distribute their works. The danger lay in a state of mutual support, and Bishop West of Ely, who had to keep his watchful eye on Cambridge, and Longland, who had Oxford within his diocese, were fully aware that the universities must be kept orthodox at all costs. The bishop of London, and all other diocesans who had within their jurisdiction ports where books could be smuggled in, would need to be vigilant if this small cloud (which in 1521 was no bigger than a man's hand) was not to turn into a storm.

Longland did not need reminding of the threat, nor any urging to do something about it. Much as he detested the erring abbot of Thame, he detested Martin Luther even more. Longland did not, like Fisher,[2] attempt a reasoned contradiction of Luther's views. He took the orator's part, and, preacher that he was, he hurled abuse across the North Sea at the arch-heretic:

> You, Luther, already turn everything upside down and confound everything preaching (as you do) neglect of everything in place of charity, for cleanliness filth, for celibacy and chastity the company of women, for obedience contempt and sedition, for a Christian life the lax and uncontrolled life of the sons of Belial. Thus you despise the church, you despise its authority, the honour of the Eucharist, all sacrifice, the priesthood, vows, religion, virginity, and chastity. You revile the holy sacraments, from which we derive every remedy and help against all the diseases of the soul. You want everything to be in common, you want the human race to be a wanderer on the earth as it was in the beginning, without a leader, without a ruler ... without authority ... without virtue, without grace.[3]

Predictably, therefore, Longland gave a great deal of his time and effort to attempting to prevent the spread of Lutheranism, especially in the university of Oxford, of which, as bishop, he was ordinary, and of which, by 1532, he was to become chancellor. In addition he put some energy into seeing that people in former centres of Lollardy were kept in fear of the stake and disinclined to risk their lives by receiving preachers or books, either from overseas or from English theologians who had espoused Luther's cause.

Within one week of Longland's consecration, there was, at St Paul's Cross, a public demonstration of orthodoxy, and Luther's works were ceremonially burned.[4] Longland lost no time at all in following up this ceremony with a purge of the university and of the diocese. He had behind him a royal proclamation, dated October 1521, and specifically directed to the problems of the diocese of Lincoln alone, thereby suggesting that its position in this regard was unique. It required mayors, sheriffs, bailiffs and other officers to assist the bishop who 'hath now within his diocese no small number of heretics' whom they were charged to aid him in finding and bringing to trial.[5] Following this proclamation, Longland wrote with considerable concern to his commissary in Oxford to alert him:

> And whereas I commanded Dr London my commissary to call the booksellers of

your university and to make search for these corrupt works as Luther and other[s] have caused to be printed and sent into this realm, he sayeth you promised you would within fourteen days make search and send such books unto me. By the law, causes of heresy be specially reserved unto the ordinary and in that cause no person is exempt from his ordinary. Wherefore in other wise such great danger and slander as might insue unto your university by such books, which young indiscreet persons will desirously read and talk of, I sent my commissary purposely to Oxford to stay all occasion of selling, bringing or buying such books whereof some he brought unto me. And [I] am informed many like be dispersed about the university, if you by our wisdom can secretly bring them in, you shall do much for Christ's church and the wealth of the university. And the truth is they be accursed especially by the Pope's Bull that retaineth, favoureth, readeth, sell, buy or otherwise keep or hide the same. In eschewing whereof put your helping hand for the redress of the same. And I pray you I may know what you do in these premises with diligence. Thus fare you well.[6]

In 1521 it was natural that the university of Oxford should be the first to be scoured of heresy, but Longland realised that it was when heresy became 'extra-mural' and worked in cooperation with dissident groups in the parishes that a dangerous situation arose. So at much the same time that he was turning the bookshops of Oxford upside down, he was also turning his attention to the long established centre of Lollardy, Buckinghamshire. John Foxe called Longland 'a fierce and cruel vexer of the faithful poor servants of Christ'.[7] His account of Longland's persecution of the Buckinghamshire Lollards is not extant among the bishop's registers from which Foxe alleged that he was quoting. But it is certain that there was a special register for the purpose, which Foxe saw and which has since disappeared. Among the Usher manuscripts in the possession of Trinity College, Dublin, are twelve lines copied 'Ex libro Detectionum Confessionum et Abjurationum haeretic' coram D. Johanne Lincolniensi episc'o. an. 1521 (In Bibliotheca Lambetha)'.[8] There is also a certain amount of corroborative evidence to the accounts of Foxe from other quite different sources. Longland seems to have rounded up between three and four hundred people who had at some point been suspected of heresy in the area of Amersham, Chesham and the Chilterns. They were likely to have been accused of heresy before Bishop Smith in 1508. They were asked by Longland a number of questions: had they come before Smith? Did they in their belief about the sacraments err in any way? Were they members of a heretical society and did they know of any person who might be? Had they been to readings – presumably of the English New Testament or heretical works – and had they had secret dealings with 'known men'?[9] Foxe suggests that as the result of these questions, and the information gathered from them, certain individuals were incriminated, and that some fifty were put to penance and sent to monasteries. His list of these monastic penal establishments is a strange one, for it includes one house at Abingdon which was not in the diocese of Lincoln, and a number of other houses which we know to have been corrupt enough (at least at a slightly later date) for the bishop to have visited them: Thame, Dorchester and St Frideswide's were all on the list. If Lollards were sent to these places they would no doubt have been confirmed in their heresy rather than wooed back to the catholic faith.[10] We might be disposed to dismiss Foxe's account as a good story but a tall one, if he had not added to it the names of four persons who were handed over to the secular arm for burning: they were Thomas Barnard, James Morden, Robert Rane and John Scrivener. Amongst the certificates of excommunication in the Public Record Office there is one dated Wooburn, 28 January 1522, giving just these names and testifying that they were handed over to the secular arm for burning 'in causa heretica'.[11] There seem, therefore, to have been in Buckinghamshire several hundred Lollards who could combine with the Lutherans of the universities and launch against the Catholic church propaganda which might well gain credence if the authorities were not quick to suppress it. In a short period of time the diocese of Lincoln could have become the all-important 'springboard for the Protestant Reformation'.

That the bishop perceived the danger is seen in his acute anxiety about the sale of books. His anxiety increased as news of the first folios of Tyndale's translation of the New Testament reached England. Throughout 1525 and 1526 the search for heretical books took on a new urgency.[12] Obviously Longland was especially concerned about the books reaching Oxford, and he impressed upon Wolsey the need for a further public demonstration of orthodoxy, crowned by a sermon at St Paul's Cross and the burning of heretical literature. His letter of 5 January 1526 mentions secret book searches and exhorts the cardinal 'to bind ... merchands and stachioners in reacongnisans never to bringe in to this Realme any such boks, scrowles or writings'.[13] In February 1526 the ceremony duly took place, with Fisher preaching and with Robert Barnes and some London booksellers as penitent heretics to provide colour.

Within his own diocese the bishop continued the hunt for all those whose opinions seemed heretical. In November 1526, the chancellor had before him Thomas Wattes of Grafton who confessed that 'ther are noo sanctes in heven', and that God is 'not in heven but withInes*'. He added that 'Or lady nor noo sancte doeth enny miracle', and some witnesses said that his language on the subject of the Virgin was obscene. He was given an immediate public penance which included prostration at the chancel steps for two Sundays during mass, and his case was also referred to the bishop.[14] Thomas was relatively harmless, but the threat which the Lincolnshire sea-board presented might not be so easily managed. Smugglers with books could land virtually anywhere along that coast and be away by morning. Longland sounded the alert to the archdeacon of Lincoln, warning him of the dangers of heresy and asking him to search out heretics, and particularly to be on the look out for heretical books which had been smuggled in and might well be in English. Priests in Lincolnshire were to pass the warning on to their congregations at Sunday services.[15] At the same time Longland took almost a sportsman's delight in apprehending preachers or intellectuals who seemed to be propagating heresy. He wrote to Wolsey that a monk had preached 'the most seditious sermonne that ye have herd of, in raylyng agenste your Grace and Byshopes for this sequestration of evyl preachers, maynteyning certayn opynyons of Luther comforting erronyous persones in ther opynyons'.[16] And again he wrote triumphantly that 'I have two Lutherans in my house, theoon is the Preste that ... wrote ... the letter ... which I delyvered to your grace, and the other is he that he wrote it unto ... The preste is a very heretyk ... I purpose to abjure them both and putt them to penance and afterward to remayne in two Monasterys in penaunce tyll your pleasur be known.'[17] The triumphant note of Longland's letters which implied that the means of transmitting heresy by book or preacher were under control was sounded a great deal too early. The following year, 1528, was to be critical for Longland and his adversaries on this issue.

Longland had to preside with Tunstall in 1528 at a trial of a heretic who admitted buying Lutheran books in London and selling them to students at both Oxford and Cambridge. He admitted preaching heresy in London, Norwich, Ely and Lincoln.[18] This was bad enough, but news came from Oxford that Thomas Garrett, a known Lutheran, had been apprehended in the city, and that books were found and links were shown to have been established between him, the parson of Honey Lane in London, and a bookseller named Nicholas in the churchyard of

* *sic* for 'within us'.

St Paul's in London.[19] Obviously the question was how many people had received these books, and how wide Garrett's influence had been. No one knew exactly, and in February 1528 Dr London wrote to the bishop of Lincoln in some alarm, since it appeared that Garrett had insinuated his way into many homes. He had been in Oxford since Easter and had cunningly sought out the young humanist scholars:

> at his being ther [at Oxford] he sowght owt all siche wiche were gevyn to greke ebrew and the polyt latyn tonge, and pretendyd he wold lern ebrew and greke. And bowght bokes of new thinges toallewer* them. After that he procured a great numbre of corrupt bokes and secretly dydd destribute them amonge his new acquayntans in sondry colleges and hallys ... Mr. Clerk wasse hys caller unto Oxford for he wasse hys familiar acquayntans.

To make matters worse Dr London had discovered that Garrett's new-fangled Cambridge ideas were being spread to the young:

> Yt ys evydently proved that Mr Clerk hath redd in hys chambre pollys† epistle to yonge men and such as were of ii, iii, or iv years contynuans in the universities. Wold godd my lorde is grace hadd never be motyonyd to call hym nor any other cambridge man unto hys most towardlye colledge ... Wee were clere with out blotte or suspicion till they come![20]

Longland, in writing a little later to the cardinal, elaborated on the infection of the university, observing that the corruption had extended to Reading. Ultimately he was able to tell the cardinal that the heretic was caught.[21] The storm in an academic tea-cup was born of the fear that Garrett and his like would infect others, most particularly priests. Between 1527 and 1532 Longland took the unusual step – taken also, as far as we know, only by the bishop of Ely (who was in the same position with respect to the university of Cambridge) – of asking suspected priests for an oath before they were admitted to a benefice. They were asked not to spread Luther's views (*Lutheranis erroribus seu ceteris per ecclesiam dampnatis heresibus opinionem non feret nec eiisdem studia verbo aut facto favebit iuratus*).[22] These oaths were not required of everyone, and it is hard to know why particular priests were singled out, but they are a reminder, along with book burning and heresy hunting, of the seriousness of purpose which the bishops of Lincoln and perhaps of Ely and Norwich, were displaying as they perceived the spread of heresy and did not trust to the force of the existing faith to stop it.

The vigilance of the authorities meant that they proceeded against the

* *sic* for 'allure'.
† *sic* for 'Paul's'.

deluded and possibly harmless as well as against the real heretic, thereby strengthening the impression of the bishop as judge rather than purely as shepherd of his flock. The case of the abbot of Sawtry's servant illustrates the point. He was up before the chancellor in the court of audience with a wild story of seeing a vision which gave a peculiar twist to his ideas of the Host. He stated:

> he had seen a vision of a man werying a violet Jaket, A tawny fustion dublet, his hose yalow tawny sylk, a pair of pynsons with a litle black spot at the ankyll [with a woman equally brightly attired in] a mustard gown, a crymson hatt, whyte kyrschyves, hyr gowne tyed up behynd with a silk blue and green drawer [Then there appeared a priest from Blackburn, his gown] full of ashes as he had been rolled in the Ashes and ther a black fella [*sic*] mett him and put hym behynd a walle and there wer many great shrykes.

This vision or nightmare would not have worried anyone if he had not also alleged that at the consecration of the Host he had another 'vision':

> He dydde see in the hoste over the preste's heade a chylde naked in fleshe and blode and his armes abrode and hys fete streght down haldyng furth his hart and all the[er] of was rede as blode except the outermost circle which was whyte as breade the thykness off a small twyne threde ... And he saith when the preste brake the hoste in the breaken yt was the color off a lawn breade and then the priest went to the lav[abo] he dydd see six grene dropes hangyng at the preste[s] iii fore fyngers whilst [*sic*] the preste whiped off with the towell. And that sight maketh hym believe that in the hoste within the circle goyng about the hoste is white bread.

We do not know whether the man was regularly deluded but quite clearly his vision was itself the result of a too literalistic interpretation of transubstantiation. Taught as he had been that the Host was indeed the Body of Christ, he thought he would see the Host bleed if 'it may happen to hyt upon a mans' tothe', but this was prevented and the faithful were spared from spilling the Lord's blood by 'a circle of breade ... to kepe in the bloode'. He alleged that voices told him to make his vision known, but the vicar general was of a different opinion; he clearly realised that the man was no heretic of the normal sort and gave him the usual straightforward penance, ordering him not to tell stories of this kind in the future.[23] It was a measure of the panic into which the hierarchy had been thrown by the advent of theologically informed heresy that the case was heard at all, and heard, moreover, in the audience court.

Longland and West of Ely were clearly on the warpath against heretics, and their sense of urgency was well understood by their fellow bishops. When the Reformation Parliament was called, convocation seemed to be quite as concerned with heresy as with the business of reforming the church.[24] Yet in 1529, in the diocese of Lincoln, all our evidence suggests that heresy was confined to the Chiltern area, at most fifty miles square, and to a few young scholars in the university of Oxford, particularly in Cardinal College. Far from being a springboard for a Protestant reformation, the heretics seemed like an irritant which might encourage the church to put more and more books on a national 'Index', and more and more innocent men and women on the rack – two developments which marked catholic reformations elsewhere in Europe. The next ten years would be decisive in determining the faith of Englishmen. Would Protestantism be stamped out or would it spread in spite of rigorous persecution?

III

1530–40
REFORM IN HEAD AND MEMBERS?

1. THE SUPREMACY AND THE BISHOPRIC

The question of authority

The diocese of Lincoln, like all other dioceses of the English Church, was caught up in and radically affected by the events of the Reformation Parliament. Not only was Longland a member of the House of Lords but he was also a member of convocation, where some of the critical debates affecting the authority of the bishops in the church were to be discussed. The story of the diocese must, therefore, move to Westminster to see what legislation was enacted which affected the church and how Longland, in particular, reacted to it.

The summoning of the Reformation Parliament was to prove the end of an era for Longland in a number of very important ways. He was, in the next five years, to be even more caught up in the affairs of state and to be even less at the disposal of his diocese. But his diocese itself became an area for the clarification of the supremacy, and whatever ideas he might have entertained about reform within it came to an abrupt halt when his jurisdiction was inhibited in 1534; thereafter the steps taken against the monasteries were to result in the removal of the part of the church in which Longland had displayed most interest. But there was no reason to suppose, in 1529, that time was not still on his side where reform was concerned. Indeed, there was considerable reason to suppose the reverse, and some evidence to suggest that individual members of the episcopate as a whole were moving towards reform, both in their several dioceses and in their ideas for the agenda of convocation.

At the national level, convocation, when it convened in 1529, set its hand to drafting, with the help of the lower house, some provincial decrees which were long overdue but which would regulate the behaviour of priests as well as their learning and clothes. They should avoid taverns, they should not play at dice and they must not pass the night in suspicious company (which in effect meant that they must not be alone with any female who was not a relative and who looked attractive). The bishops also recognised the abuses arising as a result of the appropriation of churches by the religious, and were no doubt set on discussing still more when they were interrupted.[1] Their discussion of reform was brought to an abrupt halt when Archbishop Warham suddenly asked them whether they would agree to cancel the loans they had made to the king earlier, thereby effectively making a free gift of what had been a forced loan.

This intrusion of the king's finances was an early sign of a problem which was to exercise not only Longland but other bishops as well: the relation of the king to the church and to the diocesan bishop. On this occasion the question was raised in a financial sense, but it meant that convocation went into recess with little of what Longland regarded as its really urgent business concluded: heresy had hardly been discussed at all. The prelates and the representatives of the clergy made their several ways home for Christmas, with little done and seemingly having left the business of the reform of the church to the Houses of Commons and Lords, who had passed legislation about residence, probate fees and mortuary fees.[2]

For Longland, the Christmas of 1529 had to be spent at court. But in addition to what had happened at the recent convocation, Longland had another reason to feel uneasy during this particular season of celebration. For him, the court lacked an old friend. The disgrace of Cardinal Wolsey had occurred just before the first session, and although Longland knew his successor as Chancellor, Thomas More, there is no reason to suppose that they were close friends. With Wolsey it had been different; they had been at Oxford and Magdalen at the same time, and in his letters to Wolsey Longland seems to have unbent enough to tell the cardinal of his aching limbs and tiresome duties. But Longland's evident friendship with Wolsey did not mean that he was now out of favour with the king. Longland continued as the king's confessor, and indeed there are signs in his correspondence that he performed the duty at least until 1541, if not until Henry's death.[3] In those circumstances he could hope to have royal support; and his wholehearted involvement in the king's divorce also increased the esteem in which Henry held him. What he lacked was a close friendship with the king's advisers, and when Cromwell became one of them he was to be in some difficulties.

3. Bishop Longland's chantry in Lincoln Cathedral

In the interval before the opening of the second session of Parliament, Wolsey threw a long shadow over the church. He had given up most of his best properties, offices and his great college at Oxford to the king; in his retirement to York he was kept far from friend – but not far enough from foe. In the Michaelmas of 1530 fifteen clerics, eight of them bishops, were indicted for breach of *praemunire* for their alleged support of the cardinal. The bishop of Lincoln was not among them, not (one suspects) because he had not supported the cardinal and made agreements with him about the exercise of the legate's jurisdiction in his diocese, but solely because he was a supporter of the divorce.[4] His immunity was not for long; by January 1531 *all* the clergy were accused of breach of *praemunire* through the exercise of their spiritual jurisdiction.[5]

The decision to proceed against all the clergy seems to have been taken in October 1530, and by November an officer had been despatched to arrest Wolsey and to bring him south. It was a curious twist of fate for Longland that the old cardinal died in one of the worst religious houses in the whole of the diocese – in fact among the Augustinians of de la Pré, Leicester. The abbot who ministered to Wolsey was the superior whom Longland was most anxious to remove.[6]

Whatever his own feeling about the fate of Wolsey may have been, Longland now faced a very urgent and searching question. He had to discover whether the full penalties of the statute were going to be demanded of the church and whether the spiritual jurisdiction, with powers of correction and visitation which were an integral part of the bishop's ecclesiastical authority, was going to be removed.[7]

In January 1531 convocation met again to consider the gravity of the indictment. They were given to understand that a large grant of money to meet the king's expenses over the marriage might be sufficient to buy the clergy out of trouble. They disliked the reason suggested for the grant, which seemed to prejudge the divorce question, on which there had been no debate but on which all knew there would be disagreement. They also hoped that the king would accept £50,000 instead of £100,000. They very soon learned that there was no hope of reducing the sum required, and that if they were unhappy with stating the reason for the grant, namely, that it was to meet the expenses incurred in the royal marriage litigation, they would have to accept a different prologue to their grant, one which included the recognition that the king was 'sole protector and supreme head' of the English church and clergy.[8]

In the ensuing debate it was not Fisher alone who perceived the dangers for the church of such a formula. There was prolonged discussion, and someone (probably Audley) suggested that the supremacy could be accepted *quantum per legem Dei licet*, 'as far as the law of God allows'. Longland, with the bishops of London and Exeter, accompanied Warham in seeking a meeting with the king. None could be had, and convocation spent an anxious afternoon debating the supremacy and trying to gain access to Henry. It was not until the next day that Warham did so, and the king agreed to the saving clause. Longland and seven other bishops signed their assent to the formula.

That did not end the dilemma for the bishops. They were pardoned for the past but what of the future? Could they resume their spiritual jurisdiction or would they again be guilty of breach of *praemunire*? The statute which pardoned them was retrospective, not prospective.[9] Moreover, the interpretation which the king appeared to be giving to it was in line with Roman law which had clearly been in his mind for many years. It was quite simply that no law or custom should exist which was prejudicial to 'hys jurysdiction and dignitie royall' – a claim which Professor Ullmann has shown he used very early in his reign and which he culled from the late Roman empire.[10]

The next session of Parliament which met in January 1532 raised the same question of the scope of *praemunire* yet again. The Commons presented the king with a 'supplication against the ordinaries'. The supplication complained of the grievances that arose as a result of ecclesiastical jurisdiction; it alleged that men were cited to appear in church courts on frivolous charges, and that they incurred heavy expenditure and had to pay exorbitant fees to the courts for the probate of wills. The supplication complained particularly of the procedure adopted in heresy cases.[11] More menacing still, it raised the question whether convocation could make canons without the royal assent. The king sent the supplication to convocation to consider, and, under extreme pressure, Stephen Gardiner, bishop of Winchester, attempted an answer to the supplication which both upheld the power of the clergy on the one hand and denied the abuses on the other. Clearly he had not quite grasped the fact that the king was in full cry after *any* power which could theoretically be used against his regality.[12] The reply was not considered satisfactory and convocation had to start again. The bishops conceded that convocation could not make law without the royal assent. But Longland then saw a new danger: what was the status of existing provincial constitutions which had not received royal assent but which were daily operative in the ecclesiastical courts of the land? Accordingly he compromised his own acceptance of the supplication.[13]

To the perceptive, the first three sessions of the Reformation Parliament had seen the crucial question of the headship of the church raised, and, with it, the question of the relationship which the English church had to the monarch and to the papacy. Moreover, it implicitly raised the question whether the reform of the church was the responsibility of the convocation, now answerable to the king, or of the Lords and Commons, who in the first session of Parliament had taken it upon themselves to legislate about residence, mortuary and probate fees.[14] The next three sessions, in 1533 and 1534, were to find Parliament enacting in statute form the principles which convocation had conceded, and clarifying some, if not all, of their implications. The act for the restraint of appeals removed all jurisdiction from papal interference and thereby made possible a purely English solution to the problem of the divorce.[15] By the end of 1534 Acts of Succession and Supremacy and Treason were passed which gave to Anne Boleyn and her children the succession, and gave to Henry VIII the one power which Constantine had not held and which did not have the support of Roman law: the power to decide heresy.[16] By the Act of Supremacy, Henry had the right 'to repress and extirp all errors, heresies and other enormities and abuses heretofore used ... and ... full power and authority from time to time to visit, repress, redress, reform, order, correct, restrain and amend all such errors, heresies, abuses, offences, contempts and enormities whatsoever they be, which by any manner, spiritual authority or jurisdiction ought or may lawfully be reformed, repressed, ordered, redressed, corrected, restrained and amended'.[17] The intention of the Act was clear enough in what was claimed, but how precisely such a supremacy could be implemented, whether through the existing diocesan structure or another, was yet to be discovered.

These Acts, taken as a whole, not only required the assent of a diocesan, they also needed the clarification of practice: could the church courts function as before, and could the bishop visit as before, or did the king have to give his explicit assent that both these activities did not impair his regality? Moreover, would the power to determine heresy result in any changes, and what would happen to the tentative movements towards the reform of the church which had preceded the Reformation Parliament? The answers to these questions would only come gradually as king, council, Parliament and bishops and clergy began to test the ground. Did the bishops actually believe in the supremacy or the divorce? Longland gave no indication at all that he disagreed either with the divorce or the succession oath (unlike Fisher of

Rochester) or with the oath which he took, with a number of his episcopal colleagues, renouncing the jurisdiction of the see of Rome and all allegiance to any foreign potentate.[18] He was also included in a somewhat dubious list of bishops 'not of the popish sort' who it was suggested should be let loose on the recalcitrant monks of the London Charterhouse.[19] Yet his only positive statement on the question of the authority of the bishop of Rome was made in 1538, four years after the Act of Supremacy, and at a time when Cromwell was watching him carefully as a result of his being accused by the rebels in the Pilgrimage of Grace of having been a cause of the unrest.

Longland was no lawyer and he was therefore very unlikely to have been familiar with Roman law and with the meaning given to 'imperial' in the late Roman empire, still less with the extension of that meaning by Henry VIII in his corrections to the coronation oath. On the other hand, Longland was very close to the king and likely to be put on his mettle if his royal penitent quoted Roman law at him. As a theologian he would have seen the force of both sides of the argument about the legitimacy of the marriage, and he, along with others, was likely to have been unhappy at the thought of the throne of England passing to a woman. Like the other bishops, he may have had to spend a long time adjusting, particularly to the Act of Supremacy; or, as Chapuys put it in 1534:

> The Bishop of Lincoln ... has said several times since Christmas that he would rather be the poorest man in the world than ever have been the King's councillor and confessor.[20]

Whether from base motives or from profound convictions he held his peace about what exactly he thought of the supremacy; he took the oaths, and only in 1538 did he preach on it (as far as we know), and it is perhaps important that his interpretation of the papal supremacy is that it interferes with the jurisdiction of others. Preaching before the king at Greenwich on Good Friday, 1538, he argued that there is only one great bishop and 'he dyd penetrate the hevens whose name is Jesus the sonne of god'. It follows that:

> This is the heed bushop of all bushoppes and of the worlde, named of god ... to be our greate bushop properly called *Summus pontifex* the hughest bushoppe, the bushop of bushoppes. For this he onely that is *Summus maximus* and *universalis pontifex*. The bushop of Rome therfore ought herein to be abashed, ashamed and to abhore his owne pryde. For in this he outrageously dothe offende god and blasphemeth hym in that he presumeth to take this hygh name from our bushop Christ ... Lette the bushop of Rome therefore knowledge his greate faulte, his high folye, his unlawful usurpation, his unpreestly presumpcion and humble

hymself to Chryst and god his great bushop ... Wolde god he wolde reforme himself. Wolde god he wolde kepe hym selfe within the compasse of his autoryte and no more to encroche upon other mennes iurisdictyons but diligently kepe and over look his owne diocese and be content with that.

It was the failure of popes 'to be content with thynne owne dioces, with thyne owne charge as other bushop are theyrs', which Longland condemned. At no point in this sermon does he debate the relationship between royal and priestly authority; his basic message is that a bishop has an area of jurisdiction to which he should adhere, and that bishops are answerable to the one great bishop who is Christ.

But what of the king and what of the power to determine heresy? Longland could scarcely preach to the king's face in 1538 that the king should not exceed the limits of his authority in matters entrusted to the bishops *sub Christo*. Yet that is exactly what Longland *did* do, in that sermon. In a quite unambiguous way, he emphasised that the authority of kings and emperors is also *sub Christo*, derived from the supreme authority of Christ, *dominus dominorum, rex regum*. This argument is derived from Romans xiii, and its implication could scarcely be missed: 'trespassers will be prosecuted'. All authority is legitimate because it is derived from Christ, but it must also be exercised in its own appropriate sphere. Thus Longland insisted:

He (Christ) is *pontifex potens*, a mighty bishop, myghty, and full of power. We but weyke and feble bushops, not able to doo any thynge but by his permyssyon and helpe ... No power in this worlde but of hym. *Omnis potestas a domino deo est*. All power is of hym. And as he hymself wytnesseth, *Data est mihi omnis potestas in cælo et in terra*... He is a myghtye bushop. Of hym and by hym, Emperours, Kinges, magistrates and potestates: bushoppes, preestes, with all other that hath power hath theyr power and auctoritie. Who is able to turne the wynde? to make the wynde blow or cease, but he? Who is able to say and prove, I will nowe have rayne, nowe clere: the soone to shine, the water to flow, to ebbe, with soche other, but onley he... He is the myghtye bushop. We are not so.[21]

It followed that until Henry VIII showed that he wished to intrude into the jurisdiction of the bishops of England there was no problem from Longland's point of view. Henry could be given (and was duly given) the title within the diocese of Lincoln of 'caput anglicane ecclesie *sub Christo*'.[22]

The announcement of an impending visitation of the diocese of Lincoln by Thomas Cranmer, which reached Longland in June 1534, raised exactly that issue, creating a challenge to the exercise of what Longland believed to be *his own* sphere of authority or jurisdiction. On *this* ground Longland was prepared to fight with all the verve which he also used against the pope.[23] On behalf of himself and his cathedral church, he appealed against Cranmer to the Court of Chancery which had become the only resort for appeals once they had been withdrawn from Rome.[24]

There were several reasons why Longland appealed so vociferously against a metropolitan visitation. But first and foremost was the consideration that such a visitation denied the equality of all bishops under Christ. In addition it also raised the more subtle question whether Cranmer at Canterbury had any supremacy which did not derive directly from a papal title. The bishop of London was the first to take issue with the visitation on the ground that Cranmer had taken upon himself the title of legate, which could only be derived from the see of Rome.[25] The offending title also appeared in a letter to lords, barons and knights of Lincoln from Henry VIII asking them to assist the archbishop, who was 'tocius anglie primas et apostolice sedis legatus natus'.[26] This title was not used so openly in the mandate announcing the visitation by the archbishop of the diocese of Lincoln. It was, however, implicit in it, and Longland further claimed that the power to visit *any* other diocese at all came from outside the realm and was therefore in breach of *praemunire* – he had been quick to learn the lessons of the past and the relationship of the imperial claim to the statute. Accordingly he said the archbishop was:

in derogacionem excellentissimi in christo principis et domini nostri henrici octavi dei gracia anglie et francie Regis fidei defensoris et domini hibernie illustrissimi regalie aut corone sive regie statum ... vel consuetudinem huius Regni anglie tendere videbitur.[27]

The bishops of Exeter, Norwich, and Winchester joined in the protest. For Longland there was not only the fear that *praemunire* would yet again be incurred by allowing the archbishop to invade his diocese, there was a further threat to his power as ordinary in the diocese of Lincoln. A letter survives in Lincoln which shows very clearly that the metropolitan visitation was not to be like other visitations. The archbishop's representative, Dr Gwent, was given further powers by the king:

for as much that you excersyce the visitacion of my lorde of Canterbury in dyvers partes of hys provynce by reason whereof you have a greate apparance of the clergie in thys Realme before you to gether attons [*sic*] and shall come in to dyvers Abbeys and other Collegial and cathedral churchys We wooll and strytly comaunde you that ye procure the chapter seale of every spirituall incorporacion that you shall comme unto, and the subscription of every mann of that chaptre to be put to thys wrytyng devysyd by us and our counsail the counter payme* whereoff subscribed by my lorde of Canterbury ye shall herewith recyve. And

**sic* for 'counter-part of an indenture'.

further that yow shall procure the subscriptyon of every priest by you vysited to the Article concernyng the bysshoppe of Rome hys aucthoryty with in thys Realme. And if aney parson or parsons will resiste or gaynsay so to seale or subscribe, that you do call ayed of the next Justice sheryff or other temporall officer ther abowte and cause all such persons makyng such Refusall to be kept in warde unto our Further pleasure be known therein. And faill ye not thus to do with all your wytt and diligence as ye tender our pleasure.[28]

For Longland this was an invasion of his rights as diocesan, and moreover an invasion which all diocesans were not to suffer. The oath to the succession and the oath renouncing the bishop of Rome were proceeding in the diocese of Winchester apparently unaided by commissaries from Canterbury.[29] There was no suggestion in the see of Norwich that the metropolitan visitation went hand in hand with the oaths to the succession and denouncing the power of Rome.[30] Why then should Lincoln be singled out for this special and particularly distasteful treatment?

It is perfectly possible to guess that the archbishop or his commissary had simply decided to visit the diocese of Lincoln first in any case, and that therefore no significance attaches to this marriage of the succession oath and the metropolitan visitation. It is equally possible that some bishops were thought to be less than wholehearted in their loyalty to the new regime. But we would have expected the dioceses of London, Norwich and Chichester to be in the queue ahead of Lincoln, because Longland, for all his misgivings, had not publicly opposed any of the recent legislation, and the worst he seems to have done was rapidly to have got on the wrong side of Cromwell. That mutual mistrust is evident by 1536 when Longland writing to Cromwell said he was 'bold always to trouble you with my rude pen'.[31] We know that in the following year the archbishop's commissary, Gwent, was in Chichester, where the oath-taking was not complete,[32] but we would have expected both Stockesley and Gardiner to be ahead of Longland in the line of 'troublesome' bishops. It may be that Longland's long silence and outward conformity to the supremacy was known to be the product of unease, and that factions at court, if not the king himself, prevailed on Cranmer to put the bishop under close scrutiny. If anyone hoped to silence Longland, he had misjudged his adversary.

The bishop was a tireless opponent and a good letter writer. He made no secret at all of the fact that he resented any intrusion into the affairs of his diocese. But his protests could not prevent the arrival of Richard Gwent on 4 August 1534 for the metropolitan visitation of the cathedral church. His findings do not appear to have survived, but they were said to have been in 'quadam papiri scedula'. The visitation was prorogued until 1 December, and the dean and chapter paid 66s.8d. for procurations.[33] They also made payment of 7s.6d. to the servants of the registrar, 5s. to the servants of the archbishop and 10s. to Gwent's servants and 13s.4d. to the archbishop's registrar. All in all it had been an expensive affair. But Longland was not so easily defeated. He sent off to Wooburn 'pro antiquis libris concernentibus visitationem Reverendi Patris Domini Cant'Archiepiscopi'.[34] His anger was really roused when he learned that the commissary of the archbishop had dared to admit John Gilden to Ewerby vicarage, which was in the patronage of Kyme priory.[35] On 31 August the bishop's commissary presented the archbishop's representative with letters showing that the bishop had appealed. The appeal rested on the basis that bishops of Lincoln had enjoyed, for more than eighty years, peaceful jurisdiction and the right to admit to benefices. This right was in the process of being violated in the case of Ewerby, and it was rumoured that the same thing had happened at Etton. In order to make his point doubly clear, Longland took the Michaelmas ordination at Liddington in person[36] and continued in person or through his vicar general to admit priests to benefices.[37] Against one such admission the scribe had written 'Memorandum, fuit admissus durante visitacione metropoliticani Archiepiscopi'.[38]

Longland did not win all the way. The admission by the archbishop's commissary of John Gildon to the vicarage of Ewerby went ahead; but so did Longland's protest with all its ramifications. It forced the king and his advisers to consider in practical detail what the supremacy over the church actually meant. Was the power to visit and correct to be delegated permanently to the archbishop of Canterbury, was he effectively to be the supreme head, or was the reality of the royal title to be underlined by the king's personal involvement in the affairs of the church? Indeed, could any authority be exercised in the church without royal authorisation? The bishops had asked in vain in convocation for a precise definition of the statute of *praemunire*. The implications of Cranmer's visitation made uncertainty and equivocation no longer possible.

An added urgency was brought to the question by the appointment of two new bishops; Lee of Coventry and Lichfield, and Goodrich of Ely were consecrated in April 1534 and had sworn to recognise Henry VIII as 'under Almighty God to be the chief and supreme head of the Church of England'; and they acknowledged that their bishoprics were 'wholly and only' of the king's gift.[39] This raised important questions for bishops appointed *before* 1532 – certainly for the bishop of Lincoln, who had been appointed by papal bull and whose subsequent oaths left no doubt about his allegiance, but considerable questions about the origin of his power: was authority, received from Christ, mediated through the papacy or from the king?[40] The question was most acute with reference to Cranmer himself; was his authority wholly derived from the king or from elsewhere?

It would, therefore, be in the solution to the problems of the precise powers which the supreme head, the archbishops and the bishops themselves actually possessed that Longland would learn whether his strictures against the bishop of Rome and his exhortation to him to 'be content with thynne owne dioces' applied with equal force to the king. Between 1535 and 1540, Longland learned that they could; at the same time he learned that his proximity to the king could be used to preserve the bishop's status and rights as ordinary of the bishopric of Lincoln.

The issue first became focussed on the vicegerency.[41] The precise date at which the king decided to exercise his supremacy through a vicegerent is not known. It was probably in the last months of 1534.[42] Professor Lehmberg has shown that it was prompted by doubts about the origins of episcopal power candidly expressed in a letter from two of Cromwell's agents. Lehmberg did not realise that the letter itself was the product of the fiasco of Cranmer's metropolitan visitation. The agents, though, were well aware of the problem that it had posed; they suggested that the king should take into

> his hands at once al jurisdiction and power; and, for a season, or at his plesure, exercise the same for the establishment of his subjects and a perpetual monument. Also lest the Bishops if they had alwayes enjoyed this jurisdiction without any interruption would (as in maner they do already) have supposed and reckoned, they had received the same from elsewhere than from the King's Highness; it seemed to us good that they should be driven by this means to agnise their author, spring and fountain as else they be too ingrate to enjoy it.[43]

Certainly if this was the intention of the vicegerency it cut clean against Longland's understanding of his office and jurisdiction, and it may explain why he acted with undue haste on certain occasions which we shall consider.[44] He could not stop the vicegerency, but he could minimise the inhibition of his own jurisdiction by insisting on his argument that he had specific powers *from Christ*, and not from either the bishop of Rome or the pope, which Cromwell's agents suggested were the only alternatives.[45]

On 18 September 1535 orders were sent to all bishops through the archbishop of Canterbury and the bishop of London, as was usual, inhibiting the exercise of their jurisdiction for the duration of a royal visitation.[46] Longland gave a graphic account of how he received his inhibition and, as ever, he was ready with his 'rude pen'. He wrote to Cromwell:

> It may please you also to knowe that vith daye of Octobre att vi of the clocke att night I received the kynges mooste honorable Wrytinges of inhibicyon concernynge his graces visitacion from my Lorde[s] of Caunterbury and London, And have with all diligency sent the same forthe to all my archdeacons, commyssaryes, offycers and minysters.[47]

This no doubt was a civil enough response. But Longland with his sharp eye for the main issue had already seen a basic problem in the inhibition which, if exploited, could leave important powers in his own hands and not in those of the king or his vicegerent: bishops alone had the power of ordination and confirmation, and these at least would have to be released to him by virtue of his episcopal orders. He therefore went on in his letter to say:

> Albe itt if itt maye soo stande with the kinges mooste gracyous pleasur and yours, iff I might be soo bolde, I wolde mooste humbly beseke [*sic*] the same to give me lycence for the good ordre of my dioces.[48]

He then asks for the right to give orders, to bless churches, chalices and vestments, to hold institutions and inductions and to confirm children – all these duties, except those of institution and induction, were beyond the competence of the vicegerent and would have had to be delegated to a bishop in any case. Then Longland cautiously, almost like a cat stalking its prey, asks to 'here causes of instans, correcon of synne and to prove testamentes if ye think this convenyent els not to graunte to me and myne officers the same'. In that request he had moved from episcopal duties to duties which could be performed by *other* ecclesiastics (at least until the office of commissary was opened to the laity in 1545).[49] Treading his way even further forward Longland added:

> And over this to be so good master to yor beadisman, the archdeacon of Lincoln, as to lycence his offycers to visyte his archedeaconry Els shall he lacke money to serve the kynge where he is. For this is the cheff tyme of his profites of his archdeaconry And I thynke some of the archedeacons have doon ther progresse of visitacion or [*sic*] this tyme.[50]

Longland prudently sent with the letter a 'dust box and a caste of counters' with Cromwell's arms on the side made by goldsmiths. His suit was successful and he was given back his powers of ordination and jurisdiction, whether correction, instance, or probate, provided that the value of the goods of the deceased did not exceed one hundred pounds. There was only one difference between Longland's power as bishop before the vicegerency and after it, and that was that the licence which returned him his jurisdiction stated that he now exercised it by virtue of the royal commission (*vigore hujus commissionis nostre*) and during the king's pleasure.[51]

The device of inhibiting the jurisdiction of the bishop and returning it to him by royal authority answered the questions raised by Cranmer's visitation in a clever way. Bishops were no longer simply bishops '*dei gracia*' but also with the support of the king. Longland's full title changed from '*dei gracia Lincoln' episcopus*' to '*Johannes permissione divina Lincoln' episcopus auctoritate excellentissimi in christo principis et domini nostri Henrici octavi dei gracia anglie et francie regis fidei defensoris domini hibernie et in terra sub christo supremi capitis ecclesie anglicane fulcitus*'.[52] Exactly the same formula could be used for the dean and chapter and for archdeacons. Their powers might be fully or partially restored, but always on the authority of the king and pending his pleasure.

The dean and chapter of Lincoln received their licence dated 19 December 1535.[53] But they had a bill to pay in the form of procurations to the king's visitor, Dr London, and food and tips to his servants, as well as the expense of sending for the licence, which cost them forty-five shillings.[54]

The vicegerency died with Cromwell, and this also removed for the time being a potential source of anxiety from the bishops. Their titles and those of their successors had been changed, and their authority appeared to be divine but supported by the king; but only in the event of another vicegerency was the latter a threat. But if the potential threat of an active royal supremacy had been removed, and if the purely episcopal powers of the bishop and his right of jurisdiction had weathered the storm which was personified in Thomas Cromwell, the see of Lincoln had not come off so lightly in terms of its resources, and ultimately in terms of geographical scope and size.

The threat to resources

The see of Lincoln had considerable sources of wealth and patronage: it was valued in 1536 as having an income of £1,962.17s.4d. This was made up of temporalities and spiritualities, the latter being put at £584.8s.11d.

Other bishoprics, like those of Ely, Winchester and Canterbury, were considerably wealthier, though the two which most closely resembled Lincoln in terms of size and numbers of parishes, York and Norwich, received less.[55] It is quite clear that Longland was aware of the disparity and found difficulties in meeting obligations, like that incurred by the escape of prisoners from one of his gaols.[56] But it is also clear that he watched over his money with the proverbial care of a Scot.[57] It was not that he could never give money away (we know that he gave Erasmus gifts from time to time[58]) but he seems to have had a reputation for liking to know where the money had gone and for refraining from giving until he was sure it was necessary. He made much of the fact that his post of royal confessor kept him in London, where prices were greater than they were in the country; he complained that he had to keep on servants at Holborn 'in manner . . . all year';[59] certainly in 1535 he was in debt to the king for about £600.[60]

Longland had a wide range of expenditure, both that dictated by the needs of his diocese and that which indulged his personal tastes; and there were obviously some claims for expenses made to him by his subordinates, while travelling the length and breadth of his far-flung diocese. It is clear from his will that he spent much on books, and he had a chained library at Buckden; it is also clear that he purchased very expensive vestments and communion vessels. Another expensive taste was for dials, astrolabes and clocks.[61] We do not know how many servants he had to wait on him or to accompany his deputies, but the bills for expenses submitted between 1533 are negligible. The expenses of the registrar and his servants for riding from Wooburn to London and staying there for six days were 9s.4d.,[62] and a fragment of a book of costs, undated but probably dating from 1545, includes an item 'for dinner for nine persons with the apparitor 3s.', and later 'for dinner for six persons 2s.4d.'.[63] Nearly forty years before food prices had begun to rise, in 1500, 'one quarter and two pieces of beyffe' cost the bishop 3s.4d.[64] It would not appear that deputies were allowed to submit expense accounts for lavish dinners or expensive parties.

Longland used a great deal of his income, just as West of Ely did,[65] in building a chantry on the south side of his cathedral church – a chantry which was never used as he intended. He was also concerned to help his nephew Richard Pate, who was archdeacon of Lincoln and who was on the king's business as an envoy mainly to the Emperor's court. Longland asked Cromwell not to forget that he owed Pate £115,[66] and Longland's cousin, William Robyns (who was a merchant of the Staple), seems to have acted as a banker for the sums which passed between the bishop and Pate.[67] (What Longland did not know was that William Robyns and Pate were hand in glove, and Robyns knew the bishop's character well enough to realise that if Pate could get money from elsewhere than from his uncle, he should do so. Robyns wrote to Pate in 1540, 'I pray you that such money as ye do receve from me from tyme to tyme be not disclosed to my lord of Lyncoln by you nor eny of yor servantes for hyt myght chance to hyndre you yf he be dysposed to do you eny good ... althowghe he be as yet straytely lased.'[68]) Longland had, therefore, some costly obligations which could make serious inroads into his finances, quite apart from the fact that inflation reduced the purchasing power of his income by about one half by 1540.[69]

By 1540 Longland would also be confronted with the loss of income which the dissolution of the monasteries brought and which was expressed in the diminution of his spiritualities. This was a more serious problem for the bishop of Lincoln than it was, for example, for the bishop of Ely; spiritualities accounted for nearly 30 per cent of Longland's total income at the time of the *Valor*.[70] At Ely they constituted a mere £100 or 4½ per cent of the total.[71] It has been argued that the bishops could have kept themselves and their successors from serious financial trouble in the sixteenth century by a more enlightened policy in the management of their estates. This was certainly true,[72] but what has not been appreciated is the loss to the bishops of some of their spiritualities.[73]

Theoretically, pensions due from religious houses on account of the loss of fees entailed in their appropriation of certain churches, which amounted between 1533 and 1534 to £138, should have been paid by the court of augmentations or the lay purchaser of the monastic land, but nothing made up for the fees entailed in the election and confirmation of religious superiors, which brought in £6.13s.4d., in the same years.[74] Fees for blessing superiors and installing them brought £2 per annum (or thereabouts) and procurations due from the visitation of religious houses should have brought £50; the Act for First-fruits and Tenths also took from all bishops the income from vacant benefices which could account for as much as £5 for each archdeaconry.[75] These were small sums amounting to no more than £100, but they were not unimportant as prices rose, nor could the bishop be sure that other spiritualities would not disappear – as the case of Richard Layton indicates.

In 1537 Longland alleged that Richard Layton had not paid the spiritualities due to the bishop from the archdeaconry of Buckingham, and that a sum of the order of £20 was due from the previous two and a half years.[76] Layton, writing to Cromwell to defend himself against the bishop's charges, raised the question of whether the bishop any longer had spiritualities due to him from his archdeacons. He listed all the sources which constituted spiritualities and tried to show either that they had been abolished by Parliament or that they were the archdeacon's legitimate revenue, and not the bishop's. The conclusion which Layton reached was:

For Peter's pence he can have nothing; *quia non sunt*; for procurations nothing, for synodals nothing, for fines of testaments he hath half, for vacations nothing, for installations nothing, for my pensions and indemnities nothing.[77]

Longland's reply to this summary removal of all spiritualities was to deny that the most valuable of the spiritualities paid by the archdeacons, *prestationes*, were Peter's pence, which Layton had alleged that they were, and in fact the bishop was right. An early sixteenth-century account book of the spiritualities of the bishop of Lincoln has survived. Under *de prestacionibus* sums of £108.8s.8d. are recorded as having been paid to the bishop at Easter and Michaelmas: but these were *not* Peter's pence, which appear separately.[78] It looks very much as though *prestationes* were synodals and as such worth over £200 to the bishop, since they were payable twice a year. But this was small comfort to Longland, who could not get the money out of the archdeacon and was obviously apprehensive lest other archdeacons follow Layton's lead. The debt was still outstanding at Longland's death.[79]

Further inroads into the bishop's spiritualities were made with the creation of the new diocese of Peterborough from the archdeaconry of Northampton, and the new see of Osney and subsequently Oxford. Peterborough was securely in existence by October 1541,[80] and Oxford came into being in 1542.[81] The loss in synodals was £74, and procurations for visitation would have added considerably to that sum.[82]

Faced by a diminishing income from spiritualities, it was of immense importance that Longland should make the most out of his lands and should use his patronage of offices, like that of bailiff or high steward, to the most favourable advantage. But obviously it takes time to change a leasing policy where lands are concerned, and rents which were realistic at the beginning of his episcopate were not so in the inflation of the 1540s. It was perhaps fortunate for him that few properties came up for leasing in the early part of his episcopate, and most fell in at the very end when he must have been feeling the financial pinch. The bishopric of Lincoln had lands in some forty-six places in 1521.[83] They were valued in 1536 at £1,378.8s.5½d., and it was rare for Longland to lease them at anything but their current value, though he tended to make exceptions for his family. Similarly, he rarely leased the whole of a property: at Biggleswade the mill alone was leased, and then for its value in the *Valor*, and with the demesne or the rents of assize.[84] Higher than value rents were charged if the lease was for longer than thirty years – unless to a member of the family. His cousin, Anthony Forster, received in 1534 the castle of Newark (Notts.) with the meadows at North Gate and Farndon as well as the valuable fisheries and mills, the rabbit warren at Tolney and the manor of Balderton and the toll of Newark for a rent of £96.6s.8d., and for a period of thirty years. It is sometimes difficult to identify the precise parts of a property mentioned in a lease with the parts of it mentioned in the *Valor*, or in a valuation of the see made earlier which is similar in most particulars to the *Valor*. But it seems likely that the rent was about £25 less than it should have been.[85] As a result of this lease, Forster was a power to be reckoned with in Newark, and this showed itself from time to time, as when Forster and Longland cited William Meryng to appear before the King in Council. Meryng wrote letters excusing himself on account of illness but expressing the view that if his absence was not pardoned the town of Newark would be ruined.[86]

Two other highly favourable leases were made by Longland to cousins. One was of specified demesne lands in Dorchester in 1545 to Richard and Alice Beauforeste and their sons Richard and Luke. This was for sixty years and at a rent of £19.9s.8d., for what appears to be the manor of Dorchester. The value in the *Valor* of the manor was £108.4s.4d.,[87] but the lease was ambiguous in specifying the 'house called the Bishops courte in the same town of Dorchester with these dominicall lands'. The bishop reserved to himself rents of assize, customary rents and fines, amercements and suits of court, and the lessees were to do all repairs 'as well in bearing the charge of workmanship as in finding and providing all manner of stuff requisite to the same, great timber and stone only excepted'. The house was not to be sublet nor could any change of use occur on the lands.[88] William Robyns, the Staple merchant, another of Longland's fortunate cousins, received the manor of Bishop's Norton for forty years for £4.3s.4d., with the responsibilities to do all the repairs and not to change the use of the land. This lease was only to operate when a previous one, made in 1533 for thirty years, had expired, with the result that the property was leased until 1603 at the same rent.[89] The folly of such a lease was either not perceived by the bishop or else deliberately ignored.

Another important and highly favourable lease was made to William King and Richard Curzon, neither of whom were members of the bishop's family. It was of a part of Louth, namely the mills and demesne, for a period of twenty-one years at a rent of £19.3s.4d. This was probably ten pounds lower than the property was worth.[90] The explanation may lie in the duty of the tenants to find a lot of equipment, 'mylne stones, iron geres and iron workes, cogges, wheles, spyndellys and all other maner of goyng geres with charge of all workmanship of the same'. It also appeared that roof and wall repairs were necessary, for which the bishop would give timber but the tenants were to find the flood gates; and no change of use might occur on the land.[91] Two leases of rectories were made during the life of the tenant at £40, but here inflation was recognised: they were to rise in rent to £47 when the lessee died and his executors took over the property.[92]

When and where no special circumstances such as these appear to have prevailed, properties were leased at the value given in the *Valor*. Mills at Biggleswade and Sleaford were let at exactly that level in 1524 and 1547,[93] and the leases of properties at Wooburn, Banbury, Mumby and North Weston were let at a clear profit from the *Valor* assessment.[94]

A further means of benefiting a tenant was by the length of time for which the lease was to run, as can be seen from Table 8 below:

Table 8. *Duration of leases of episcopal lands*

1–20 years	...	0
21–30 years	...	4
31–40 years	...	5
41–50 years	...	3
51–60 years	...	3
over 61 years	...	1

By the end of his episcopate, Longland was leasing for longer periods. But there is a suggestion that these long leases brought with them entry fines which in their turn brought to Longland an immediate cash relief. The longest lease of all, for ninety-nine years, was made in 1547, a few months before the bishop's death, to Sir John Williams. That this lease was extraordinary is shown in Longland's will. He says:

> Item I borowed of Sir John Williams knight one hundred markes who covenanted with me for the renewing of his lease of North Weston, to agree with me for the fyne because the years were lxxxxix I demaunded the hoole hundred markes and he offered xl^{li} And as moche as we were at noo full poynte he left my obligacion in the custody of my Stewarde till we were at more leasure to have more communication and soo remaynes.[95]

This lease is particularly important in showing the personal interest which Longland took in his financial affairs. It also shows that entry fines were charged even though no record of them survives. It therefore highlights the difference in estate management which Longland displays from that of his contemporaries. Unlike Booth of Hereford he did not increase his holding.[96] Equally, unlike the bishops of Ely and Chichester, he did not keep back areas of demesne which were in one place only and therefore easily managed[97] and which could provide him with food. Nor did he make long leases of between sixty and one hundred years in any number, as did the bishop of the new diocese of Chester.[98] For his episcopate alone, unprofitable exchanges were also avoided (though they were immediately imposed on his successor), and so he escaped the greedy designs of his monarch, unlike the archbishops of Canterbury and of York.[99] The policy which he adopted with regard to his own authority he seems also to have held in estate management, namely that there should be no interference with his see – a policy particularly marked in his latter years.

Table 9. *Dates of leases of episcopal lands*

1521–30	....	1
1531–40	....	2
1541–7	....	13

His success in keeping off the vultures, at least for a time, may well have owed something to his patronage of the offices at his disposal; they do not appear to have been particularly lucrative but they appear to have been much sought after. The office of bailiff of Dorchester, Thame, Wooburn and Fingest brought its recipient £6, as did the custodianship of Sleaford Castle.[100] The most valuable of all such posts seems to have been that of the bailiff of Newark.[101] In 1545, Longland vested the post with his cousin Anthony Forster and his son Giles for seventy years.[102] To this post he added others as they became vacant or as they became near enough to vacancy to warrant a reversion, a gift on the death of the present holder – a practice used by Crown and landowner alike.[103] Anthony Forster and his son were also given the reversion of the custodianship of Coleby and Stow at £3 and £2 respectively.[104] The device of reversion was used on other occasions by Longland to forward his family, strait-laced though his nephew believed him to be. William Robyns received the post of bailiff of Sleaford Castle on reversion,[105] and that of Liddington went in 1534 to his nephew John Pate and John Joseph, 'kinsman' and servant to the bishop.[106] As well as Coleby and

Stow, the post of keeper of Stow Park, Newark, went to Anthony and Giles Forster.[107] But these posts could also be used to curry favour or secure protection at court: the post of bailiff of Biggleswade went in 1531 to Francis Bryan, a member of the king's household.[108] Thomas Cromwell was slightly sweetened by the gift on reversion of the post of custodian and bailiff of Banbury Castle in 1536; Cromwell was eager for the post and Longland seems to have enjoyed keeping him waiting.[109] The most valuable of these offices was that of high steward of the diocese, worth £20, which Longland granted first in 1529 to the Duke of Norfolk and then in 1547 to William Paget.[110]

Of themselves, Longland's modest grants of office or of the few leases at his disposal were not enough to save him from the pressure for exchanges or favourable long leases to members of the court. He saw in his family a barrier against damage to the church, but the very fact that he survived so long as a bishop also assisted him. Holbeach, his successor, immediately agreed to an unprofitable exchange of manors which deprived the bishops of Lincoln of some of their better residences.[111] But Longland was an old dog, not inclined to learn new tricks, and he seems, like Goodrich of Ely, to have kept the clamour for church lands away from the diocese. Superficially, he may seem to have been a blatant nepotist, but he clearly thought that his family were as good custodians of the lands of the church as any, and certainly he at least knew his family well enough to know which of them was trustworthy. The proof of this wary policy can be seen in the fact that when he died no part of his inheritance had been alienated by exchange and only one lease had been made for the duration of a full century.

No survey of the revenues of the see, comparable to the *Valor*, survives for the time of Longland's death, and changes in its income from land accompanied the translation of his successor. We may assume that his landed income, though eroded by inflation and some favourable leases, was similar to that which he enjoyed in 1536. His predecessors were likely also to have made favourable leases, and it is unlikely that Longland's outnumbered theirs. But his spiritualities had certainly declined by one fifth, and in Layton's threat to synodals the bishop could lose a further two fifths. A similar threat faced his fellow bishops, but few had sees and expenses of the size of Lincoln. The removal of Oxford and Northampton from the see did not make the travelling very much easier or cheaper. Longland and the diocese of Lincoln may have come out of the Henrician period reasonably well financially, but it was not well enough.

The threat to the ecclesiastical courts

It was one of the ironies of the Henrician Reformation that the issue which had, more than any other, precipitated the break with Rome, that of the bishop of Rome's right to judge the instance case of the royal marriage, and which had developed into a condemnation of all prelates for their exercise of ecclesiastical jurisdiction, did not bring to an end the English ecclesiastical courts (although it changed them);[112] nor did it see the end of some supposed abuses which were allegedly disliked by the Commons and condemned in the supplication against the ordinaries. Longland had to work hard to preserve his episcopal powers, and in that he largely succeeded. He also had to work hard to defend the finances of his see, and in that he was not wholly unsuccessful. But his audience and consistory courts, and those of his commissaries and archdeacons, were suspended for only a few days whilst he awaited the appropriate licence from the vicegerent. It is very difficult to assess, however, what happened to the courts in the diocese between 1530 and Longland's death in 1547. The books of the court of audience cease in 1527 and only a few folios survive for it between 1543 and 1545. There is no consistory material at all for Longland's episcopate, but we do have a court book for the archdeaconry of Lincoln from 1536 to 1545 and some rather scrappy (certainly incomplete) material for the archdeaconry of Leicester.[113] Some further material, chiefly relating to Oxford and Northampton, does not go beyond 1540 and covers too short a chronological span to be useful for comparative purposes.[114]

In the archdeaconry of Lincoln between March 1536 and March 1537, there were thirty sessions of the court and sixty-eight appearances (as distinct from cases) made at it;[115] between March 1544 and March 1545, in 28 sessions 267 appearances were made, a dramatic increase in the business of the court which seems to be paralleled in Lancashire.[116] Since we have no evidence of the number of cases heard by the court of the archdeacon of Lincoln in the 1520s, it is impossible to know whether 1536–7 marked a decline in the usual business and whether 1544–5 represented a return to the normal. Dr Lander suggested that in the diocese of Chichester, court business was at its lowest in 1533–4 and there was only a return to the pre-Reformation level of business in 1556.[117] Similarly, Dr Houlbrooke has shown that instance business in the courts of the diocese of Norwich dropped to its lowest point in 1534 but that it recovered, with a few lean years, by 1545. Less complete evidence survives for the diocese of Winchester, for which 1547 seems to

Table 10. *Cases in the court of the archdeacon of Lincoln, 1536–7, compared with 1544–5*

Type of Case	% of total cases 1536–7	% of total cases 1544–5
Tithe	4.4%	29.5%
Testamentary	10.2%	17.6%
Defamation	44.1%	32.2%
Marriage	32.3%	13.8%
Delapidations	2.9%	0.3%
Dues of church	2.9%	2.9%
Not given	2.9%	3.7%
Office case	0%	0.3%

mark the lowest point in instance business. We do not know when business was at its worst for the ecclesiastical courts in the archdeaconry of Lincoln, but it is quite clear from Table 10 that it increased dramatically in a certain sort of case between 1536 and 1544. As office cases were so rare, it is impossible to assess whether the censures of the court were losing their force, as Dr Lander suggests and as seems to have been the case later in the century in the diocese of Norwich.[118] Office cases only found their way into the archdeacon's court book by accident. We can see an increase of business in this period chiefly in tithe and testamentary cases. In contrast, the defamation actions which are a feature of the early Lincoln and the Leicester court books had declined, and so had marriage cases. The diocese of Norwich, though not of Winchester, shows a similar rate of decline.[119] Marriage and defamation cases normally arose as a result of *lay* initiative. Tithe cases in Lincolnshire (the significance of which will be discussed later), like those in Chichester, were mainly brought by the clergy.[120] What does, however, emerge from the slight evidence which we have is that penance was used not only as a deterrent but as an admonitory exercise. Richard Wellys, who admitted defaming one of his neighbours in June 1541, was required to stand up before the whole congregation between matins and mass and say: 'Where I have spokyn slaunderous wordes of one Jenet Broxolme of malice owther wise than I ought to I am sory therefore and desyr you to gyff no credence therunto and so aske her forgiffness.'[121] Money payments were used more extensively in Northamptonshire than elsewhere.[122] Fees seem to have remained constant. If the laity had gone through a period of disillusionment with the church courts in the 1530s, it did not last long and could not extend to testamentary business. Marriage cases had always proved a somewhat cumbersome way of dealing with a variety of personal preferences and legal claims – not least that of prior contract which was abolished by statute in 1540 – and the decline of the use of the courts in consequence was usual in other dioceses beside that of Lincoln.[123]

Old age and the dangers of heresy had the effect of driving Longland back to preside in his court of audience. During the tense years of the 1530s he seems to have perceived that the priorities of his early years, his exclusive concern with the religious and with the secular colleges, had come to an abrupt conclusion. By 1543 we find him dealing in person with erring clergy in his court of audience and watching carefully over preaching.[124] The survival of his courts owed nothing to him; he was fortunate in that they seemed to have fulfilled a need which for the time being they met sufficiently well for the storm of criticism to which they were subjected in the early 1530s to leave them unshaken.

It is unfortunate that for the see of Lincoln, unlike that of Norwich, we have so little court material for the 1530s and 1540s, and that so few trends can be perceived. Meaningful comparisons with an earlier period cannot be made. The structure of the courts in the Lincoln diocese differed from that of Norwich and Chichester, but – slight though the evidence is – it would seem that the cases brought before the courts ebbed and flowed in a similar way, if with a slightly different chronology, to that already observed elsewhere, notably in the diocese of Norwich.[125]

2. THE SECULAR COLLEGES AND THE MONASTERIES

Longland had kept to a minimum the incursions into his own jurisdiction by the archbishop and the vicegerent. When he regained his right to visit in 1537, it does not seem to have extended to monasteries, but it did extend to the secular colleges, and he would have seen the effects upon the colleges of the supremacy and its accompanying acts. The dean and chapter of Lincoln and the great cathedral church itself were all marked by the events of the 1530s, and much of what the cathedral suffered could never be repaired or restored, even under a severely Catholic prince.[1]

The dean and chapter were represented in convocation by John Rayne, the vicar general, and like the bishop himself, they probably had little idea, when the Reformation Parliament commenced, how greatly its proceedings would touch on the life of the cathedral church. It took the dean and chapter some time to note that Parliament had laid down a new scale of probate fees, for instance (which limited the amount to be paid to the registrar so that the chapter clerk would have to alter his charges accordingly). It was not until September 1537 that they debated

> whether the chapter clerk should have his fees for them [wills] according to the ancient custom of the cathedral or according to the royal statutes lately provided and put forth on that behalf. At length, considering that that statute was penal, and that they could by no means have or receive from any will beyond the fine limited thereby, they willed and decreed that for the future the chapter-clerk should have his fees as limited and assigned by the said statute without resistance or opposition from the chapter.

It had taken seven years for the statute to be implemented.[2]

They were somewhat quicker in appreciating that they had been indicted, along with the rest of the clergy, for breach of *praemunire*, and on 26 May 1531 they bound themselves under the common seal to pay £100 to the treasurer of the king's chamber.[3] They were not quite as put out as was their bishop by the metropolitan visitation, not least perhaps because they were used to it whenever the see fell vacant. Not only did they pay their procurations of 66s.8d. to Richard Gwent, but they promised '*consciencie*' to preach that the king was head of the church in England, and that the bishop of Rome '*qui in suis bullis pape nomen usurpatet summi pontifici principatum sibi arrogat non habet maiorem aliquam Jurisdictionem collatam sibi a deo in hoc regno Anglie quam quivis alius exterior' Episcopus*'. The pope should not be held in private esteem and no one would pray for him '*tamquam papa sed tamquam Epis' Romano*' [*sic*]. In future, loyalty would be to the king alone and to his heirs and his laws; scripture would be explained in this sense, and the cathedral chapter would pray publicly for the king and Anne '*cum sua sobole*' ('her offspring'), and for the archbishops of Canterbury and York.[4]

Hardly had the archbishop left them than the dean and chapter had to face the prospect of a royal visitation through the vicegerent. Quite how expensive this could be is shown in the cathedral accounts for the common fund: the payment of procurations for the archbishop of Canterbury's visitation had figured in the commons accounts for September 1533–4; those to his servants had figured in the accounts for 1533–4 as well, and in the years 1534–5 the chapter repaired its losses by spending little on that which was out of the ordinary except two shillings on the binding of books.[5] But in 1535 to 1536 the extraordinary expenditure which was comprised in the inhibition of their jurisdiction began again. The local inn was used to house the royal visitors; and in consequence 52s.11d., was paid to Thomas Wilson of 'Lee Angeell in Ballio Lincoln'. The inn was well known, and situated in what is today

Bailgate. The payment was for '*expensis Thome Bedell visitoris domini Regis per tres dies mensis marcii*'.

Thomas Bedell was not the only one who needed warmth and food in Lincoln that year. His servants had to be tipped, and in the accounts of the subsequent year (to spread the load) they were paid 32s.5d.[6] This activity was not without the orchestration of messengers riding to London to query the points at issue between the visitor and the chapter. Between 1535 and 1536, £12.5s.2d., was paid to Roger Pett' for riding to parley ('*ad loquendum*') '*cum visitore Regis pro negociis capituli*'.[7]

But despite the activity and the payments, the dean and chapter, like their diocesan, had their jurisdiction inhibited from 8 October, when the inhibition reached Lincoln; and in their case the inhibition continued until 19 December 1535.[8] No wills were proved by the dean and chapter in the autumn of 1535, and the jurisdiction of the archdeacon of Stow was also inhibited.[9] But the courts of the archdeacon of Lincoln, for whom a special licence had been sought by his episcopal uncle, show no such break.[10]

Even this was not the end of the interruptions for the dean and chapter. The bishop was anxious that they should not forget his particular authority, and so he visited the cathedral between the visitations of the archbishop and the vicegerent, possibly in an informal capacity. His aim was the usual one of indicating that the diocese of Lincoln was his god-given cure, and that no matter how often his jurisdiction was inhibited he would assert his concern and his rights at the end of the day. The close in 1535 seems to have resembled a celibate Barchester, with all parties bent on establishing rights and duties where before there had been privileges and obligations. The bishop sent his cousin William Robyns to Cromwell, saying that he himself had been very weak in his limbs and feet since Easter but intended to ride at some time in the next week to Lincoln, to view the cathedral and his other spiritualities.[11] Nor was this the end of the disturbances suffered by the chapter. In March 1537–8 the dean once again had to promise that no authority was exercised and no other allegiance owed 'aut prelato aut romano pontifici', but to Henry VIII to whom alone the chapter would give duty and obedience, and whom they accepted and recognised 'pro supremo in terris ecclesie anglicane immediate sub christo capite'. They added that all monies going to the pope would be discontinued. In fact that had been the case for some time.[12] However, what the dean and chapter actually believed and what they were preaching was of immediate concern to the bishop, who announced his intention of making a formal visitation in 1539.[13]

That visitation, of which only the injunctions survive, seems to have been concerned with a certain lack of decorum in bell ringing, candle lighting and in the escorting of the dean, on high feasts, by the vergers. It seems to denote a concern by the bishop, not only with the statutes governing residence, which had already been shown to be central to the whole life of the cathedral, but with the proper reverence to be displayed in a church and especially in the most prestigious one in the diocese. The problem of the cathedral clergy in the 1530s was not only one of their role (which has been a problem for them ever since); it was also one of combining, in a dignified and legitimate way, the duties of its several parts. In the morning, there were for example, a large number of masses to be said by different priests at different altars. Some of these obligations had accrued to the cathedral from its chantry bequests, some were the product of its own obligations as 'Mary Masses' which were daily masses in honour of the Patroness of the cathedral. The timetabling of such events was understandably difficult. We have seen that Longland found the vicars choral and poor clerks, many of whom were chantry priests, hard to keep to their obligations.

It was not so much the brawling, the dice and the dogs which worried the bishop on this occasion. It was more serious: he was concerned at the lack of patient dedication to a vocation of liturgical prayer displayed by the lower clergy of the cathedral. This was understandable enough: they were poorly paid, and the renewal of faith which might occur in a parish when a priest recognised the spirit by its fruits was not theirs. Many of them can have known little or nothing of those for whom they interceded, and in these circumstances it is hardly surprising that masses were rushed, priests were late for statutory duties, and bell ringers soon recognised that bells no longer announced a set of masses but merely wakened the priests who were supposed to be saying them. Longland had preached often enough on the theme 'the letter killeth and the spirit giveth life' to recognise in the poorer clergy of the cathedral the signs of boredom which manifested themselves in a tendency to frivolity and unpunctuality, common enough in the religious orders. Whether he tried to quicken the flagging spirits of the clergy we do not know; he certainly issued a timetable of masses and bell ringing to which they were ordered to adhere. Unlike Bishop Sherburne of Chichester, faced with a similar problem, he did not see fit to help the vicars choral and choristers, in particular, by employing laymen to assist in singing the offices, which may well (as any choir boy knows) turn the liturgy into more of a privilege than a penance. Longland's list of bells and duties which were to be performed by priests, night watchmen, bell ringers and vergers was far less imaginative.[14]

The residentiary canons did not escape his displeasure. He was, as he had always been, concerned with the all-important matter of residence. It had been Longland's wish that the dignitaries of the cathedral reside.[15] The Reformation Parliament in its first session had passed an act ostensibly to promote residence and to allow only certain persons to have chaplains who in turn need not reside in a benefice. But cathedral dignities might be kept without the obligation to residence, provided that in the prebendal church there was a vicar who would serve the cure of souls.[16] Effectively this made the cathedral offices that much more desirable because it was possible to have a vicar as deputy and still derive a sizeable income from the living, even though the priest was not in one of the categories of persons exempted in the statute from holding only one living. Until 1536 there were six canons in residence, each of whom received a stipend from the common fund, which varied because it was divided between them only after all other claims on that fund had been met: in 1533 to 1534 it was as low as £22, but when the number of canons in residence fell to four between 1536 and 1537, each received £31.11s.10d. Of those four, one was in London on chapter business, and when the remaining three tried to share out the duties between them, they had to ask each canon to take on more than one office 'considering the fewness of the canons in residence'.[17] The chapter itself gave some thought to the problem, but to no purpose. They merely gave their approval to a statute made in 1520 which allowed anyone dying during a period of major residence to receive the emoluments from the common fund as though he had lived to the end of the financial year.[18] This was clearly of advantage to the frail, but hardly helped the basic situation which arose because too few canons wanted to reside.

It was for Longland to appoint canons who would reside, and in 1539 the numbers in residence went back to six; Christopher Tamworth was appointed precentor and protested major residence, and so did Henry Lillilow. Another addition to the residentiaries was John Cottisford, an Oxford theologian of some distinction who had helped Longland hunt out heretics in Oxford in the 1520s.[19] In addition to this new blood, Longland, at his visitation of 1539, made a serious injunction about residence. He clearly had in mind the speed with which his treasurer, Richard Parker, had moved from major to minor residence and to requesting an annuity – all in a mere five years.[20] Longland ordered that in future no one should transfer from major to minor residence unless he had fourteen years of major residence behind him. The only exception was to be made in the case of a canon detained by 'notorious and continual infirmity or bodily weakness so as to be unable personally to perform the duty of major residence'. But even this exception could not be claimed by a canon who had done less than three years in major residence, that is to say residence within the close of two thirds of the year. It is apparent that Longland was concerned to see that there was an adequate number of canons to lead the offices, and, in the case of dignitaries, that they should in turn sing the antiphons and in turn 'feed' the choir.[21] The bishop's injunction coincides with the confirmation of James Crawe as organist on what appears to be an increase in stipend, and certainly with a clear statement of what he should teach the choristers:

> the science of singing viz playnsonge, prykedsonge, faburdon, diskante and countor and also in playing the organs in the cathedral especially two or three of them whom he or his deputy shall see fit, docile and suitable to be taught to play on the instruments called calvicordes in future.[22]

Bequests to the cathedral remained constant throughout the 1530s and 1540s, and that in effect meant that the accounts relating to the fabric show an income which varied only slightly between 1535 and 1547 – though inflation had eroded its purchasing power.[23] In contrast, the offerings at the High Altar of the cathedral, which usually totalled about £30,[24] fell from the highest total reached in this period (£39.9s.1½d. in 1522[25]) to nothing at all by 1538–9.[26] The decline was gradual throughout the 1520s and was reversed in 1528 and 1529 when offerings were just over £36.[27] In 1530 they fell to a mere £15.9s.7d., but they were up to just over £38 in 1532. A dramatic fall in offerings occurred between 1536 and 1537 when only £18.2s.1½d. was given, followed in 1537–8 by a bare £5.4s.1d. Thereafter there is an annual entry of '*nulla*'.[28]

It would seem highly unlikely that these sums reflect a move away from pilgrimage and justification by works. In that event we would expect a *gradual* decline continuing into the 1540s. The timing of the decline in offerings at the High Altar goes hand in hand with the dissolution of the monasteries, and it would have been a dull man indeed who did not recognise between 1536 and 1538 that an offering to the church might rapidly become Henry VIII's pocket money. The point was brought home with dramatic clarity in Lincoln when the shrine of St Hugh, the great glory of the medieval cathedral, was razed to the ground, and with it the lesser known shrine of John Dalderby. In 1520 a list of the jewels and other treasures belonging to St Hugh's shrine was made, and though it is incomplete, it gives some idea of the magnificence of the shrine. The head of the saint was encased in silver gilt with enamel; the bishop's mitre was of the same, and the pontifical of St Hugh was made out of gold with precious stones and relics. There were a number of rings with precious stones on them, including one 'with one orient sapphire' standing at the top of the mitre on St Hugh's head. There were also branches of gold with coral on them, and cruets, chalices and pattens of silver. Additionally there were loose jewels, one of which was 'a sapphire pale'. There was also a large collection of books, one of St Hugh's life, 'chained'.[29] Offerings were made at the shrine as well as at that of John Dalderby.

The chapter appears to have appreciated that the jewels of these shrines and of the cathedral itself were in some danger. This is clear from a list of the treasures of the shrine made in 1536. Its author, Henry Litherland, wrote beside some items that they had been removed by the chapter: 'an Image of owr savyor sylver and gylte stondying upon vi lyons voyde in the breist for sacrament for Estur day havying a berall before and a diademe behynde with a cross yn hand weyng xxxvii[oz.]' is noted as being 'extrahitur per Capitulum'. Various crosses, small in size, appear to have the same entry by them, and a number of corporals were kept by the dean and chapter. Furthermore, other items reappear in the cathedral during the reign of Mary, which suggests a policy of prudent preservation on the part of someone.[30] There was also a list, in what looks like Longland's hand, of 'the stonys and perlis in my myter', which suggests that Longland, like the dean and chapter, was anxious not to let the king have too much.[31]

The stripping of the shrines took place in June 1540. A royal commission was issued to the effect that the shrine detracted from the true worship of God:

> Forasmuche as we understande that there is a certen shryne and dyverse feyned reliquys and juellys in the cathedral churche of Lincoln wherwith all the simple people be moche deceyvyd and brought in to gret superstition and idolatrye to the dishonor of god and gret slaunder of this our realme and perill of ther soulys. We lett you wyt, that therfor beyng myndyd to brynge our loveying subjects to the right knowledge of the truths takeyng awaye all occasions of idolatrye and superstition ... [the king had 'appointed certain commissioners' to] take downe as well the sayd shryne, superstitiose reliques as superstitiose juellys, plate, copes and other suchelike ... and to see the sayd reliques juellys and plate salvely and surely to be conveyd to our tower of London unto our juell house ther.[32]

The 'loot' from Lincoln apparently amounted to 2,621 ounces of gold and 4,285 ounces of silver, with numerous pearls and precious stones, and there is mention of a great amethyst and certain cameos which came from Lincoln cathedral.[33] But though the king succeeded in getting a lot, the treasurer and chapter had retained a certain amount for themselves and their successors. Moreover, the devotion of the people of Lincoln did not cool just because the glitter of precious stones no longer honoured the saint. In 1541 the bishop was obliged to pass on to the dean and chapter a letter from the king which stated:

> Yt is lately come to our knowledge that this our goode intente and purpose notwithstandyng, the shrynes, coveryngs of shrynes and monuments to these thyngs doo yett remayne in sondry places of our realme, moche to the slaunder of our doyngs and to the gret displeasure of allmighty God, the same beyng meanes to allure our subjects to their former hypocrysye and supersticion ... For the due and spedy reformacion whereof we have thought mete by these our lettres expresly to will and commaunde that incontynently upon the recepte hereof ye shall not oonly cause due serche to be made in your cathedral churche for these thyngs, and if eny shrynes coveryng of shryne, table, monuments off myracles or other pilgrimage do there continue, to cause it to be taken away as there remayn no memory of it.[34]

There was little the bishop could do to mitigate a royal command of this kind; it had to be sent out, and he performed that duty without comment. But what he could not do openly, he tried to do in other ways. In particular he did his best to give to the cathedral precious vestments and plate which would go a little way to make good the spoliation of the shrines. An inventory of the jewels and valuables of the cathedral survives for May 1557, and many of the items are listed as being 'ex dono Johannis Longland'; a number of richly embroidered chasubles, tunicles and copes were given by him, together with some chalices and pattens as well as silver and gilt phials for use in his chapel or elsewhere.[35] He also gave the cathedral in his will 'all my bokes lying and being at Bugden [*sic*] of the greatest and best sorte' and these were 'to furnyshe their Lybrary with all'. Additionally, he left them his mitre, cross and staff and sandals with two books for the giving of orders and the consecration of bishops, and a book of 'benedictions covered with cloth of golde'. A cope of 'fyne clothe of Tissue' and a complete set of silver vestments for celebrant, deacon and subdeacon were given by him, as well as hangings for his chantry chapel. He emphasised that he gave these things 'to minystre, celebrate and serve god within the same churche' for the bishop when 'he cometh thider and not otherwyse'.[36] No one individual could put back into the cathedral the quantity of plate which had been taken to the Tower. But some effort could be made to try to ensure that plunder on that scale did not occur again.

There were effectively only two ways of achieving that objective. One was to try to put pressure on the government, at least on the council and the men closest to the king at court, to use their influence to protect the treasures of the church; the other was to remove all that incited ideas of plunder. The problem, however, was that if a courtier was to be bought off with a right of presentation or a favourable lease on cathedral lands, this at once excited interest in the remaining lands. As was to be the case with the monasteries, once any monastic property appeared to be for lease or sale, then there was pressure to release *all* for lease or sale. The fatal mistake would be to fail to follow a carefully planned strategy in the alienation of either offices or lands. It would be easy enough to squander them, but in the long run it might be more rewarding, and serve the long-term interests of the dean and chapter better, if all gifts were made with the good of the cathedral in mind; and this meant, for Longland, the preservation of the offices and dignity of the cathedral and the preservation of the seven sacraments and with them an ordained ministry. That such things would be called into question was not immediately obvious when Longland made a very bold and, at the time, high-handed order. On 18 January 1533, he wrote to the dean and chapter of Lincoln:

> I require you that you suffer not my chapiture sealys to passe of any of my prebends or landys unles ye have eny especiall lettre from me for the same. And that a note may be mayd in your registre of thys my requeste concernyng my landys and prebendys.[37]

It would appear that even as early as 1533, Longland was anxious that the chapter should make no grants without his knowledge. There was nothing especially new in that, but the intention of the order becomes clearer when we examine its consequences. Only one lease is known to have been made of prebendal lands between 1521 and 1532; there may have been some which have left no mark on the records, because leases by the dean and chapter were not fully registered until 1559.[38] Between 1533 and 1545 no less than twenty-two were made of all or some of the fifty-eight prebendal lands. It is clear that Longland's order that he should approve all grants had the effect of their being entered either in the cathedral act book or in his register or in both. We may, therefore, be faced with an optical illusion caused by the failure to register leases in the 1520s. But the question remains why Longland made that particular order at that particular date. It is quite clear that in his leases he followed a similar policy to that which he had pursued with his own lands: where possible his family, or his registrar, or someone of known probity, appears as the recipient. It looks, therefore, as though the bishop was concerned that the prebendal lands were under threat of being confiscated, and that he was anxious that they be leased in such a way that they would be reserved to the chapter for some years to come. We do know that a plan of confiscation was in being by the autumn of 1534,[39] and it seems very likely that gossip at court which preceded the drafting of a formal plan may have reached Longland. In any event, Longland acted as though to avoid confiscation between 1532 and 1545, and a large number of leases were made in that period when the plan for confiscation may have been discussed in court circles and, thereafter, when the dissolution of the monasteries appeared to be bringing it closer to becoming a reality. His leases are dated as follows:

Table 11. *Dates of leases of prebendal lands*[40]

1521–1531	...	(1)
1532–1541	...	14
1542–1545	...	8

In contrast to other bishops, notably those of Bath and Wells, and eventually of Chester, and in contrast to the archbishop of Canterbury, Longland appears to have tried to keep his leases comparatively short and to confine those of more than fifty years to lessees who were of his theological persuasion;[41] his leases were normally for the duration of twenty to forty years, as can be seen from Table 12. The longest of these leases was of Haydor, leased in 1534 with episcopal consent by William Frankleyn, junior, to his father, William Frankleyn, senior, for sixty-one years.[42] The bishop's cousin Anthony Forster was granted the prebendal lands of Stoke in 1544 for fifty years.[43] Edward Longland, a nephew of the bishop, also granted Forster his prebendal lands at South Scarle in 1545 for thirty-one years.[44] Another of the bishop's cousins, John Pate, received in 1533 lands at Thame, Sutton and Buckingham – all were leased for fifty years.[45] Longland's trusted servant and registrar received the lands of Banbury in 1536 for thirty years.[46]

As in the case of the rented episcopal lands, there is no mention in any lease of entry fines, but they were almost certainly paid, though they may not have been very high because the lease was normally at a rent just above the valuation of the prebend given in the *Valor*.[47] The exceptions are easily explained. The prebendal lands of Carlton with Dalby were

Table 12. *Duration of leases of prebendal lands*

1 to 10 years	0
11 to 20 years	1
21 to 30 years	5
31 to 40 years	11
41 to 50 years	3
51 to 60 years	1
61 to 70 years	1

leased by the prebendary William Fleshmonger to Thomas Dymock for £5.6s.8d., and they were valued in 1535 at £14; but Dymock had to find the stipend for two priests for all forty years of the lease.[48] The only other lease at less than the *Valor* was of Stoke in Nottinghamshire, and this went to the ubiquitous Anthony Forster.[49] On occasions some piece of land or unit of accommodation was withheld in the lease, thereby ensuring that the prebendary could, if he so chose, come to his prebend and preach or visit. Edward Longland, in his lease of South Scarle, agreed with the lessee that he 'and his successors shall have at all times one honest chamber to lie in for him and his servants and stable room with hay straw and provender for their three horses by the space of xiiii days and xiiii nights once every year whensoever it shall please them to come thither'.[50] The prebendary of Sutton and Buckingham withheld 'all the mancion place of the sayd parsonage in Buckingham, two courtes, th'orcharde, the ponds, the hacney stable and hey barne next unto the sayd stable'.[51]The lease of the prebend of Dunham was to be only of the 'canon's lands', and no house or tenement was involved.[52] Care seems to have been taken in many cases to keep the advowson of the vicarage for the prebendary himself, thereby ensuring that members of the collegiate body were able to appoint vicars of a theological persuasion similar to their own. The advowson was retained at Thame, Stoke, South Scarle, Sleaford, Farendon and Balderton and Cropredy.[53] The advowson was alienated only in one case, that of Haydor, which was the prebend given by son to father.[54]

Longland has been severely criticised by historians for leasing, with the full support of his dean and chapter and the canons of the cathedral, so much prebendal land. The editor of the chapter acts sees Longland as using lands and offices to his own advantage and he is described as 'unscrupulous'.[55] Dr Walker writes of his ill stewardship of the see.[56] But there is clearly another interpretation which can be put on his actions, particularly with regard to the dean and chapter. If prebendal land was leased in large enough quantities and for long enough, there would be little immediate gain to be had by its confiscation. Moreover, it might come up for renewal at a time when England had returned to a more obviously Catholic stance than Cranmer and Cromwell were giving to it in the 1530s. Just as we shall see that monasteries were 'salting away' treasures for the return of happier times, so Longland seems to fight to put all he can beyond the reach of a greedy king or an ambitious minister. Moreover, there is no reason to suppose that just because of his order about the custody of the seal, Longland imposed terms of leasing on (or suggested lessees to) either prebendaries or the dean and chapter. Apart from the lease of Thame, which was by one of his cousins to another, the prebendal leases follow Longland's visitation of 4 September 1533, when he would have had an opportunity to explain to the dean and chapter what he had in mind.

The leasing policy of the dean and chapter when left to their own devices is difficult to reconstruct. Frequently the duration of the lease and the rent were omitted, and the clerk simply recorded the lease and added 'as will appear in the indentures more fully thereupon'.[57] The majority of leases were made for twenty or thirty years or the life of the lessee, and there seems to have been no attempt at all during the period to make very long leases at low rents; the only exception was of a chantry which was leased for over seventy years.[58]

It was one thing to attempt to put out of the king's reach the lucrative prebendal lands, but it was quite another to claim his favour for the cathedral church of Lincoln, particularly after the Lincolnshire rising of 1536, which gave the shire a bad name. Longland seems to have appreciated this fact and to have recognised that he could gain friends at court by granting away for a limited time the advowson of certain prebends, a practice which was usual with parish churches. This could be regarded as a diminution of his own power, but, if done with care, it could achieve other and more desirable objectives. The combined effect of leasing prebendal lands so that the prebendary could not exploit them in any way, taken with the statute of 1529 which allowed priests to hold canonries in plurality provided a vicar was appointed, made the non-residence of prebendaries exceedingly likely. Equally, Longland's insistence on fourteen years in major residence before minor residence could even be requested made the residence of canons in the close rare except for those who were dignitaries of the cathedral or who were old and perhaps infirm. It seemed, therefore, relatively safe to give away the next presentation to a canonry and prebend and still safeguard the close from the cool wind of protestant thinking: few would venture to reside in either the prebends or the close because it had now come to involve such a long commitment. Additionally, if some patronage was given to persons in whom Longland had complete trust there would be a high enough number of conservatives to ensure that tradition was represented in the cathedral.

On a small scale, Longland had begun to make grants of advowson before 1537. He granted away three: those of Caistor in 1531 and of Aylesbury in 1534 to Thomas Boleyn, Earl of Wiltshire, in a mistimed attempt to ingratiate himself with the Boleyn faction at court;[59] the third grant was of Louth which went in 1535 to the king.[60] In 1538 the patronage of Leighton manor was put into Cromwell's hands on the express condition that a suitable priest should be presented and that Richard Layton – the obstinate archdeacon of Buckingham (who had kept from Longland his spiritualities) – was not given the prebend. Exactly the same condition was attached to the gift of the advowson of Ketton to Anthony Knyvet.[61] Other gifts were made to those whose ecclesiastical sympathies he could trust, and they were obviously of value if the recipient outlived the bishop. The ghost of Longland would still walk the cathedral cloister and whisper his condemnations of Martin Luther! He gave the advowson of Sutton in the Marsh to Stephen Gardiner,[62] and advowsons of Biggleswade, Caistor and Norton Episcopi went to his cousins Robyns, Forster, Pate and Beauforeste; the retired dean of Lincoln, George Henneage, received those of Corringham, Haydor and Nassington.[63] Out of fifty-eight possible advowson grants, Longland actually made thirty-two, though some of these were of the same prebend for another turn.[64] This policy kept the active residentiaries conservative and pacified a few courtiers. But Longland made one bad mistake.

The defection of his spoilt nephew, Richard Pate, archdeacon of Lincoln, to the Pope's cause as represented by Reginald Pole, resulted in an attainder being passed against Pate in 1542, and his archdeaconry was then in the king's gift. Unusually he bestowed it on George Henneage, who had already been dean of Lincoln. But Henneage had resigned the deanery in March 1539 for no apparent reason – a full three years before Pate's defection.[65] There is some suspicion that Cromwell 'persuaded him out' on the promise of a future reward, which, in the event, he was not there to give. It is clear that Cromwell wanted the deanery for a more pliant cleric. He seems to have planned a neat device to get the vacant deanery for his own nominee. He wrote to Longland for a prebend for a clerk who would be suitable for the deanery. As it happened, one of very little value was vacant, that of Bedford Minor; and Longland in granting it to whomsoever the king would name as dean debarred himself from any discussion of the matter; he thought it was to go to a certain Dr Day.[66] In fact the prebend and the deanery went to John Taylor, a fellow of Queens', who had become master of St John's College, Cambridge.[67] Not only was Taylor a cantankerous man, but he had strong Protestant leanings and was eventually to be deprived of all his livings by Mary. He was installed personally as dean in August 1539, but he did not go into residence in the close until August 1546, by which time he and the Fellows of St John's were at loggerheads.[68] As dean, he had the patronage of the vicarage of Wirksworth in Derbyshire, and he showed his ecclesiastical sympathies in granting it away to the one known Protestant patron in the diocese, Charles, Duke of Suffolk.[69] The next living which came his way was that of Rushden in Hertfordshire. He gave it to Richard Cox, the famous Marian exile and ultimately bishop of Ely.[70] The bishop was impotent to stop him, though it could be that his stringent ruling on major residence, which was the product of his visitation carried out a mere two months after Taylor's admission to the deanery, was a fierce attempt to keep Taylor out of the close.[71]

Longland could not keep out of his cathedral all signs of change. In 1540–1 the chapter purchased Bibles for its churches of Gosberton, Alesby and St Nicholas, Newport, at the sum of 6s.8d. each, and two copies were purchased for the cathedral itself for 26s.[72] In 1542 Longland issued an order to the dean and chapter and to all rectors, vicars and chaplains of his diocese to read the Scripture, and for the chapter clergy to be present at its reading on Monday, Wednesday and Friday of each week.[73] He did not live to see the dissolution of the chantries, though some had ceased to function in his time. Though the certificates which followed the first act of dissolution do not survive for Lincolnshire, it may be assumed that, within the cathedral as well as outside it, many had ceased to function. In any event, when the commissioners for the *Valor* came to Lincoln cathedral, they found fifty-three chantry priests serving some thirty-six foundations. In 1548, when the commissioners looked into the chantries and how they were financed, they found a mere seventeen chantry priests left in the cathedral serving eleven foundations. It is no accident that those which survived longest were the best endowed: the Burghersh and Cantilupe chantries could pay their priests well over £7;[74] the works chantry and John of Gaunt's chantry, both of which had disappeared, could only provide just over £4 and £6 respectively.[75] It is highly dubious to connect the disappearance of chantries solely with a disillusionment with prayer for the dead or a disbelief in purgatory.[76] The *economic* reasons for dissolution were very great and in some cases overwhelming: in the 1540s, when the full force of inflation was beginning to be felt, it was impossible to live on a salary of £5 or less without any additional benefits in kind; nearly all of the Lincolnshire chantries which disappeared between the making of the *Valor* and the 1548 commission can be shown to have been under £6. Chantries at Normanby, Fulstow, Croft, Belchford and Stamford were all valued at less than £5 and all gave up.[77] The reasons which account for the survival or disappearance of any individual chantry are complicated by the possible possession of private means by its cantarist, but it is also clear, if we look at the secular colleges in the diocese, that intimidation as well as financial difficulty played their part in bringing a foundation to an end.

The secular colleges tended to be treated like the monasteries by the commissioners for the suppression, and when a pension, usually of £6, was offered to inmates who would surrender the foundation to the crown, the pressure to give up was considerable. The ownership of the estates with which Cotterstock was endowed was called into question and it surrendered in 1539, and the colleges of Higham Ferrars and Fotheringhay followed in 1542 and 1547 respectively; in both the emoluments of the fellows were £7 and verging on the inadequate.[78] We do not know why Tattershall surrendered in February 1545, but it was well before the new dean, who may have disapproved of its foundation, took up residence.[79] Ironically, the longest lasting of the colleges was Newarke. It did not cease to exist until Easter 1548 in spite of considerable pressure to capitulate earlier.[80] No chantry or collegiate foundation is known to have ceased either because it could not give allegiance to Henry as supreme head or because it expressed a disillusionment with its purpose which caused a conscientious revolt. In this the colleges differed from the monasteries. Newarke also survived the smear campaign which the royal visitors attempted to conduct against it. It did so less because of the intrinsic virtues of the college than because of the inept criticism of the visitors.

The notorious Richard Layton visited Newarke and he thought that the hospital was well kept, but that the canons were exceptionally taciturn. He reckoned the abbot was honest, but how, in the conspiracy of silence that surrounded him, he even formed that conclusion, we are not told. He planned to get the canons to talk by objecting against them buggery and adultery.[81] In 1538, just over two years later, when the college was visited by Anthony Draycott, vicar general to the bishop, there was evidence enough of a neglect of the offices, of women being received without the permission of the dean, and of hospitality being lacking – but in all the troubled history of that college, there was never a suggestion of buggery or adultery. Layton was on the wrong track altogether; he should have objected against the canons their hunting and drinking and misappropriation of the facilities of the hospital, which though built for the poor was full of their ageing relatives – the offences in fact which run through the history of the fifteenth and sixteenth century college.[82] Layton's gross method allowed the college twelve more years of life.

The college fared better than the monasteries which were visited at the same time, but some of the monasteries had fallen out with the king before his visitors so much as crossed the threshold of the house. The oath which required a sworn statement that 'the bishop of Rome has no greater jurisdiction in England than any other foreign bishop' was asked of the monasteries in the eastern part of the diocese in the summer of 1534.[83] By August the commissioners had moved into Lincolnshire, Leicestershire and Northamptonshire, and by September they were in Buckinghamshire and Oxfordshire.[84] Only two of the religious houses of these counties objected to the oath. The Carthusians of the Isle of Axholme had consulted with their London house and with the superior of their house at Beauvale about the supremacy. All three superiors took the same line: after asking for an exemption from the oath, they were refused and had to take or reject it. They rejected it, and after trial in Westminster Hall in April they were executed at Tyburn in May 1535 by the barbaric method of hanging, drawing and quartering.[85] The Axholme house did not follow their superior, but there was at least one monk in the diocese who thought the Carthusian priors were right in their witness. He was the abbot of the Cistercian house of Woburn in Bedfordshire. Originally he had taken the oath, as had his brothers, but in 1538 he became sick, and when the pain grew intolerable it exacted from him the confession that he wished he had died with the Carthusians. Examinations were conducted in the house in May 1538, and it seems clear that the abbot and others, though they prayed for the king as supreme head of the church, had read a book entitled *De Potestate Petri* which they had caused to have copied. Witnesses said that the abbot in his illness had cried out that he wished God would take him out of the world and that he had died with the good men who had suffered heretofore. But they said 'he neither spake that it grieved his conscience nother [*sic*] of the Pope'.[86] One of his monks had said 'neither thou, nor yet any of us shall do well as long as we forsake our head of the church, the Pope'.[87] Another monk said he had heard the abbot say that the Carthusians and More and Fisher were taken away that 'naughty heretikes may have their swynge'.[88] The abbot himself said that when in his preaching he neglected to declare the king as head of the church he had done so, not of malice 'but for a scrupulous conscience that he then had, considering the long continuance of the bishop of Rome in that trade being, and the sudden mutation thereof'.[89] The abbot had obviously discussed the matter with local clergy of theological repute, and he had been heard to say (and admitted it) that 'It is an unmerciful thing thus to put down the houses of God and expulse the inhabitants from their living, yea and many one from life too'.[90] He and two monks and the sub-prior were executed in 1538 for such sentiments.[91]

The oath was followed, where the monasteries were concerned, by two things, both of which occurred in 1535: the commission to assess all ecclesiastical property, whether of monastery or church, for first-fruits and tenths (the commission which ultimately produced the *Valor Ecclesiasticus*), and the royal visitation of the monasteries which resulted from Cromwell's vicegerency and which was actually begun before the inhibition of episcopal jurisdiction in October 1535. It was from the wholly false and misleading marriage of the findings of these two separate commissions that the case for the dissolution of the monasteries would be made. The *comperta* of the visitation provided the case against the monasteries contained in the preamble of the act for their dissolution, but it was the *Valor* which provided the first of several valuations which determined whether a house should be dissolved or not.[92] The *comperta* of the royal visitation into the life and standards of observance of the religious have not survived in any number for the monasteries of the diocese; none survives for Lincolnshire, and those for Leicestershire are incomplete.[93] As a result it can be very difficult to find a record of visitation near enough in point of time to that of the royal visitors with which to evaluate the royal findings. Additionally, the royal visitors had access to all houses and the bishop did not. Chicksands, for instance, was exempt from episcopal visitation, and while accepting Professor Knowles' dictum that Richard Layton (the archdeacon of Buckingham) wrote to Cromwell accounts of the monasteries 'with ... racy phrasing and unfailing verve',[94] some of his statements were not so far from the findings of the bishop of Lincoln himself, although Longland was more measured in his tones. Layton reported two nuns at Chicksands as pregnant,[95] but it is clear that his sources of information were not good; he got the tale from 'one old beldame', since the prioress and her nuns shut the door in his face and told him tartly that they were bound by their religion to confess only to their own visitor. At best his story was based on secondhand information. Harrold, a priory of Augustinian canonesses, also had two suspected pregnancies amongst their number. Such things did happen, as the former priory of Littlemore indicated,[96] but if we compare this house with other houses of that order visited in 1530, we find that no such report came from Gracedieu, Goring or Bushmead.[97] It would seem, therefore, that if Layton's report was true, it was nevertheless unusual, and it is clear that Sir John Mordaunt, who had tricked the prioress of Harrold into sealing a writing in Latin which she did not understand, was probably up to tricking her sisters into answering questions and admitting guilt of indiscretions (also suggested to them in Latin) of which again they had no knowledge.[98]

Layton reported that St Andrew's, Northampton, was in debt, and he mourned the fact that the prior was so good![99] The Leicestershire house of Garendon, which was said by Leigh and Layton to have five inmates noted as sodomites, one religious allegedly with ten boys,[100] seems to betray a vivid imagination on the part of the visitors: four months later the monks were described as being of 'good conversacion and (they) all desyre ... to continue in ther religion'.[101] The Augustinian nuns of Gracedieu were visited by the vicar general in 1528;[102] their unanimous verdict of '*omnia bene*' looks a trifle suspicious, but it is hard to see how the commissioners were so certain in February 1536 that two nuns were incontinent and had produced (*pepererunt*) young, when a mere four months later there was no gossip of this kind and, among the nuns, simply a desire to continue within the religious life and at the same house.[103]

John Tregonwell, who visited the houses in the diocese in Oxfordshire and Buckinghamshire, reported well on Godstow, and found in Eynsham a 'raw sort' of religious who were guilty of every kind of offence, including '*etiam crimen pessimum*', but he noted that they had been punished by the ordinary and that the abbot, though virtuous, had abandoned the unequal struggle of correcting his brethren.[104] He had good things to say of Chacombe where there was a new prior 'well learned in Holy Scripture'; he was Henry Austen, who had succeeded Thomas Saunder in 1534. But his view of the house differed not at all from that of the vicar general in 1530.[105] He found the nuns of Catesby 'free from suspicion' but he could not resist a jibe at Longland's expense. He reported that he found the house 'under the jurisdiction of the bishop of Lincoln, by usurpation, I suppose, as the order has always been exempt'. At Bicester he discovered that a monk had run away as a result of having been punished for incontinence, but basically the prior looked after his brethren well.[106] The same prior had been at the helm when in 1530 the house had been visited by the vicar general, but the signs of fabric decay on an extensive scale which were drawn to the vicar general's attention had obviously passed unnoticed or been ignored by the royal visitor – unless, of course, money had been found in the intervening years to rebuild.[107]

Yet even if Tregonwell was more reliable than Layton, in the event the reports of neither mattered. The injunctions which the King gave to the monasteries in 1535 were not made to any *individual* house, as the injunctions of former bishops had been; they were given to *all* houses, and their impact on the Augustinians of de la Pré, Leicester, who drank much and kept greyhounds with which to hunt,[108] and on the canons of Dorchester, would be startling enough. In place of the illicit book on fishing at Dorchester, Holy Scripture was to be read,[109] and the bloodstock at Leicester was likely to be seriously affected by the requirement that no monk or religious brother leave the enclosure. The disguise of Roger Palmer of Great Missenden, which he put on to hide his monastic profession, would now be more than ever necessary. How would he or the abbot reach the warmth of Margaret Bishop's bed, in the light of the visitor's injunctions to adhere strictly to the limits of enclosure? Margaret's own chances of climbing the fences of the monastery were similarly limited. Monasteries were to have one gate, and Dorchester villagers would have to find other ways of reaching the mill.

The injunctions were clearly meant for male rather than for female religious but they were well beyond the competence of either. As a result, Cromwell received a lot of letters pleading for the mitigation of one or more of the injunctions. The cries of the abbot of Osney were amongst them: how could he, he asked, visit monastic property if he was confined to his monastery; and if that argument did not melt the vicegerent's heart, what about his health? For, he added, 'Osney stondith verye lowe all combrid with waters where in youth I was notte brought uppe but was brought uppe in a holesome grounde, the kinges grace college which sometymes was called the kinges monasterye of Saynt Frydeswide, where if I shuld contynuallye nowe in my Age be constrayned to tarye allwayes in Osney hit wold no Dowte abbreviate my lyffe and be my utter confusion.'[110]

But the findings of the visitors did not matter for another reason. The preamble of the Act of Suppression admittedly made use in the most generalised possible way of the so-called *comperta* of the royal visitation, and it therefore dwells on the decline in numbers of the religious, their neglected lands, and 'unthrifty and carnal abominable living' with 'yet nevertheless little or none amendment it hitherto had, but their vicious living shamelessly increases and augments'. In contrast the king desired the 'total extirping and destruction of sin'. The king was concerned with the vices of the religious, and not his own; but the conclusion reached by the statute was not that there should be a dissolution of the most corrupt houses but that the king should have and enjoy all monasteries with their lands 'tenements, rents, tithes, portions below the value of £200'.[111]

That value and virtue, and rents and religion, were not the same thing, and that meticulous observance might be found in the poorest of houses is the contradiction which runs right through the statute. Suppression was to be by wealth alone, and the assessment placed on a house by the commissioners for first-fruits and tenths and found in the *Valor* was to be checked and re-examined.[112] A large number of the houses in the diocese of Lincoln were in danger.

If we work from the *Valor*, which tended to underestimate the demesne, there were three houses in Bedfordshire under £200 and six over that value. In Buckinghamshire eight were below the line and one house only was above it; in Huntingdonshire five were below £200 and two above it; in Leicestershire eight were below and four above; in Lincolnshire thirty-nine were below and eleven above; in Northamptonshire seven were below and five above; and in Oxfordshire eight were below and four above the all-important value. In the diocese as a whole seventy-eight houses were threatened with dissolution and thirty-three seemed to be safe.[113] Among the so-called 'safe' houses which had incomes of more than £200 were houses which were amongst the worst in the diocese and which Longland had been at pains to visit and reform himself; yet he had achieved no real sign of a massive change of heart.

The means by which a house continued to exist even though it should have been dissolved were often highly dubious. The prioress of Legbourne near Louth wrote to Cromwell in some bewilderment; she says:

> whereas we doo here that a grete nombre of abbyes shalbe punysshid, subprest, and put downe, bicause of theire myslyvyng, and that all abbyes and pryoryes under the value of cc^{li} be at oure moste noble prynces pleasure to subpresse and put downe, yet it may pleas youre goodness we trust in God ye shall here no compleyntes agaynst us nother in oure lyvyng nor hospitalitie kepyng. In

consideracion whereof, if it may please youre goodness in oure great necessitie to be a meane and sewter for youre owne powre pryory, that it may be preserved and stond... We have noon othir comfort nor refuge but oonly unto youre goodenes.[114]

The house was dissolved in the autumn of 1536.[115] Even though the visitors found a house in good order, it was dissolved. Catesby, according to the commissioners for Northamptonshire,

we ffounde in verry perfett order, the priores a sure, wyse, discrete and very relygyous and devoute and with as good obedyencye as we have in tyme past seen or belyke shall see. The seid howse standyth in sueche a quarter muche to the releff off the kynges people, and his graces pore subjectes their lykewyse mooche relewed... Wherefor yf yt shulde please the kynges highnesse to have eny remorse that eny suche relygous house shall stande, we thynke his grace cannot appoint eny house more mete to shew his most gracious charities and pitey one than one [sic] the said howse of Catesby.[116]

So rare a report, which tallies so well with that of the bishop's vicar general in 1530,[117] did not win the house a reprieve. The commissioners were simply accused of bribery, or as they said 'itt was like that we had receyved rewardes'.[118] Chacombe was not spared, though not found wanting,[119] and even a plea by Cranmer to spare the house of Epworth in the Isle of Axholme only met with favour beoause it was over the value anyway.[120] Catesby and Chacombe were dissolved in July 1536.[121]

Yet certain houses were saved: in Lincolnshire, of the thirty-nine houses threatened with suppression, only about twenty were suppressed.[122] Stixwold, a Cisterican house of nuns, was suppressed, only to be refounded.[123] Kyme bought itself out of immediate disaster.[124] Two monasteries fell to the king because of the treasonable participation of the superiors in the Lincolnshire rebellion in 1536, those of Barlings and Kirkstead,[125] but most of the worst houses from the point of view of monastic observance stayed. The prolonged attempt to bring a vestige of adherence to the rule in the monasteries of Leicester, Missenden, Dorchester, Nun Cotham and Thame was apparently to continue, and the visitor, be he royal or episcopal, would have the added problem that their numbers were increased by the arrival from dissolved houses of those who wished to continue the religious life.

It was perhaps because he knew this all too well that Longland, normally so ready to lift his pen, particularly when his jurisdiction was inhibited, remained uncharacteristically silent during the dissolution. He is not known to have pleaded for any single house. Either he knew it was useless to do so, or, in the light of his own attempts at reform, he recognised that monasticism as represented in his diocese was sick unto death. He had held up to the monks of Westminster the model of the virtuous religious and had found few in the diocese who would follow his advice:

> What greater scandal or disgrace can there be than that men, consecrated and bound by solemn vows to God alone and divine workship, should buy in the open market meats, fish and all manner of other dainties for the table and dispense their purchases at home? ... You must keep the chosen way, you must walk among the snakes and scorpions of this world with your loins girt, your feet shod and your staff in your hand, you must make your way through the snares and poisons of the world, that having a pure conscience, truly saying with the psalmist 'Lord, I have loved the habitation of thy house and the place where thy honour dwelleth', 'One thing have I desired of thee, that I will seek after, that I may well in the house of the Lord all the days of life', you may come at last to those sweet waters of Jordan, enter that land of Promise and ascend to the house of the Lord.[126]

Longland knew few in the houses of Thame, Dorchester, De la Pré, Leicester, or Missenden who had exhibited any sign at all that they understood this message, or were prepared to enact it.

As the dissolution of the monasteries moved from being a matter of implementing the act of 1536 to becoming a matter of voluntarily surrendering and so receiving a pension, Longland would come to recognise that so comprehensive a dissolution would have some severely practical consequences for individuals and for the diocese as a whole.

The immediate problem was one of personnel. Monks and nuns who had chosen not to go to another house but to receive capacities, or the right to be considered as seculars, had to find employment, and that meant, before pensions were introduced, employment in competition with the seculars. Before 1538, it was normally only the superior of a house who received a pension, and thereafter one group of ex-religious, the friars, did not receive them. Mr Hodgett has estimated that in the diocese of Lincoln after 1541 there were some 277 friars or ex-religious without a pension, and about 429 who had got pensions because their houses were dissolved after 1538.[127] For those 277 there was the problem of livelihood and the hostility which they encountered because of the threat they posed to an already competitive benefice market. The friars were in particular trouble, as one agent pointed out to Cromwell after the suppression of some twenty houses in Grantham, Grimsby and Hull. He asked Cromwell 'to be good lorde for the pore ffreyrs capacytes; they be very pore and can have lytyll serves withowt ther capacytes. The byschoyppys and curettes be very hard to them withowtt they have ther capacytes.'[128]

In contrast, those who belonged to the houses which were dissolved after 1538 had not only a small income which the pension provided, but they had also had time to use the patronage and in certain cases the wealth of a house for their own purpose. At Launde the visitor noticed that the 'howshold stuf was sold and coveyed away ... And as concernyng the plate, the prior told me that he made hit awey a good whyll agoo to the intent to have redemyd his howse... And as for horsez, he told me that he had gyven to dyvers of hys servauntes every of them a geldyng'.[129]

The advowson of monasteries could also be used to place monks before the dissolution of the house. William Asewell, who was a monk of St Albans, was presented by Thomas Manningham to the rectory of Caldecote in 1540; the presentation by Manningham was on a grant from his old house.[130] Other grants helped monks of the same order if not the same house: Thomas Colson, who was formerly prior of Merton, was presented by the prior and convent of Dunstable to the vicarage of Pulloxhill in1539.[131] In 1540 eighteen ex-religious were presented to benefices. But they remained a fortunate few, and at no time did the religious gain a large share of benefices[132] (see Graph 2). The female religious were hardest hit. They were not at first permitted to marry, and they had much smaller pensions than the men: 60 per cent of them had £2 per annum or less, and 28 per cent of them had between £2 and £5. After 1549 they were allowed to get married; five out of seven of the nuns of Sixhills married, and some ex-religious set up house together.[133] In that event there was some possibility of continuing at least the offices and prayer life of a religious, though the full richness of community life was absent. Longland seems to have encouraged this attitude. In May 1540 he licensed Agnes Jordan, recently abbess of Syon, to have holy offices and mass celebrated by suitable chaplains in an oratory or chapel within the manor of Southland in the parish of Denham.[134]

Obviously some ex-religious acted as curates or, for a while, chantry priests. These are hard to trace because a pension and a cure were incompatible in most cases. Occasionally, however, a scribe notes the former house of a curate if he is an ex-religious. In the deanery of St Ives there were some sixteen curates or chantry priests.[135] Two incumbents in the deanery were ex-religious, one from Huntingdon and one from Leicester.[136] Three curates appear to have been ex-religious; Ralph Cockes, formerly of Wroxton, was a curate at Houghton,[137] Thomas

Felde of Ramsey held Wyton,[138] a chapel of Houghton, and John Nicolles was a curate of Somersham.[139] Returns for the deanery of Huntingdon are incomplete, but ex-religious are recorded as pensioners in three curacies out of four.[140] It is rare to find this sort of information about the lower clergy of the diocese, but obviously the ex-religious and ex-chantry priests were an asset as ordinations declined, and as the number of ordained priests became insufficient to minister to the parishes of the diocese, let alone – had they continued – the chantries. The Protestantism and avarice of the court which first dislodged the monasteries and then the chantries also made possible the employment of some of their former inmates because it took such a toll of the aspirants to the priesthood.[141]

The fate of the monastic lands lies beyond the scope of this study, but one aspect of their alienation concerns us. Frequently the monasteries had appropriated for their perpetual use the greater tithes of a parish and had let the cure be served by a vicar, often on a fixed stipend, or receiving other, lesser, tithes. It is estimated that 648 of the rectories of the diocese of Lincoln were appropriated in 1535.[142] The number represents about one third of the parishes of the diocese. Tithe, never popular, ceased to have any meaning at all when it was no longer paid to the church in its institutionalised form. But one of the results of the dissolution and the subsequent grants and sales of monastic lands was that tithe became due to the laymen who now controlled monastic estates. We have noted that there was a dramatic increase in the tithe cases in the ecclesiastical courts, a phenomenon not confined to the diocese of Lincoln.[143] It would seem that the lay farmer who took greater tithe for lay and absentee landlords had some difficulty in getting his dues just as the monasteries had before him. But in the discrediting of tithe, all the clergy were involved – especially the rector for whom it was part of his stipend. The transfer of appropriation as part of the monastic lands threatened the incomes of parochial clergy who were, for other reasons, already in financial difficulties.[144]

As, in the first years of his episcopate, Longland was to devote the main thrust of his time and effort to the religious and his cathedral church, so also in the second decade he had to spend part of it in securing his authority as diocesan. In effect this meant that he could not visit the monasteries until 1537 when his licence to visit was returned, and by that time some of them had disappeared. But he is not to be found in these years pleading the cause of a given house. He seems to have realised that the effort of his former years was largely wasted and that if he was to use his hard-won diocesan authority to any advantage, he had to turn his attention to the parishes and to the rising tide of heresy at court.

3. THE SECULAR CLERGY

Residence

No one single statute passed by the Reformation Parliament (with the possible exception of the Act for First-fruits and Tenths) of itself changed the social and economic position of the secular clergy. But taken as a whole there were few acts relating to the church which did not in some way affect the parochial clergy. Change came upon them gradually, but the mark left by the legislation of Parliament on the lives and expectations of priests and intending priests was very considerable.

In the very first session of the Reformation Parliament an act was passed with the intention of limiting pluralism and non-residence. Absenteeism seemed in the eyes of members of the House of Commons to affect the quality of preaching and teaching within a parish, the maintenance of hospitality and the supervision of curates. There is no reason to suppose, as did the bishop of Rochester, that Parliament had become infected with heresy to be interested in such matters.[1] Preaching was seen to be particularly important not only to those who wished to begin a reformation but to those who wanted to prevent one. In the middle ages, clerks had preached quarterly, in theory if not in practice, but before the arrival of the printing press it was not altogether likely that the preaching of the priest or his curate would be criticised or questioned by his parishioners. He shared with them a common lack of knowledge and common difficulty in remedying ignorance by adequate schooling.[2] But by 1530 this assumption of popular ignorance and of the priest being only a little better informed than his congregation was breaking down. Not only were there more schools, but there was an ever increasing volume of works in the vernacular, many of which were aimed at increasing the knowledge and piety of the laity.[3] It was in these circumstances that the Commons, in particular, saw that there was something to fear: a curate might be too ignorant to be able to combat heresy if he confronted it in a parishioner who had read the works of Tyndale or even Luther – a danger clearly perceived by the king in his proclamations banning such books, and by convocation.[4] But if it was easy to see the dangers of absenteeism, it was also difficult to prevent it.

Parliament could not enact that there should be no pluralism and that all priests should reside, for the simple reason that the incomes of royal servants and episcopal officers, to say nothing of the stewards and the chaplains of the gentry and aristocracy, were paid largely from parishes to which they gave no attention or at best a yearly visit. The Houses of Parliament, therefore, enacted that clerks should normally have only one benefice with cure of souls. But there were exceptions. Parishes which were worth less than £8 could be held in plurality, and clerks who already possessed more than one benefice could keep four of them; priests serving at the court, and chaplains to specified dignitaries, might have two benefices, and the privilege of non-residence was extended to pilgrims, servants of the king who were abroad, scholars at the universities, and some chaplains. Cathedral dignitaries might hold another benefice in addition to the canonry or prebend assigned them, but no emolument should be taken by the beneficed for singing requiems.

The concerns of the Commons, as well as the difficulty of their task, are clearly expressed in the other clauses of the act. The house of a parson or vicar, for instance, must be well maintained and 'sufficiently reparell'd', and someone should be charged with serving the cure and dispensing hospitality.[5] Reforms of this kind had been attempted before, and the question which confronted reformers in this area was whether they would be enforceable: so many clerks could and did claim legitimate exemption from the operation of an act limiting non-residence and pluralism that the level of absenteeism might remain completely unaffected by legislation designed to curb it.[6] One way or another, a whole host of clerks could excuse themselves from the feast – from residence – and clerks from the highways and byways were compelled to come in and take their places. The question raised by the parliamentary legislation of 1529 was whether it would be any more successful than its precursors.

The Reformation Parliament itself was undeterred by past failure in this area, but the reality of the obstacles to limiting pluralism and absenteeism becomes apparent if we look at the effect of their legislation in the diocese of Lincoln. In the year following the act, sufficient evidence survives for the archdeaconries of Bedford, Buckingham, Oxford, Huntingdon and Lincoln to suggest that there was an immediate decline in non-residence and pluralism in the early 1530s.[7] The rate of the decline, and perhaps its causes, vary considerably from archdeaconry to archdeaconry, and 'non-residence' did not denote the same problem in all areas. The areas in closest proximity to London or the universities of

Oxford and Cambridge sustained pluralists who may also be classed as non-residents or absentees, but who might nevertheless hear confessions at Easter, preach, and exercise a notional supervision over the curate. Absolute absenteeism or insufficient residence to benefit the parish in any way at all was clearly the worst fate for the parish.

In Lancashire, Dr Haigh has shown that before 1520 the absenteeism of the clergy was lower than that prevalent in the Lincoln diocese, but he shows also that it was increasing and that by 1520 it had reached 30% and by 1550 33%.[8] A similar pattern of increase has been suggested from the subsidy returns of 1526 for the diocese of Lincoln,[9] but the overall increase did not continue at an equal rate (and in some cases did not continue at any rate at all) in the diocese in the years subsequent upon the 1529 act. There are problems in estimating the exact rate of increase or decrease following the act because the evidence for each archdeaconry is not always of the same kind, or of the exactly similar date; and sometimes in any one archdeaconry parishes are left out which reappear in a later record. This is clearly true of the episcopal visitation of the archdeaconry of Bedford in 1530 which reported only one non-resident, a figure which is highly unlikely to represent the real total. In these circumstances the rate of non-residence and absenteeism is best represented as a percentage of the parishes from which a return was made, by archdeaconry. If this strategy is adopted a decline in non-residence is noticeable in all the archdeaconries from which we have evidence after 1530, followed by an increase which varies in chronology and size.

Table 13. *Parishes reporting non-residents as percentage of parishes visited*

Archdeaconry	1518[10]	1530–3[11]	1540[12]	1543[13]
Oxford	35%	9.7%	15.8%	no longer in diocese
Lincoln	19.6%	15.4%	no record	no record
Huntingdon	22%	16.6%	26%	26.5%
Bedford	14.8%	0.95%	14.8%	9.6%
Buckingham	25%	6.6%	30%	17%

The archdeaconries of Huntingdon, Bedford and Buckingham furnish us with the best evidence of absenteeism, but that of Lincoln actually gives more details about the effects on the parish and the reasons which allowed the incumbent not to reside at all. These reasons are also best given in tabular form – Table 14 (pp. 116–17).[14] It is immediately obvious that the reasons for absenteeism varied between archdeaconries, and that individual archdeaconries also supported more absentees with one reason for absence rather than another. By 1543 royal and episcopal servants were heavily represented in Huntingdon; pluralists who gave no specific reason for their pluralism accounted for a lot of non-residence in Lincoln, while the number of non-resident incumbents in Oxford livings declined between 1518 and 1540. What are the factors at work, over and above the actual reasons given, which help to explain the differing pattern of non-residence?

Many of the reasons defy explanation as they are the result of the preference of individuals who decided to live in one parish rather than another. John Rede, for instance, rector of Broughton Astley in Leicestershire, preferred to reside in Derby; John Denham, rector of North Kilworth, resided in his parish of Barnack, and the rector of Market Bosworth, Maurice Adams, was at Wells.[15] The individual reasons which determined the residence of a pluralist in one rather than another of his livings were usually a matter of taste, but the demands of other commitments were also important. Livings near London were sought after, and this may account for the low rate of non-residence in the diocese of Canterbury in 1538–9 (14 per cent).[16] Similar considerations could apply to the universities. Morgan Johns preferred to reside at St Giles Northgate rather than Dunton in Buckinghamshire while he studied, but thereafter his native Wales claimed him.[17] If these considerations had been the only ones in operation we would have expected a lower rate of non-residence in Oxford and Huntingdon due to their proximity to the universities than in the other archdeaconries. In reality the reverse is true, and remained so, and this may be explained by the value of benefices in those areas. The archdeaconry of Huntingdon had the largest number of benefices valued at over £20 of any archdeaconry in the diocese, and this probably accounts for the fact that, in spite of its proximity to Cambridge, the level of non-residence within it remained high. Its livings were the besought rewards for royal and episcopal service.

The act of 1529 intensified this pressure on the more valuable benefices. If pluralism were limited to two or three livings, depending on the cause of dispensation, then it was important that these livings yield to the recipient an income comparable to that which he had enjoyed when a greater number of livings were available to him. The long term tendency of the act was to tie the most valuable livings to pluralism and in some cases absenteeism, leaving the latter in the perpetual care of a curate. Such livings owed their value, in the case of rectories, usually to their glebe land, and the resentment of the parish against the farmer of the

Table 14. *Specific reasons for non-residence as a percentage of all reasons for non-residence, by parish*

	Royal service	Not given	Pluralist	Episcopal diocesan service	Scholar–university	Religious	Pilgrim-age	Aged or infirm	Total non-resident
1518									
Oxford	2	25	10	3	6	2	0	1	49
Lincoln	5	22	13	0	4	2	0	0	46
Buckingham	1	16	14	3	3	1	0	0	38
Bedford	0	19	8	0	1	0	0	0	18
Huntingdon	2	15	7	2	4	1	1	0	32
Total	10	87	52	8	18	6	1	1	185
%age of total non-resident parishes	5.4%	47.5%	28.1%	4.4%	9.8%	3.3%	0.54%	0.54%	99.58%
1530–3									
Oxford	2	6	7	0	1	0	0	0	16
Lincoln	8	12	13	5	7	0	0	0	45
Buckingham	0	5	0	0	0	0	0	0	5
Bedford	0	1	0	0	0	0	0	0	1
Huntingdon	3	5	5	1	0	0	0	0	14
Total	13	29	25	6	8	0	0	0	81
%age of total non-resident parishes	16%	36%	31%	7.4%	9.9%	0%	0%	0%	100.3%

1540									
Oxford	4	1	19	3	2	0	0	0	29
Lincoln				NO RECORD					
Buckingham	8	2	11	1	1	0	0	0	23
Bedford	6	3	9	0	0	0	0	0	18
Huntingdon	11	0	14	2	5	0	0	0	32
Total	29	6	53	6	8	0	0	0	102
%age of total non-resident parishes	28.4%	5.9%	52%	5.9%	7.85%	0%	0%	0%	100%
1543									
Oxford				OUT OF DIOCESE					
Lincoln				NO RECORD					
Buckingham	7	1	9	5	4	0	0	0	26
Bedford	5	2	14	0	3	0	0	0	24
Huntingdon	11	6	10	6	3	0	0	2	38
Total	23	9	33	11	10	0	0	2	88
%age of total non-resident parishes	26.1%	10.2%	37.5%	12.5%	11.4%	0%	0%	2.3%	100%

Sources: *LR.S., 35* L.A.O., Vj. 11, Vj. 12, Vij. 1

land who would also collect the parish tithe might be very great. This was not a wholly new phenomenon,[18] but the act gave to the fight for the rich benefice a new urgency and a possible source of continual friction.[19]

A further effect of the act was to increase the occasions when the non-resident was bound himself or by proxy to give the reason for his absenteeism. It is noticeable that by 1540 servants of the crown or chaplains to a grandee (specified in the act) were taking a larger share of the parishes than they had in 1518–19 or in 1530. Even the poorer archdeaconry of Bedford had parishes which sustained their share of courtier priests: Newnham was held by a chaplain to Lord Bray.[20] Dean, which was worth over £33,[21] went to one of the Duke of Suffolk's chaplains, Henry Slyfield, who was not resident and therefore unlikely to be able to spread his patron's Protestant sympathies.[22] The Lord Chancellor's chaplain held Shillington, valued at over £85.[23] Roger Dyngley, who was a doctor of theology, was vicar of Banbury and rector of Conington;[24] he was brought to Cromwell's notice for his papal leanings but he cannot have 'vexed his parishioners', as he was alleged to have done, very often, as he was said to be a non-resident and in the royal service.[25] It looks as though his parishioners of Conington, which had sustained a non-resident for ten years, were making trouble in the hope of getting a resident incumbent. It was worth more than £16, and on Dyngley's death the patronage of it passed to the bishop. As it was one of the wealthier parishes, he gave it to one of his chaplains, also a non-resident.[26] Long term non-residence, which had been a problem on a limited scale before 1520, now threatened to be the permanent fate of a wealthy parish.[27]

The act had recognised that one parish of £8 was insufficient to live on, and discounted from its operation the first benefice a priest received if it was below that value. It followed that one benefice of less than £8 could be combined with another of any value provided that the poor benefice was the first to be received. In the archdeaconry of Huntingdon, one fifth of those said to be pluralists held livings below £8.[28] But such combinations of poor with wealthier livings tended to be exceptional. This was important to the lower clergy, as Dr Zell has suggested, and as all the Lincoln evidence confirms, because a living brought independence even if its stipend was small. Moreover, the possession of a living of this kind still left the incumbent free to hunt for another.[29] This would take time while the competition continued to be severe, but, as we shall see, it eased, and put poorer clergy in a better position.

Certain pluralists were left untouched by the act: those who had acquired their livings before the statute were allowed to keep four of them. Robert Appulby had acquired Hamerton in 1517 and was able to keep it, in spite of having another parish acquired before the act;[30] Thomas Horley held Graveley, and he too combined it with other livings.[31] By 1543, in the archdeaconry of Huntingdon, of the ten priests who were said to be pluralists, no less than four had gained their livings prior to the act. The full effects of the statutory limits placed on pluralism were therefore unlikely to be felt until the generation of clergy who had acquired livings before 1529 had died out. Some of them may have been fortunate enough to get a benefice in their twenties, and there then was a possibility that they would keep it until the reign of Elizabeth, unless marriage, or convictions which brought upon them the attention of the government, intervened.[32]

In one area of the thorny field of pluralism, the act seems to have succeeded in its intention, though that was because bishops, the faculty office, and perhaps patrons co-operated. The non-residence of vicars had always been regarded as highly exceptional but it had nevertheless occurred, particularly in the case of wealthy vicarages valued at £20 or more.[33] The vicarages of Burford and Charlbury in Oxford, or of Long Sutton in Lincolnshire, were glittering enough prizes to have had an intermittent history of non-residence.[34] By 1543 things were changing. Between 1518 and 1519, in the archdeaconries of Huntingdon, Buckingham, Bedford, Oxford and Lincoln, 18 per cent of all non-residents were vicars; between 1530 and 1533 only 11 per cent of all non-residents were vicars; by 1540 the percentage had again risen to 12.6 per cent, but in 1543 it was 10.2 per cent.[35] It is of course highly doubtful whether a resident vicar was any better than a resident curate acting for him. But as the pressure came for the official faith to be defended – whether this defence took the form of proclaiming the royal supremacy or keeping registers of births, deaths and marriages – a higher and higher premium was put on education, and in areas where the incumbent was of some influence, especially in towns or large country parishes, graduates might be an asset.

Graduates were always prone to be non-resident. They were more likely than others to be wanted for royal or episcopal service, or they might be furthering their studies in an attempt to rise to the level of high office. Obviously the actual number of graduates in residence in any one year varied as death removed some and institution admitted others. A very large number of graduates were presented to the livings of the diocese (see Graph 2), but it is often apparent that they would be seen by their parishioners rarely if at all. In Lancashire, Dr Haigh has found that the total of graduate incumbents who were non-resident never fell below 63 per cent in the first half of the sixteenth century.[36] As the need to defend one version of Christianity rather than another became more pressing, this represented a loss of talent which might have dangerous consequences. The diocese of Lincoln was fortunate in having more *resident* graduates than did Lancashire. If we look at the three archdeaconries for which the material is fullest, we find:

Table 15. *Graduate residents and non-residents, 1540–3*[37]

Archdeaconry	Graduate non-residents shown as % of clergy in the archdeaconry	Graduate residents shown as % of clergy in the archdeaconry
Buckingham	8.5%	15.2%
Bedford	12.1%	21.0%
Huntingdon	20.1%	25.9%

These figures suggest that because of the attraction in terms of remuneration and proximity to London, Oxford and Cambridge, which many deaneries in these archdeaconries offered, there were a greater number of resident graduates than there were non-residents. The number of resident graduates was not as low as it was in Lancashire. The explanation is the obvious one: the nearer a living was to a centre of learning or to the capital the greater the possibility of a priest using it as a base from which he worked rather than purely as a source of income. But there may be other explanations as well: an overall increase in the number of graduates coming out of both Oxford and Cambridge was beginning to create an employment problem;[38] graduates increased their numbers of non-residents as well as residents. They had only a 35 per cent share of parishes from which absenteeism was reported in the first two decades of the sixteenth century, but by 1540–3 they had a half share of it in Buckingham and Bedford, and a three quarters share of it in Huntingdon. Graduates were, therefore, increasing their hold on the usual posts, such as government service, episcopal administration and the administration of the university, all of which necessitated a level of non-residence (albeit not a total one if the parish held was near to the main place of work); but graduates were also settling down in the parishes. This was to be of the greatest importance to the progress of the Reformation in the diocese of Lincoln. Resident graduates would prove to be the main support in Longland's defence of his diocese against the inroads of Protestantism. The graduate incumbent was expected to provide the mainstay of the preaching in the diocese, and leading theologians of the universities who had taken to the parishes seem to have furnished Longland with a formidable amount of support in publishing the Six Articles and defending their content.[39]

Ordination, promotion and education

Many of the established landmarks in the progression from acolyte to priest, and ultimately to beneficed priest, changed as a result of the legislation of the 1530s. The cumulative changes represented by the idea of the royal supremacy, in the requirements of residence and in the new assessment and taxation of the clergy, were bound to raise questions about the security not only of benefices valued at under £8 (which might be held in plurality) but also about the opportunities for the unbeneficed. If there was to be a cut back in pluralism, and if the rate of non-residence fell and more priests resided in their livings, then fewer unbeneficed clergy, and fewer curates, would be needed – but there would be a greater opportunity for curates to become beneficed. Equally, from 1536 monks with capacities which enabled them to seek for cures alongside unbeneficed secular clergy swelled the queue of the unbeneficed waiting for the prize of a parish of their own.

Much of the legislation of the 1530s, therefore, put greater and greater pressure on jobs and, at the level of parish *or* curacy, that pressure could be acute. Moreover to cast doubt on the efficacy of masses and intercession for the departed might not only cut down the potential number of jobs, it would also release onto the benefice market yet more needy priests. In such circumstances change, whether towards a return to the *status quo ante* or towards the Protestantism of Geneva, took with it profound social consequences. Protestantism might require the cutting back of jobs; Catholicism did not. Viewed in this light the midway position of the English church by 1536 was putting the clergy, both beneficed and unbeneficed, materially speaking, into a state of anxiety.

Just as the Act for First-fruits and Tenths put a very heavy burden on some, and subsidies made that burden intolerable for others, so the dissolution of the monasteries put a different kind of obstacle in the way of priests or intending priests. The whole basis of the ordination title was changed, and, in a large number of cases, moved from being a matter of making an arrangement with the local monastery to suing for a title from the gentry who had acquired monastic land or suing for one from the court of augmentations. The last monastic title given to an ordinand appears in the ordination lists for February 1540, when John Trewelove gave his title as that of '*dissoluti monasterii de Thame*'.[40] Thereafter ordinands cited a title from the king, from the lands of gentlemen, or from the court of augmentations: James Proctor of the diocese was ordained '*ad titulum quinque marcarum de terris Roberti Cansfeld armigeri*',[41] Former religious with pensions gave titles from the king,[42] and Oswald Slemaker of Banbury gave his title as '*titulum annuitatis sibi concessi ex terris Willelmi Danvers de Banbury*'.[43] How precisely any individual got a title before the dissolution, and whether they were largely legal fictions, since the monastery whose title was cited often appeared to have no further dealings with the priests they promoted, is unknown.[44] But the advantage of the monastic title was that it was usually a local house which obliged. A local boy might even have received rudimentary schooling in the house and would, therefore, have found it easy and natural to ask the superior for a title. It was quite a different matter to ask one of a magnate whom the would-be-ordinand had never seen, or to take on the expensive and laborious process of suing for one either from the court of Augmentations or from the king.[45]

More serious than the change in titles at ordination was the change in patronage. Before 1536, patronage was largely in the hands of the religious orders, though eminent laymen had a good deal of it. The religious were accessible, and even if they did not have a living vacant they had means of recording aspirants for livings; and they were not, of course, peripatetic. No expensive suit was needed only to receive a negative answer. The dissolution of the monasteries changed this, and a considerable share of the patronage of the diocese went to the king. How great the change was, is apparent in Table 16.[46]

The transfer of power to the king, although it was temporary, since he tended to exchange advowsons for episcopal manors, represented in practical terms the need for a suit to be made at court for a living, either in person or by letter. Moreover, the king was apt to give beneficies either to those who had already served him well or to those from whom he expected future service. In effect this profited the graduate and those likely to be non-resident at the expense of the non-graduate who might lack some of the expertise but not necessarily the pastoral skills which the village would require. The religious had some benefices at their disposal after 1536 because all had not succumbed to the pressure to

Table 16. *Patrons of incumbents shown as a percentage of all patrons*

Patron	Church	1521–Dec. 1535	1536–May 1547
King	rectories	4.7%	12.7%
	vicarages	0.3%	8.7%
Laymen	rectories	31.7%	38.9%
	vicarages	4.1%	16.1%
Churchmen	rectories	6.5%	5.6%
	vicarages	5.9%	3.8%
Corporations	rectories	3.2%	2.7%
	vicarages	2.9%	2.3%
Religious	rectories	15.2%	3.8%
	vicarages	25.4%	5.0%
Not given		0.1%	0.1%

surrender even as late as 1539. During the intervening years they could, if they chose, use their patronage to benefit one of their own number, either by advancing him into a living or by giving the living to the chaplain of an important layman who would help the inmates of the house at a later date. Very few of the religious orders were farsighted enough or worldly wise enough to adopt either policy. Of the Augustinians, Leicester gave Lilbourne, a wealthy parish, to a former Dominican in 1538; though there were four other vacancies between 1536 and 1539, this was the only presentation they made to benefit a fellow religious.[47] Of the three vacancies which Marton had at its disposal, one was given to a royal chaplain but the remaining two do not appear to have gone to ex-religious.[48] Newnham had four vacancies but used none in this way. The Benedictines were equally unaware of the needs of their brother religious; Crowland, Peterborough and Westminster had opportunities to help, but, though identification of ex-religious is difficult, it would appear that their patronage was not used for their own number. St Albans, in 1539, presented Campton in Bedfordshire to a Benedictine of Norwich who had become abbot of St Albans, but no other religious was assisted in the same way.[49] The Cistercians and Carthusians, with all the other orders, totally ignored the use which could be made of their patronage. The only exception was the Premonstratensians who gave three of their livings to canons, but as this was the regular practice of the house it cannot be attributed to farsightedness.[50] Quite how much the dissolution of the monasteries took the inmates by surprise, how unready they were for the final axe to fall, and how trusting they were in the value of a royal pension, could hardly be more clearly demonstrated.

Yet for the religious after 1536, as for the secular priests, the quest for a post which might provide lodging and companionship in addition to the bare but essential stipend on which a man could live was never an easy search. And there are suggestions that it was going to become more difficult than it had ever been. Between 1527 and 1535 (but omitting 1531 for which the ordination lists are incomplete) a total of 643 seculars were ordained priest, averaging just over 80 per annum.[51] During the same period, but also omitting 1531, 355 livings became vacant by resignation and 508 became vacant by death: this made a total of 863 vacancies or 107 per annum.[52] Before the dissolution of the monasteries, there was, therefore, an excess of vacancies over those ordained. Admittedly, the vacancies might be filled by a priest who already held a parish or by one who held a curacy, but this would normally produce a vacancy at *some* level even if at the humble one of curate; there would also be further vacancies for curates caused by deaths among curates and other unbeneficed clergy.

Dr Zell has shown that in Kent between 1520 and 1550 there was a decline in the number of subsidiary clergy employed in a parish. He demonstrated that in 1521 in the diocese of Canterbury there was an average of 1.7 clerks per church; in Rochester in 1533–4 there were nearly two clerks per church. He suggested that such a high number of unbeneficed priests continued until the 1550s; then the dissolution of the chantries took away many opportunities on the one hand and increased the number of clergy seeking beneficed or unbeneficed posts on the other, with the result that in the diocese of Canterbury the ratio of employed clerks to parishes fell to 1.17.[53] This was clearly a situation in which catholics might be made, less by their belief in purgatory than by their need for a job, and, if nationally applicable, this would greatly have assisted the Marian reaction.

In Lincoln, and probably elsewhere, the position was different because ordination declined with job opportunities. This was not because initially in the Lincoln diocese the ratio of priests to parishes was notably dissimilar to that of Canterbury. If we compare the job opportunities available in 1526 with those in 1543 in three archdeaconries we find:

Table 17. *Clerks in parishes in 1526 and 1543*[54]

Clerks per parish in	Archdeaconry of:-		
	Bedford	Buckingham	Huntingdon
1526	1.7	1.5	1.6
1543	1.8	1.6	1.9

It is apparent that in the diocese of Lincoln, as in those of Canterbury and Rochester, there was no shortage of posts for priests prior to 1545. But this could be changed by the dissolution of the chantries, which might remove opportunity and release onto the benefice market a large and unwanted work force. Fortunately, a large pool of unemployed priests did not exist in the diocese of Lincoln. Between 1536 and 1546 a total of only 246 men were ordained priest, averaging 22.36 per annum (see Graph 1); a total of 217 priests resigned, averaging 19.7 per annum and 714 incumbents died averaging 64.91 per annum. If, with Dr Zell, we may assume that the mobility of the clergy into any diocese was matched by that of the clergy leaving it, an extraordinary situation was developing in the diocese which a comparison with the previous decade will reveal:

Table 18. *Vacancies and ordinations, 1527–46*[55]

	Total ordained	Vacancy through resignation	Vacancy through death
1527–35	643	355	508
		Vacancies exceed ordinations by 220	
1536–46	246	217	714
		Vacancies exceed ordinations by 685	

It could be argued that this was a regional development which could be remedied by an exodus of priests from other dioceses. But it does not look as though ordinations had kept pace with jobs elsewhere. There were few ordained at Durham after 1531 and none at all between 1536 and 1544; at Exeter only thirty men in all were ordained between 1539 and 1544; and at York after a marked decline in 1529 there were apparently no ordinations between 1547 and 1551. In the diocese of London numbers had declined in 1536 and were just beginning to pick up in 1537 only to drop sharply again.[56] Whatever the explanations in the several dioceses for this decline, it is clear that it was highly unlikely that the deficit of priests in the diocese of Lincoln could be reversed by an influx of surplus priests from elsewhere.

Not all these vacancies could have been filled by the ex-religious. Mr Hodgett suggested that there came on to the job market, between 1536 and 1541, 277 unpensioned and 429 pensioned religious, making a total of 706,[57] a number not far short of the vacancies arising from the drop in ordinations: between 1536 and 1546 there were a total of 931 vacancies (whether caused by death or resignation) and only 246 men were ordained. If all the ex-religious had survived and had been willing to take the vacant posts, no difficulties would have occurred. But the reality was otherwise. A death rate, usually estimated at 5 per cent per annum, would have severely reduced the number of religious to 423 instead of 706. It was precisely this gap between vacancies and ordinations which gave the unbeneficed curates as well as the ex-religious their chance. The drop in ordinations transformed the quest for benefices: 18 per cent of those ordained in 1537 had a benefice by 1544, and 22 per cent of those ordained in 1538 also had one. Equally, a sample of those ordained before 1521 suggests that 44.5 per cent got a benefice *after* 1536.[58] On the most basic level of subsistence there was enough in the changing pattern of clerical life under Henry VIII to endear tenure to a priest and to go far towards making him a vicar of Bray. It was after all better to be the vicar of Bray than the curate or stipendiary of Bray.

Once a priest had a living, even before the doctrinal tenets of the church of England were changing, there was a strong probability that he would stay in it. Zell has found that in the Canterbury and Rochester dioceses this was the case, but the unbeneficed or lower clergy, notoriously difficult to trace, were always on the move from one subservient position to another.[59] A similar picture emerges for the diocese of Lincoln: for a large number of priests, tenure meant staying in one parish and dying in it. If we look at the archdeaconries of Bedford, Buckingham and Huntingdon we find the following position:

Table 19. *Percentage of incumbents staying in parish, 1526–43*[60]

Archdeaconry	Parishes	Incumbents staying 1526 to 1543
Bedford	120	30.8%
Buckingham	121	28.0%
Huntingdon	169	26.0%

Over a quarter of all incumbents stayed in a living once they had got one. The reasons were understandable enough, but in addition, the statute which placed a new obligation on *new* incumbents to the pay the king first-fruits, or *one whole year's stipend*, was enough to deter all but the wealthy few from moving (see Graph 3). It was not the same for the unbeneficed, who had less to hold them and every incentive to move to new posts. Among the unbeneficed of the archdeaconry of Huntingdon only 6.4 per cent stayed in the same place between 1526 and 1543; in

Buckingham only 8.2 per cent and in the archdeaconry of Bedford 8.0 per cent.[61] These figures are very similar to those for Canterbury and Rochester. But where did the rest of the 'migrating' unbeneficed go? Most unbeneficed clergy seem to get 'lost'. As in Kent, so in Huntingdon, Buckingham and Bedford, well over 50% disappear, and of the remainder some become beneficed and some simply move on to other unbeneficed posts.[62] At least by 1536 the chances of spending a lifetime as a curate or stipendiary were not as great as they had been twenty years earlier.

We do not know the individual reasons which deterred men from offering themselves for the priesthood in 1536 and thereafter; there may have been a silent protest against the changes which had accompanied the break with Rome. This may also have been informed by anxiety about the ways and means of acquiring a title or a benefice after the dissolution. It may have been further informed by the knowledge that the church no longer offered such rich prizes in terms of stipends, and that taxation of the clergy through first-fruits and tenths took a toll of their resources. In any one case the balance of spiritual value and material gain would differ. But what can be seen is that the decline in the number of ordinands in the diocese of Lincoln, and elsewhere, made possible the advancement of many unbeneficed clergy, and this fact alone would be of importance in forming their attitude to change. Many would be at least in middle age and for that reason less adaptable to innovation; for those ordained before 1521 the possession of a benefice after so many years of moving from curacy to curacy would possess a significance which would not be missed; tenure would colour their theology, and may well have allowed them to bend with the prevailing wind.[63]

For Longland the changing conditions under which the clergy were ordained or presented to him for admission to a benefice brought a problem all its own. It was for him to see that the priest in the parish, whether incumbent or curate, not only could celebrate mass and visit the sick and hear confessions (as he had always done) but that, as the royal supremacy moved from being a statement of presumed fact into an active and reforming headship, he could explain changes and reassure the old or bewildered as the landmarks of their traditional religious practices were removed. But, as we have noted, only about 25 per cent of the parish clergy who were resident were graduates, and in the remaining 75 per cent of parishes which were held by residents, the king and the bishop needed to rely on priests who had been examined at ordination, and would be examined again at institution, but whose examinations were directed to ascertaining their knowledge of Latin and their understanding of their duties. An *apologia* for the Henrician church would not have been part of their test, and if they were to grasp the changes which were taking place well enough to put them into effect as well as to explain them, they had to be able to read with ease and (once registers were ordered) to write as well as to preach if thought fit to do so.

The link between learning and defending the new order was made by the bishop himself in an attempt to get one of his chaplains a benefice; he wrote to the king in 1535, 'he is a singular lerned man as well in dyvynytie as in Laten and the Greke as fewe other within yor realme. A man mete to serve your highness. And hathe as well and notably ... preached to ... the confutacion of the usurped power of the Busshope off Rome.'[64] In another letter Longland commended a priest on the grounds that he was 'wise well lerned and virtuouse'.[65] Both these men were graduates, and it is more difficult to discover the educational standard of those who were not, yet much depended on them.

Some priests who were not (as far as we know) graduates possessed books, and this may suggest their scholarly interests; but equally it may not, for books may be possessed without being read, and where the title of a book is mentioned it is usually one of scholastic theology which would not help its reader in the defence of the Henrician supremacy. Thomas Wallessie, who was not in fact a graduate but who was a royal chaplain and rector of Aston Clinton in Buckinghamshire,[66] left the works of Nicholas of Lyra, an early fourteenth-century theologian, with concordances and glosses, as well as those of Haymo of Faversham who had revised the ordinals for the Roman breviary and missal in the mid-thirteenth century.[67] Thomas had the library with which to defend the old order but hardly the new. Others were rather less specific in their bequests. Thomas Potrell, parson of Conisholme, left 'all his books of scripture',[68] and one of the unbeneficed clergy of Winthorpe had books valued at 3s.4d.[69] The curate of Market Deeping left 'books' as well as money to scholars, which suggests he ran a local school, but we are not told what the books were.[70] John Rowte, a former monk, left sermons and an exposition of the Gospels which he had acquired from James Richardson, rector of Cold Ashby.[71] But these examples are few and far between, and most priests make no mention of books at all in their wills, perhaps because the changes of religious stance adopted between 1540 and 1560 made one day's theological tomes into another day's bonfire. We have no idea of the percentage of book owners, or of book readers. We are still left with the fundamental problem of how many unbeneficed and beneficed clerks were not up to explaining the *rationale* of the *old* order, let alone a new one.

No thorough test of all the clergy of the diocese of Lincoln was undertaken by Longland, and the earliest date at which we can gain some insight into the educational accomplishments of the clergy is 1576. Obviously, many of the priests beneficed under Longland and many of those who held curacies or chantries, had died by that date, but the officials in the archdeaconries of Lincoln, Stow and Leicester give us the age or the date of ordination of the candidates who were examined in 1576. The results of the examination of 118 priests who were ordained during Longland's episcopate, either by him or by one of his contemporaries on the bench, survive and give some idea of the general level of competence. The examinations were in Latin and in theology, and were formidable enough for two priests to have withdrawn themselves from them before even starting. The standard may well have varied from archdeaconry to archdeaconry and there are doubts about the impartiality of examiners: a clerk ordained by the conservative Bishop Bonner was identified as 'Bonner's clerk' (in the margin) and pronounced 'mere ignorant'.[72] Within these obvious limitations, the 1576 examination does give us some idea of the learning of the clergy and does suggest that those ordained before 1530 were not of the same calibre as those ordained later in Longland's episcopate (see Tables 20 and 21). There is obviously a considerable discrepancy between the archdeaconries, and between the standard reached in sacred learning and that achieved in Latin. It is surprising that so many Lincoln priests did well in theology although their

Table 20. *Knowledge of Latin in archdeaconries of Lincoln, Stow and Leicester*[73]

Dates of ordination	Graduates*	Category I (sufficient knowledge)	Category II (moderate)	Category III (insufficient knowledge)	Category IV (ignorant)
Archdeaconries of Lincoln and Stow Knowledge of Latin only					
1520–9	3	2	2	10	9
1530–9	4	12	4	9	6
1540–4	2	8	2	2	1
Total	9	22	8	21	16
(Not given 2)					
Archdeaconry of Leicester					
Age					
over 70	0	0	0	1	5
65–70	2	1	0	4	5
60–4	1	2	0	3	10
55–9	1	0	0	4	0
Total	4	3	0	12	20
(Not given 1)					

*Graduates were not examined.

Table 21. *Knowledge of sacred learning in archdeaconries of Lincoln, Stow and Leicester*[73]

Dates of ordination	Graduates*	Category I	Category II	Category III	Category IV
Archdeaconries of Lincoln and Stow Knowledge of sacred learning					
1520–9	1	3	4	17	1
1530–9	2	11	9	12	0
1540–4	0	6	4	2	1
Total	3	20	17	31	2
(Not given 5)					
Archdeaconry of Leicester					
Age					
over 70	0	0	0	1	5
65–70	1	0	1	6	4
60–4	1	0	1	6	8
55–9	1	0	0	3	1
Total	3	0	2	16	18
(Not given 1)					

* Graduates were not examined.

examination in it, at ordination in Longland's time, must have been very different. The questions likely to have been asked in 1576 by examiners who were apt to be imbued with the ideals of Calvin's Geneva would require exact Biblical knowledge. Examinees had clearly managed to move with the times, which suggests a high enough standard of literacy to cope with vernacular works of theology. It is more surprising that they performed rather less well in Latin, in which they would have been examined both at ordination and at admission to a benefice if this took place before 1547 or in Mary's reign. However, they would not have had to use their Latin for fifteen years or more, and their performance may owe more to their age and forgetfulness than anything else. But it would appear that Longland ordained rather more of

Table 22. *Comparison of results achieved by those ordained in diocese of Lincoln with those ordained elsewhere*[74]

	Category I	Category II	Category III	Category IV[74]
Bishop Longland:				
Lincoln	32.8%	11.9%	31.3%	23.8%
Leicester	5.2%	0.5%	36.5%	47.8%
Blythe, Lee, Sampson:				
Coventry and Lichfield	0%	0%	33.3%	66.6%
Nix: Norwich	0%	0%	50%	50%
Bonner: London	0%	0%	50%	50%
Bird: Chester	0%	0%	25%	75%
Lee: York	0%	0%	100%	0%

those who passed successfully either test (Categories I and II) than did his contemporaries. Percentages with this size of number exaggerate the national picture. Only a dozen candidates for examination were ordained outside the diocese of Lincoln. It is highly unlikely that Lee of York ordained only men who would have fallen into Category III if they had lived to 1576, but the comparison by percentage has one use; it shows that those who entered the diocese from another and whose ordination or age suggests they came into the ministry between 1520 and 1540 were likely to be less well educated than those who were examined by Longland or his deputies.

It is, however, clear that to examine men all of whom were over fifty and some of whom were in their seventies was likely to elicit many lapses of memory and some signs of senility. The picture portrayed by this examination, therefore, has to be regarded as the worst possible rather than the 'normal' or the 'highest' standard reached by priests ordained in the Henrician period. In their prime, the examinees might well have done better, especially in Latin. But even allowing for the ravages of time, men like these might well have viewed examinations, *any* examinations with alarm. None were graduates (since graduates were not examined) and it is hard to believe that those of them who were in the priesthood in 1536 were unaware of their own limitations; this may well explain why they were so afraid of an examination in Lincolnshire in that year.[75] It would also help to explain why Longland felt it necessary to write declarations and print them if he was to fulfil the vicegerent's wishes, as well as doing justice to his own desire to be the pastor and teacher of the flock which was given to him. Quite apart from the disincentives already present, this examination would help to explain the paucity of ordinands, particularly after we know that Longland had begun to examine all of them. If the drop in the ordination figures made a vicar out of a curate of Bray, so in the fight to preserve tenure were new definitions of credal statements to be shunned. Protestantism asked for an agility of mind, a grasp of precepts and an understanding of the difference between old and new. Catholicism of the Henrician variety asked only for a measure of conformity to a creed and a practice which differed little from what had gone before. In these circumstances we should perhaps be surprised that a change in the tenets of the faith was possible at all.

Innovation could spell disaster, and this was particularly true if we look at the changes which were occurring in the expectations of the clergy. But if Catholicism, as a priest saw it, meant more jobs, local patrons and limited tests, so it was also to mean a very low standard of living, with punitive taxation.

Finance and conformity

Longland can claim little responsibility for increasing the educational competence of his clergy, and if lack of other posts forced the graduate back to the parish, and legislation kept him there, so the bishops were impotent to prevent the progressive impoverishment of their clergy in face of inflation, increasing taxation and decreasing tithe. In the diocese of Chichester, Sherburne had augmented vicarages and endowed prebends, and although the livings of the see were not outstanding for their wealth, they were less in danger of amalgamation for their poverty than those of Lincoln.[76] There are no records which suggest that Longland made any attempt to augment vicarages, though his predecessor had done so. By 1534 it was too late to remedy the defect on a serious scale. The clergy entered a period notable for the stringency of its taxation and the pitiless hounding of all clerks, with the result that all were taxed at the same rate and exemptions were kept to the minimum. Those with incomes of less than £8 were no longer allowed to pay one fifteenth instead of one tenth, and those who were not resident were no longer allowed to count the stipend of a curate against tax. In 1534 Parliament enacted a statute by which the first year's revenue of any benefice which became vacant for any reason should go to the crown.[77] A new incumbent could not be expected to live on nothing for his first year of tenure, and so compositions for first-fruits were arranged and the new rector or vicar would space his first-fruits by instalments over a three-year period. For a short time new incumbents were liable for the tenth of their revenue in taxation in addition to the first-fruits, but this was subsequently amended.[78] In these circumstances resignations were expensive; rarely could a priest be sure that the resignation of one living in favour of another was worth his while; if death occurred in the first three years of tenure, while a composition with the king was in being, then the loss could far outweigh the expected but thwarted gain.

Yet more threatening to the clergy was the appointment of commissioners to assess livings so that tenths and first-fruits would be paid on a realistic estimate. Their findings in the *Valor Ecclesiasticus* show how little was exempt from taxation, and how, for the first time, pluralism was taxed. It is, however, hard to know how accurate an assessment of the value of a living the commissioners made. Often it has to be accepted, as no other valuations are available, but for the diocese of Lincoln we have a useful check in the subsidy valuation of 1526 which returned the amount received by individuals in a benefice (rather than the flat valuation of the benefice as such) from income from tithes and customary emoluments and, where appropriate, from arable, pasture and meadow lands. Though it is valuable to know the *sources* of income which the *Valor* provides, all too frequently the area of meadow or arable is not given, and therefore the effect of inflation on the benefice is hard to assess. Dr Stephen Lander has attempted to circumvent this problem in his study of the diocese of Chichester by using later glebe terriers to assess the size of the glebe, and he indicates that, unless enclosure had occurred, it is very unlikely that a change in the glebe, be it of rector or vicar, occurred between 1536 and 1600.[79] For the diocese of Lincoln this ingenious strategy is valuable in showing whether the incumbent had glebe but it is only a rough and ready indication of its size and the real value of the benefice.

Glebe terriers for the county of Lincoln dating from 1579 survive and they are earlier than those for Chichester; and though the county experienced enclosure this occurred mainly between 1585 and 1616.[80] At Thimbleby there is mention of an enclosure made by Thomas Panton in 1573,[81] and idiosyncracies of this kind may account for the totally different valuations which sometimes occur between those for the subsidy of 1526, those in the *Valor*, and the landed wealth suggested by the terrier. The arithmetic of assessing clerical wealth rests on much difficult and often irreconcilable evidence. It is often very hard to see how incumbents of livings valued at £8 and with little or no glebe could keep solvent, yet they seem to have done so in spite of, and not because of, legislation which allowed some benefices to be held in plurality. The vicarage of Cawthorpe Parva was valued for the subsidy of 1526 at £3.6s.8d.,[82] and in the *Valor* at the same sum.[83] In 1579 the vicar certified in a terrier that he had 5½ acres of arable, 2 acres of pasture and 3 furlongs of meadow.[84] If we take one of the suggested rates of valuation, namely that of an acre of arable at 5s.9d., of pasture 11s.1d., and of meadow 19s.6d.,[85] we can approximately reach the same valuation even allowing that a furlong is not a square measure and therefore probably a strip of that length but of slight width. The church would seem to have been far too poor to provide the vicar with an income even though he was supposed to have all tithes, yet the same incumbent stayed in it for the whole of Longland's episcopate and does not appear to have held it in plurality. Obviously the glebe was all important. In contrast, the vicarage of Theddlethorpe All Saints was valued in the subsidy at £7,[86] and in the *Valor* at £8,[87] but the incumbent had only a house and a furlong of land, and it is hard to see how he could survive the inflation of the sixteenth century. He was on the statutory limit which might allow plurality, yet there is no evidence of the living being held by a pluralist between 1533 and 1538;[88] thereafter the living changed hands a number of times and eventually came to Nicholas Bonner, who did combine it with another benefice in 1549.[89]

The diocese of Lincoln does not seem to have had so many wealthy livings as other dioceses: in London only a third of the clergy had livings worth less than £15 and half had parishes worth more than £20.[90] In Lancashire the average stipend of rectors and vicars was over £22,[91] but it has been suggested that three quarters of the livings in England were worth less than £15.[92] All these estimates are taken from the *Valor Ecclesiasticus*, and, from it, Dr Walker calculated that in Lincolnshire rectors averaged a stipend of £11.12s.0d., and vicars £8.3s.0d.;[93] yet it is clear that the subsidy of a mere ten years earlier provided a different picture. In Lincolnshire one third of the rectors and one half of the vicars were valued at less than £8. Savine noticed how far the *Valor* differed from the valuations made by the court of augmentations, and it is often extremely hard to trust its figures. In Stickney the value of the rectory was changed between 1526 and 1536 by the lease of the rectory, but in nearby Thorpe what explanation can there be for a valuation in 1526 of £8 and in 1536 of £21?[94] It has been thought that the differences lie in the calculation of the value of glebe, but this too is often hard to prove, since the subsidy never states the area of glebe and the *Valor* rarely does; we are driven to the later glebe terriers to get some indication of the extent and value of the glebe, and that can add to the problem rather than solve it. The vicar of Roxby was said to have 116 acres of arable land as well as tithe on corn and hay in 1579,[95] yet in the *Valor* he is assessed at £6.3s.4d.[96] The glebe in this case may have been acquired later. Yet the possession, or otherwise, of glebe is the crucial factor which alone gives meaning to the stark figures of valuation. A vicarage with five acres of glebe might weather the inflation of the sixteenth century by careful farming, whereas a vicar on a fixed stipend of higher paper value but without glebe might be in greater difficulties. Though Cranmer thought £10 a sufficient stipend for a priest,[97] it is doubtful if it would suffice after 1540, when inflation and royal taxation would bite hard, unless income was derived from good farm land. And in Lincolnshire by 1579 in a random sample of 134 parishes only just over half had more than five acres of glebe and of these most were rectories; the remainder had either less or none.[98] In contrast, in the diocese of Chichester nearly two thirds of the livings had over five acres of glebe.[99] Difficult though the evidence is, it would seem that the livings of the diocese of Lincoln were worth less and had less glebe than those of Lancashire and the diocese of Chichester, and so Lincoln clergy were more vulnerable to the pressures of inflation than their fellows elsewhere.

Under these circumstances, the abolition of the different scale of taxation which followed the Act for First-fruits and Tenths was disastrous. In 1526, livings valued at less than £8 only paid one fifteenth in tax while those valued at more paid one tenth. Hardship was expressed in arrears of payment or ultimately in a refusal to pay, and books full of the names of those in arrears survive in plenty for the diocese of Lincoln from the 1530s, though the most complete survive for 1547. These list, under each archdeaconry, all priests in arrears and all who refuse to pay, and it is noticeable that of the refusals many would have had to pay only one fifteenth in the 1520s. From 186 parishes listed from the archdeaconry of Stow twelve incumbents and four lower clergy refused to pay; of these sixteen refusals, half would have paid only a fifteenth twenty years before. From the archdeaconry of Lincoln, of 184 parishes listed there were twenty refusals of which twelve were from priests earning less than £8.[100] The diocese as a whole owed about £4,000[101] and the pure labour of collecting that sum was great.[102] But there was a certain poetic justice in Longland's concern in his will that he trusted 'all well accomped I remayn in litle debte unto the kinges grace'.[103] Bishops who had put more effort into augmenting vicarages and caring for their parochial clergy should have had a clearer conscience.[104]

An incumbent faced with inflation and the payment of the tenth was in no position to be charitable to his neighbours where their debts to him were concerned. And it is against the deteriorating picture of clerical finance that the evidence for increasing tithe litigation which comes from Lancashire, Chichester and Lincoln must be viewed.

In the diocese of Lincoln, as in Lancashire and the diocese of Chichester, there was a sharp increase in the number of tithe cases in the 1540s. In Lincoln, tithe cases increased from 4.4 per cent of all instance litigation in 1536–7 to 29.5 per cent of all cases in 1544–5. Farmers brought over a third of the cases recorded but, as in the diocese of Norwich, the bulk of the cases were instigated by rectors.[105] The ability to bring a suit at all argues a certain wealth on the part of the litigant not least because tithe cases were often complicated, and, accordingly, protracted.

From the bishop's court of audience records it seems clear that one of the problems in the Lincoln diocese, as elsewhere, was the right of a party to tithe; and another, which was often more complicated, was the *modus decimandi*,[106] the way in which tithe was to be paid. Richard Barker (clearly released from the Tower to which he had been committed for his support of Queen Katherine[107]) brought a case against Joseph Turner of Chesham in 1542 for withholding the valuable tithe on corn; apparently Joseph had either left no tithe at all or in the case of tithe of barley he left it in 'swathes nether bounden nor cocked contrary to the custom of the county'. In addition he had taken advantage of the rector's imprisonment to pay no tithes of wool or lambs; the bishop found that he was proved to have defaulted on those of corn and barley, and two arbitrators were appointed to assess what was due to the rector.[108]

The precise amount owing was hard to work out in some cases, not least where the principal place of pasture determined the rate due to the incumbent. In 1545, for example, the vicar of Turville alleged that the custom of the parish was that if any parishioner had seven lambs or seven bullocks, he should give one lamb or bullock to the vicar; this was more than a strict tenth, probably because the livestock grazed in his parish. One Thomas Este had seventeen lambs according to the vicar, but Este said he had only sixteen and 'no wife' (as though she were titheable); he was ordered to give only one lamb to the vicar. The lambs probably grazed outside the parish as well as in it, and therefore the full tithe was not required. In an order made at the same time Este was to remove a certain lady from his house. Clearly his tithes and his morality had become part of a running dispute with the incumbent.[109]

Cases of this kind had always undermined relations between the priest and his people, and in the circumstances of the 1540s, when some tithe was going to the lay impropriators of the parishes, the *raison d'être* of tithe was at stake. The royal proclamations which urged the customary payment, while they may have served to increase the pressure to pay, did not yield results; it was noted in Lincolnshire, by the church-wardens of a parish whose name has not come down to us, that 'Michael Shorte caryd a whay x [loads of hay] and tythed non ... and whe [*sic*] pray you loke scharly [*sic*] a pone y^t for the kinges hainys gosse ... upon the punyschement ther off.'[110]

The tithe statute of 1549 did not substantially ease the problems of levying certain sorts of tithe, especially personal tithe. It vested tithe cases in the ecclesiastical courts but forbade the use of the *ex officio* oath in the investigation of a failure to pay personal tithe. The animosity which could arise between priest and parish over payment was aggravated on both sides by poverty and the price rise, and a rector or vicar must often have been severely torn between his duties as a pastor and his pecuniary needs as an incumbent. The use of a lay farmer, who probably understood the agricultural practices of the parish and did not need to search his soul to ask whether the levying of tithe advanced or detracted from his profession of faith, was a useful expedient which appears to have gained ground in the second half of the sixteenth century.[111]

In the Henrician period, however, the pressures on the secular clergy in terms of finance constituted a disincentive to entering the ministry for all but the very poor, who were accustomed to much worse than clerical poverty and sought the status which the cloth afforded. Yet, ironically, the change in the ways of acquiring a benefice and particularly the change in the time needed to get one, taken with the changing patterns of education and residence which accompanied it, made the ministry in real, if secular, terms, more attractive and not less. This would not be perceived in 1536: it would take a decade for the improvement in the prospects for the unbeneficed to make itself felt and known, and the anxiety about the standard of education of the ministry and about the patronage necessary to gain access to it were yet to be proved ill founded. In such a situation, there was much to be said for securing a foothold in a benefice and keeping out of trouble. Some priests might find that the improved career prospects which the priesthood increasingly offered were offset by the decline in living standards. Others who would normally have presented themselves for ordination did not do so. Their reasons were many, but among them would surely have figured a doubt about the Henrician church, both in its theology and in its changes to the established pattern of clerical life. For some, the changes of the 1530s were too fundamental to be covered with the sugar of improved career prospects. Theirs would not be a silent *non placet*. For them opposition took the form of an overt attack upon the supremacy or upon the demands which went with it. It was an attack which ultimately took a number of the clergy and laity of Lincolnshire into open rebellion against not only their bishop but their king.

4. REFORM AND REACTION IN THE PARISHES

The oath which required the clergy to assent to the royal supremacy by renouncing Rome was asked, and in most cases given, in the summer of 1534, but its full significance was slowly recognised in the years that followed. Only gradually were the differences between a royal and a papal supremacy perceived, and the dissent felt and voiced by priests and religious, and ultimately by laymen, took some time in many cases to find expression. The succession oath and the oath asked of priests and religious which stated, in a very negative way, that the bishop of Rome had no more authority in England than any other foreign bishop, began to be required in March 1534.[1]

Few in the diocese saw the marriage and the supremacy as important issues in themselves. As in Lancashire, clerical protests against the marriage and the assumption of the headship were delayed until the use to which the supremacy would be put became clear.[2] A few in the diocese were members of Queen Katherine's entourage, and their protest against her treatment was distinct from the protests made against the supremacy by locally based priests. Her protégés were unable either to take the succession oath or to maintain silence in face of the treason act.[3] Thomas Abell, Katherine's chaplain, who had been presented by her to the wealthy rectory of Berkhamstead St Peter, as well as receiving other benefices within the diocese and elsewhere, was unlikely to keep quiet.[4] In the attainder against Elizabeth Barton, the nun of Kent, he was described as having given 'constante credyte to (her) said false and feyned revelations and myracles'; convicted of misprision and concealment of treason, he was imprisoned at the king's pleasure, and deprived of all his benefices.[5] He was responsible for one of the best defences of Katherine's marriage, the *Invicta Veritas* which was published abroad in 1532.[6] Not actually executed until July 1540, he seems to have spent some of the long hours in the Tower of London carving his initials on a bell.[7] He was not the only clerk beneficed in the diocese who was an admirer of the nun of Kent and a supporter of the queen. John Addison, rector of Loughborough and chaplain to Fisher of Rochester, was included in the attainder, and, like Abell, he was imprisoned in the Tower, though he appears to have escaped the final penalty.[8] Other priests in the diocese who openly favoured Katherine's cause included Richard Barker, also a protégé of hers, who refused the succession oath and refused to allow the queen the disparaging title of Princess Dowager. He was imprisoned.[9] James Mallett, who held many benefices and was for some time precentor of the cathedral and a resident within the close, was charged as late as 1542 with speaking treasonable words. He was alleged to have said: 'Woo worth them that began the devorce between the Kyng and Quene Kateryne for syns we had never good world.' To these sentiments he added hopes that the king of Scotland would burn and ravage England. It is hardly surprising that he was executed at the end of the year for his views.[10]

The great majority of the Lincoln clergy took the succession oath without any apparent qualm and most of them took the oath declaring the bishop of Rome to have no more authority than any other prelate equally easily.[11] Doubts about the supremacy came only as it was translated into practical reality in the form of the vicegerency, the injunctions, the statutes and the proclamations which were aimed at the duties, income and ultimately the belief of all the English clergy. For many, their often confused dissent was expressed in the Lincolnshire rising of 1536 and the Pilgrimage of Grace.[12] But others who took no part in the rebellion only gradually began to regret their oath. George Croft held the rectory of Broughton in the diocese of Lincoln, in which he appears to have resided until 1538.[13] He was royal chaplain in 1531 and had a choice between a career at court, at university or within the diocese. In 1538 he became chancellor of Chichester, but in November of that year he was arrested for saying to Sir Henry Pole, Lord Montacute: 'The King is not supreme head of the Church of England but the bishop of Rome is supreme head of the Church.' He also added 'There [was] none act or thing that ever he did more grieve his conscience than the oath which he took to renounce the bishop of Rome's authority.' He was indicted for high treason and executed in December 1538.[14] The Lincolnshire vicar of Barton on Humber, William Duffield,[15] who was a friar and suffragan bishop serving in the dioceses of York and Lincoln, came to the same conclusion and met the same fate.[16] Thomas More's chaplain, John Lark, who was rector of Polebroke as well as having livings in London, did not realise that the papal supremacy was the best bastion against innovation until 1544; he was executed at Tyburn.[17] The bishop's nephew, Richard Pate, archdeacon of Lincoln, repaid Longland's financial generosity and frequent solicitation to Cromwell on his behalf by defecting and joining Reginald Pole in Italy. He and William Pettow, the famous Franciscan friar and also rector of Sharnford, were included in the attainder against Pole himself.[18]

The Lincolnshire rising of 1536 brought many different grievances together, among which there was certainly some concern about the supremacy. But even apart from the rising, the diocese produced a steady supply of martyrs for the pope or the Spanish queen. Some twelve rectors and two vicars were formally attainted, excluding those who were implicated for their part in the Lincolnshire rebellion.[19] It is not certain that all of these were actually executed,[20] and indeed other clergy in the diocese with similar views escaped even being deprived of their livings. Roger Dyngley, rector of Conington, was summoned before the council to answer for his views concerning the bishop of Rome, which did not appear to tally with the oath or with the Act of Supremacy. He was certainly dead within two years of expressing papal sympathies, but not apparently at the executioner's hands.[21] A former friar of Southampton had views about the supremacy which he expressed openly in his preaching and which were in support of the papal supremacy. He was examined by Cromwell and let off any further process. It is perhaps indicative of the attitude of the bishop of Lincoln to such offences that he gave him a wealthy benefice – perhaps in the hopes that his sacramental views were also conservative.[22] Thomas King, rector of Fenny Drayton, told his parishioners in 1527 that he was brought up in the 'old ceremonies' and shunned the works of Luther, Melanchthon and Tyndale. In 1535 he further informed them that he was bound to obey the Pope on 'pain of damnation', and as though this were not enough, he also spoke against the king's marriage. No action appears to have been taken against him and he remained in his parish and may even have become chaplain to Catherine Parr.[23] Arthur Bulkeley, who was to become bishop of Bangor in 1542 and held the living of St Peter in the Bail, Oxford, was accused of breach of *praemunire* for upholding the authority of the bishop of Rome. He was pardoned and no further action was taken against him.[24] John Harding, rector of Norton Twycross, was also leniently treated in spite of his papal leanings.[25] John Holyman was described as a 'privy fautor to the bushop of Rome' and to be 'marvellous familiar' with the abbots of Eynsham and Reading as well as with Dr London, warden of New College. He moved in high and dangerous circles, but he kept his vicarage at Wing and lived to become bishop of Bristol under Mary.[26]

Essentially, the treatment meted out to those with papal leanings, or to those who had not obeyed all the injunctions, reflected not the gravity of the offence so much as the power of the offender to influence others. Treasonable words spoken in private, or in his cups, by a priest of little consequence were better ignored than advertised by prosecution. John Gurle, who held the church of Manton in 1534 and moved to Eynsham in 1540,[27] was guilty of saying 'the king used too many women to be able to get a child of his Queen'.[28] He was fortunate in being ignored; a trial for those words might be embarrassing even if it deterred others.[29] Similarly, there were other priests whose offences might arise from ignorance rather than malice. Walter Browne, rector of Harston in 1537, was found bidding the beads in the old form and praying for the bishop of Rome. To arrest him might be a petty gesture and one which would create more ill-well than conviction.[30] Thomas Burley, rector of Glooston, who also held parishes outside the diocese, was accused in 1536 of not amending the books in the church by deleting the pope's name from them, nor declaring the king to be supreme head of the church. Again, no action was taken against him, possibly because he appears to have been a pluralist, and so idle a one that he was unlikely to show any harmful zeal for any cause, whether that of Rome or Spain.[31]

Those who had a record of previous co-operation were also likely to be given another chance. William Buckmaster, the Lady Margaret Professor of Divinity at Cambridge, gave scholarly advice over the divorce;[32] he was later thought to be of 'the popish sort' and to have had 'a grete pertinacite to ... olde blindnes'.[33] He forbade Latimer to preach on a contentious issue in Cambridge, and the worst that became of him was that he was let out to grass. He was allowed to pass his last years in the rectory of Shorton in the diocese of Lincoln, where his conservative opinions were unlikely to be of wide effect.[34] The rector of Stukeley, Gilbert Rouse, who was accused of calling the king and council 'Lollards' and of praising the Carthusians, appears to have come to no harm.[35]

The numbers of those dissenting to the marriage or the supremacy seem small and the 'protest' harmless, but they were not as insignificant as might at first sight be supposed. The diocese of Lincoln, like the county of Lancashire, was exceptional in having *any* deprivations and executions of conservative parish clergy in the 1530s. In London, as in Kent, there were *no* deprivations at all.[36] The reasons for the difference are not hard to find. Obviously several Lincoln dissidents were well known figures with benefices in a variety of places. Thomas Abell, John Lark and William Pettow belong to the diocese of Lincoln in name only: they had benefices in the diocese, but were unlikely to visit often since they were with the court. The death of Abell was part of a political stratagem, and the indiscretions of Fisher's chaplain were not caused by his affiliations to the diocese of Lincoln, but rather by his loyalty to the bishop of Rochester. But if we look at the genuine parish priest who, even if a pluralist, worked and resided within the diocese, we find that none was executed before 1537. Richard Barker, who had refused the oath, was imprisoned in the Tower in 1534, but he stayed there.[37] What made his fate different from that of other dissident priests within the diocese was that he had not been at large during the Pilgrimage of Grace. Though none of these dissidents from the diocese (with the possible exception of Mallett) had anything to do with either the Lincolnshire rising or the Pilgrimage, they were apprehended precisely because the government had been made more vigilant and less merciful by the fact of rebellion. Dr Haigh suggests that in Lancashire in 1533 one priest railed against Anne Boleyn and was certainly examined but appears to have gone free.[38] A similar picture emerges from Lincoln: before 1536 the supporter of pope or queen was at worst imprisoned. But the Pilgrimage of Grace not only flushed out into the open some hitherto unnoticed offenders but saw the beginning of execution for those who held views which were at odds with the Treasons act or with the Act of Supremacy. London had not offended its monarch by rebellion; nor had the dioceses of Rochester and Canterbury. That of Lincoln had, and Lincoln priests, who in other dioceses might have been shown more leniency, paid with their lives after 1536. The toll, however small, was steady from 1537 to the end of Henry's reign; but there were no sudden outbursts of zealous orthodoxy in favour of one or other doctrinal stance as Dr Brigden suggests for London.[39]

The protests of the few against the oaths showed that an oath denying the authority of the bishop of Rome was not enough; nor was an oath affirming the succession of Anne's issue. The reasons for both had to be put forward cogently.

In the summer of 1534, Cranmer and the bishops of London, Winchester and Lincoln appear to have agreed to inhibit from preaching all persons in their dioceses, and to ask even curates who were authorised by law to preach to seek from Cranmer new letters licensing preaching.[40] In the meantime Cranmer sent out to both provinces a new order forbidding the beads and ordering every preacher to preach once in the presence of as large a number of people as possible against 'the usurped power of the bishop of Rome'. Additionally Cranmer warned against preaching about purgatory, honouring the saints, pilgrimages, miracles, the marriage of priests and justification by faith. Preachers were also to explain why the marriage of Katherine was invalid.[41]

By 1535 Cromwell through circular letters to J.P.s, and by June with a printed announcement which was to be read in church, made the first attempt to put forward the supremacy positively within the parish. But the initial means of ascertaining acceptance of the supremacy were far from satisfactory, and others were necessary. The bishop was to send a copy of the announcement of the supremacy to every apparitor in his diocese; the apparitors were to take a copy for each deanery; from there it was to go to all religious houses. Priests should have offered to them 'an example of the said wrytinges' and those who wished to do so should 'write them oute'.[42]

The chaos of clerks jostling one another to copy 'the wrytinges' with all the attendant difficulties of quill pen and ink greatly perturbed the bishop of Lincoln, who sensibly realised that if priests did not have their own copies to read from they might either conveniently 'forget' to make them known, or render an account so garbled that severe misunderstandings might follow. Longland, therefore, wrote to Cromwell on 25 June 1535 asking permission to have 2,000 copies printed 'for as much as the last letter of declaration in English which your mastership sent unto me last, must go into so many several places with my diocess, that al the Clerkes I have are not able to write them in long process of time'.[43] Cromwell clearly approved of the idea and either offered the suggestion (or Longland himself made it) which Thomas Bedell also suggested in August, namely:

where it is written 'they shall preach and declare', I have altered it through the book thus 'I declare unto you' or this 'Ye shall understand'. For else, I suppose, many of the curates be so brute, that they would read or speak every word as it was written, and say of themselves in the pulpit 'They shall preach and declare', as a talk runs of a collier that did so in a stage play.[44]

In any event, the text declaring the supremacy printed by Longland begins 'Ye shall understand' and contains none of Bedyll's other amendments. It was a succinct and hard hitting document which had to be read to all parishioners and to be used by all schoolmasters. It survives in Longland's register and appears to be the only copy that has survived of this crucial piece of propaganda (for the text, see Appendix, p. 157).[45] In addition to declaring the king to be the 'supreme hede immediately under god' of the church, the letter ordered that the pope's name was to be deleted from all books and omitted from all prayers. Orders to this effect were sent out with the declaration by the bishop to his whole diocese on 19 June 1535.[46]

But neither the declaration nor the changing of the old form of bidding the beads of themselves guaranteed credence. For the declaration to be positively believed rather than passively accepted, it must be accompanied by informed preaching. Yet it was precisely that kind of preaching that Cranmer had forbidden in 1534,[47] and which the new generation of bishops like Goodrich of Ely were impatient to advance, supported by Thomas Cromwell in mutual exasperation at the slow pace of reform. In January 1535, Goodrich had written to Cromwell on behalf of Dr Feley, commending him as being in favour of preaching against the bishop of Rome and against the Aragonese marriage. But he remarked on the scarcity of preachers 'in this corner of the diocese of Lincoln'.[48] He was, of course, referring to the archdeaconry of Bedford which, as we have seen, had 21 per cent of its clergy resident graduates but a high 30 per cent of incumbents who had been in their livings a long time and who were too old to change their ways.

Longland kept to the letter of Cranmer's instructions and inhibited from preaching anyone who preached '*temeratie, indiscrete, et arroganter, sepius questiones dubias, variasque et ambiguas opiniones nec adhuc publica auctoritate diffinitas*'. He accused two Bedfordshire priests of preaching on such matters and inhibited them from further preaching in March 1536.[49] One, Vyall, was a friar who held a living in Kent, which may have formed his reforming instincts.[50] A running battle raged between the parishioners of All Hallows, Oxford, and the bishop. The curate had preached without a licence. Longland inhibited him from preaching and wrote a stiff note to the Rector of Lincoln College, of which Longland was visitor and ordinary, 'marvelling' that the Rector had allowed a preacher at All Hallows who was neither learned nor a graduate; the Rector was tartly reminded to be more careful in the future with livings appropriated to his college.[51] The parishioners of All Hallows wrote later to Cromwell on behalf of the 'silenced curate',[52] but to no effect. Longland probably knew all too well that the curate preached not only against the pope but against 'ungodly papistycall superstytyon' as well.[53] It is clear in this case that Longland perceived that a battle for minds, and with them souls, was being fought from the pulpits of the realm. He was a very tough adversary, and he appears to have pursued unrelentingly those whose views veered towards Protestantism.[54] He attempted to silence Garrett, who was one of Latimer's chaplains, after he had preached in Lincolnshire which, he said, 'the countrey of Lincolnshire much grudgeth'.[55]

By 1536 Longland had written to his archdeacons, drawing their attention to the requirement of a licence and instructing them to see to it that they

> have such an eye, dyligent oversight, and inquyrye in these premysses that I maye with spede be certefied by you the names as well as such as hath transgressed the said ordre and commaundment, as of them that dothe preache any contencyous doobtefull matters or without authoryte.

Curates must note the names of all preachers, and sermons were not to be on 'matters and doubtes as dothe radre gendre countraytie and dissencion than necessary thinges apte for his audience or for the encrease of vertue and truthe'.[56] Theologically conservative preaching, supported by licence, and eventually certified in a preacher's book, was obviously guaranteed to keep the laity of the Lincoln diocese out of sympathy with ideas of justification by faith and the sacramental views of Lutherans and Lollards. If successful, this preaching would mean that the reformation in England had to stop at the supremacy and the dissolution of the monasteries.

But the diocese of Lincoln bordered on those of Ely and London, and it had within itself the university of Oxford. The universities were precisely the places where the truth or falsehood of Lutheran claims were debated and taught, and London was an all-important area for heretical book distribution. The question facing Longland and other conservative bishops was one of time: had he got long enough to reassure and teach his flock before Protestantism infiltrated his diocese? He seems to have recognised the danger with characteristic clarity.

The line separating conservative Catholic and Lutheran Protestant could be a crucial one, as a fracas at Stamford on 22 August 1535 showed. On that Sunday Richard Quaenus preached on justification by faith, and when he came down from the pulpit certain Dominicans attacked him so fiercely that if Richard Cicell had not defended the cause of 'faith', the effect of his sermon would have been destroyed; Quaenus asked Cromwell to intervene in order to build on the foundations he had laid. But to no avail: the abbot of Thame, suffragan of Lincoln and later to be bishop of Oxford, was next in the pulpit and he inveighed against those who tried to overturn the order which had lasted 1,500 years and pulled down images of saints, and who denied that the Virgin and Saints were mediators. Quaenus complained that this was the sort of preacher usual in the north and that he would not dare write to Cromwell without witnesses on account of the power of the bishop.[57] Longland was determined to keep what he viewed as heresy out of the diocese. He wrote in February 1536 to Lord Lisle with pride that 'this penetrable cold that ye write of hath not yet penetrated any one that belongeth to my church'.[58] He might have added that it had penetrated Buckinghamshire but that he was lighting the faggots to drive it away. In Buckinghamshire, if anywhere in the diocese, Protestantism could be promoted and spread, and not surprisingly Buckinghamshire Lollards were harassed and hunted down.

The Buckinghamshire Lollards had been undeterred by persecution in the 1520s[59] and one of the most notable of them, Thomas Harding, who had been accused and found guilty before bishops Smith, Atwater and Longland, was up before the bishop's vicar general again in May 1532 as a relapsed heretic who had clearly become very dangerous. He had in his possession and had read Tyndale's *Obedience of a Christian Man*, *The Practice of Prelates*, the *New Testament in English* and the *Sum of Scripture in English*. With such a library Harding was able to read to and teach his fellow Lollards some of the salient Lutheran tenets and encourage them to persist in their own views. Lollardy had ceased to be the creed of the weavers and threshers, and was now to be fed and changed by the graduates who supported Luther and who, like Tyndale, went abroad in order to publish books for their fellow countrymen. As a result, men like Harding were in a position not only to practise their creed but to evangelise and defend it. This comes out very strongly in his examination before the vicar general: he asserted that there was no mention of purgatory in Scripture and that the Virgin and Saints should not be adored, since salvation lay through the Lord's passion and not their intercession. He told his judge that he had never believed in holy water and 'could not find warrant for it in Scripture'. His views, while differing little from those of other Lollards, had gained in clarity and power because of the recourse made to Scripture.[60] John Foxe has a somewhat garbled story that Harding was burned in the presence of Roland Messenger, vicar of High Wycombe. The bishop's register suggests that he was excommunicated and absolved as well as being handed over to the secular power as a relapsed heretic.[61]

We know no more of him, but he is a glaring example of the difficulties facing bishops in the 1530s. The printed word was easily disseminated, and the Lollards of Buckinghamshire were encouraged in the beliefs which Longland wanted them to repudiate. Twelve were accused of heresy in 1531, and the Chilterns provided a convenient refuge for those *en route* to Oxford. Longland recognised this, and in a letter to Sir Francis Bryan in August 1535 he thanked him for the good order he had 'taken in Buckinghamshire in redressinge and punyshinge of such heresies and errores as hath been used in this woddy countrey of Chiltern'.[62] When a preacher was needed at Great Missenden, Longland took the pulpit himself,[63] and in this way he seems to have prevented the open Protestant evangelism which was a feature of Kent and Gloucestershire.[64] He was helped by the fact that the diocese had no obvious sea port through which books could be smuggled, but he kept a very careful eye on the Lincolnshire coast. Edward Dawson of Whaplod was accused of being a common merchant and talker in church and of possessing books in English: '*Nonnullos libros in vulgari prohibitos*'.[65] A commission was sent to several Oxford scholars to enquire into heretical books in the university, especially those of the 'the former house of St Frideswide'.[66] With a bishop so diligently guarding the pulpits of his diocese and so determined to root out heretics, it is hardly surprising that the laity of the diocese show no trace at all in their wills of Protestant inclinations.[67]

The wills of the archdeaconries of Lincoln, Huntingdon and Buckingham continue to display differences, but in no archdeaconry did a testator depart from the usual formula of bequeathing his soul to Almighty God, His mother and to all the saints. This may be an indication less of the orthodoxy of the faithful than of the scribe, but a very high number of testators continued to leave money to their parish church and for requiems, which suggests that they still believed in purgatory and the necessity for intercession for the departed. In the archdeaconry of Lincoln the number leaving money for intercession for their souls is higher in 1536 than it was in 1530. The bequests to the cathedral are down in Huntingdon and Buckinghamshire, but in the archdeaconry of Lincoln this is compensated by the increase in the bequests to the parish church. But interest was waning in parish churches (other than one's own) in all the archdeaconries; there is no longer a bequest to the church in which the deceased got married or was baptised. It is significant that even at this late date bequests to religious orders remained on a similar scale to those between 1520 and 1530, but the support of both the friars and the guilds had fallen away. In Lincolnshire this was compensated for by an increase in the number of bequests for intercession for the departed, in Huntingdon by an increase in gifts to the poor and in Buckinghamshire by nothing at all except by gifts to family and friends (see Table 23, p. 148).[68]

The signs of change which can be traced through wills are, it would seem, still slight by 1536. Yet by the summer of that year there were visible changes taking place in these very archdeaconries. By that time the monasteries of less than £200 in value were beginning to be demolished. Lincolnshire was unique in the diocese in having some forty houses scheduled for suppression – though not all were, in fact, demolished.[69] These monasteries did not resemble those of the religious of Lancashire, for instance,[70] in the quality or quantity of their services to the community, but they were nevertheless useful. We have seen how they might give a local boy the necessary 'title' to launch him into the ministry. They also possessed a sizeable amount of patronage and were responsible for 22.7 per cent of presentations to livings in the diocese between 1521 and 1536. Of the tithe cases recorded in the archdeaconry of Lincoln in 1536, none involved a religious house.[71] East Lincolnshire

Table 23. *Bequests for specific purposes in three archdeaconries, 1535–6, rendered as a percentage in a sample of 50 wills in each archdeaconry which included bequests to that purpose*

	Arch. of Lincoln	Arch. of Huntingdon	Arch. of Buckingham
	1535	1535	1535–6
Works of the cathedral	86% (93%)*	70% (92%)	71% (98%)
Other bequests to cathedral	10% (25%)	0% (0%)	0% (2%)
Own parish church	80% (76%)	74% (92%)	75% (86%)
Other parishes	22% (29%)	10% (24%)	11% (16%)
Religious orders	10% (11%)	8% (8%)	0% (0%)
Friars	14% (22%)	6% (16%)	0% (0%)
Guilds	16% (14%)	16% (10%)	4% (2%)
Intercession for departed	32% (22%)	42% (60%)	21% (26%)
Bridges and roads	0% (0%)	4% (16%)	7% (10%)
Poor	6% (0%)	14% (2%)	0% (0%)
Orphans and sick	4% (0%)	0% (0%)	0% (0%)

* Figures in brackets are those for 1521–30: see Table 3, p. 48 above.

was also distinctive in that it formed the greater part of the archdeaconry of Lincoln and had suffered from having Richard Pate as its archdeacon. Pate, like other archdeacons and bishops, had been inhibited from visiting during the royal visitation of 1536,[72] but his licence allowed the collection of procurations which might keep him in the style to which he had grown accustomed as a royal emissary in Germany.[73] His archdeaconry may well have had to pay two lots of procurations in 1536.

The southern counties of the diocese were nearer to London and were perhaps less mistrustful of change than Lincolnshire; they boasted no famous shrines threatened by the commissioners for first-fruits and tenths, as did Lincoln, and they had fewer religious houses than Lincolnshire. Certainly they did not have the experience of being subjected to three commissions simultaneously as well as two visitations in quick succession, which we shall see befell parts of Lincolnshire. That was the fate of east Lincolnshire, and it was from Louth and Caistor and Horncastle that a revolt against much of the legislation of the Reformation Parliament arose.

The Lincolnshire Rising was short and sharp, but it was the harbinger of more extensive unrest in the north of England – unrest which manifested itself in the rebellion known as the Pilgrimage of Grace. Lincolnshire was first to rise and as such elicited from its monarch a blistering response,[74] and a degree of panic for which the participants paid with their lives. A less jittery government would have played the rebellion more coolly, but for one brief week Lincolnshire confronted the government, which, if we take the propaganda seriously, was *expecting* opposition, with all that it feared.

The rebellion in Lincolnshire, which may have begun too early for support to come from Yorkshire, was quick to start and finish. It began at Louth, the town in which the people were conspicuous for backing their devotion to the church with their money, of which the outward sign was a magnificent spire. On a small scale, Louth was a sixteenth-century Chartres.[75] On Sunday 1 October Thomas Kendall, the vicar of Louth, preached a sermon, the text of which has not come down to us, but is reported as having affirmed that the church or its faith, or both, were in danger. The result of his sermon was to alert and fire the commons of the town and to inspire them to take issue with all manifestations of central government, which happened, in different forms, to have coincided in the area at this time. As a result, on Monday 2 October the commons of the town seized the bishop's registrar and marched on the nunnery of Legbourne where the commissioners were hard at work demolishing what had, it would seem, been a god-fearing house. On 3 October Caistor was also rising, helped by Louth but also by the fact that the gentry were awaiting the subsidy commissioners and the clergy were expecting a deputy of the bishop. At the same time Horncastle rose because the bishop's deputy, Dr Rayne, had reached them. He was brutally murdered amid scenes that savour more of the Third Reich than the Gospel. Each of these three centres provided contingents of priests, religious, commons, and sometimes gentry, to march on Lincoln. By 10 October the cathedral was reached, and the walls of the chapter house and cathedral rang to the squabbling and reading of terms and conditions. But rumour was rife, too, and the insurgents heard that the Duke of Suffolk was a mere few miles away at Stamford with an armed force. As this news spread, the commons and the clergy and religious seeped away to their homes, but not necessarily to safety. The rising in Lincolnshire provided the signal for Beverley, York and Lancashire to rebel, but the men of Lincolnshire lacked the stamina to keep going, partly at least because their grievances were so diverse.[76]

Of the immediate causes of the Lincolnshire rising there can be little doubt: too much innovatory action was taking place in so small an area that on 2 October 1536 it might well have seemed that the relentless efficiency of the Henrician state was being concentrated upon a mere ten square miles. The commissioners responsible for the dissolution of the monasteries had reached Legbourne in spite of the pathetic plea of the prioress 'that it may be preserved and stond',[77] and at Caistor the subsidy commissioners were expected.[78] At Louth, where the trouble began, it was the transferred feast of the dedication of the churches, which while not of importance to the church of Louth itself would have been observed in adjoining parishes. It was a weekend when harvesting was thought to be over and jollification might be expected to begin. The harvest was an average yield and something to celebrate after the poor one of the previous year.[79] The talk in the village and the towns was likely to have been of rumours of further confiscation of ecclesiastical property, and those rumours may well have been fed in the preceding week by the visit of Dr Pryn in his capacity as official of Lincoln, and of his registrar Peter Efford, who had been in the area for some time.[80] They were at Belchford on 25 September, at Louth on 26 September and at Muckton on the following day, visiting for the absent archdeacon.[81] Additionally, as we have seen, the unfortunate Dr Rayne (vicar general to the bishop) and the episcopal registrar were in the area during the last week in September. We do not know exactly why they were there, but it looks as though among other things they were giving notice of the order for the abrogation of holy days.

Convocation on 19 July 1536 debated the abolition of certain saints' days, and reference is made to them in a general way in the Ten Articles.[82] What the holy days were was stated unambiguously in a letter from the king to the bishops in August 1536.[83] Longland notified his diocese in the most general way that saints' days were to be curtailed, and his letter is dated 3 September 1536. He does not seem to have forwarded the royal schedule which he mentions. He certainly passed on in his letter that the date of the dedication of churches was in future to be 1 October and that there would be four offering days which should continue to be Christmas, Easter, the Nativity of St John the Baptist, and Michaelmas. Other saints' days which were permitted or abrogated were, he stated, contained in the royal schedule.[84] The royal schedule is in Longland's register dated 16 February 1536/7. Cranmer's own order about holy days was not made until 10 September 1537.[85] It looks, therefore, as though Longland had given his diocese, and particularly Lincolnshire, just enough information to warn and alarm them and not the full list (which effectively abolished the holy days occurring in harvest time and in law terms, with the exception of those days which were feasts of the apostles, the Virgin and St George, together with those of the Ascension, the Nativity of St John the Baptist, All Saints and Candlemass).[86] Longland's action would have had the effect of provoking speculation and directing anxiety to the one date mentioned in his letter, 1 October, the feast for the dedication of the churches.

Longland, in making this 'interim' order, was not actually innovating. His predecessor, Bishop Atwater, had made the same one, though it was probably ignored.[87] But there would have been many churches in Lincolnshire which the order affected and which were celebrating their feast of dedication on 1 October for the first time. Ironically, Louth, where all the trouble started, was not among them. It was dedicated to an apostle, St James, and could keep its feast on the proper day. But if this interpretation of events is correct, it would account for the speculative rumour on the subject of holy days which accompanied the Lincolnshire rising.[88]

Rayne was clearly bringing with him orders for more than the abrogation of certain holy days; he must also have been carrying the Ten Articles and their concomitant injunctions. The articles also date from the convocation of July 1536,[89] and the injunctions were reputed to have been issued in August.[90] Whether Longland issued them earlier than his fellow bishops is hard to establish. Circular letters from the king to all bishops ordering the reading of the articles, but implying that earlier orders had been neglected or disobeyed, survive for November 1536.[91] One priest involved in the Lincolnshire Rising in the first week of October 1536 reported that he and others 'grudged at the new erroneous opinions touching Our Lady and Purgatory';[92] these opinions in the case of purgatory are explicit in the Ten Articles, so it is probable that in addition to orders about saints' days, the vicar general was bringing and reading the Articles and injunctions. He was involved in something else as well. He was checking the valuation of livings made by the commissioners for first-fruits and tenths, and is therefore frequently described as valuing livings.[93] The bearer of so many novelties in his luggage, all of which seem to have been regarded as bad news, was obviously the target of considerable animosity; this would go far to explain why Rayne, a seemingly harmless diocesan official, was murdered apparently spontaneously by the mob.[94] But the fact that he had visited the previous week and apparently come to no harm begs the question of why Lincolnshire rebelled in the first week of October and not in the last week of September.

It was obviously important that the harvest was in by then and that the risk of destroying crops had disappeared; moreover, that weekend was one which saw a permitted holiday on Friday 29 September for the feast of St Michael and All Angels, and on Sunday the feast of the dedication of churches brought men together, and they were no doubt rendered more reckless by the feasting (and drinking) that marked the end of harvest. They could also exchange gossip. The clergy, too, were brought together to Louth by 2 October ready to meet the bishop's commissary. This was a good time for them to exchange grievances and co-operate in an agreement to ring the bells and raise their parishioners to rebellion should the rumours which were circulating prove well founded. The gentry were also assembling at Caistor on 3 October and they, too, would have the occasion to talk.

But at the centre of this discontent was a graduate priest, Thomas Kendall. His preaching on 1 October in Louth church fired the congregation by indicating that the bishop's commissaries would be in Louth next day, and he advised the people to 'look well upon such things as should be required of them in the said visitation'.[95] He had in mind a somewhat garbled report of the visitation of the deanery of Bolingbroke by John Rayne. Thomas Kitchyn reported:

> Sir Symond Maltby parson of Farforth was before Doctor Reynes at Bollyngbroke the Satturday befor the Insurrecion or there Abowte, the said chauncelor syttinyng in the courte of consistori for the valuacyon of ther benyfyces which courte fynysshed the forsaid Sir Symonde Maltby returned home to hys parishe and reported amonge his neyghbors that the churche goodis shuld be taken from them and he said ther was dyvers challyces made of tyne which shold be delyvered to them in exchange for sylver chalices and sayd sylver chalyces to be had to the kynges ...[96] And further the forsyad Sir Symond said that he (herd) the preystes ware determynyd that (yf) the said chauncelor dyd sytt any more thay wold styk hym down...[96] theyr neybors wold take ther partes in that behalf.[97]

This was not the only rumour spreading about Rayne's visit. Another of less interest to the commons was that churches within five miles of one another as well as chapels were to be 'foredone'[98] – a threat which if true would curtail the employment of the lower clergy. More threatening still to the clergy was the rumour attested by Thomas Tailboys:

> That the prestes of the deanery of Louthesk whois namys he knowethe nott, were present at Bullyngbroke the day that the bisshop's chauncelor dyd sytt at Bullyngbroke to here and perceve what order the said chauncelor dyd take ... and when they perceyvid that the prystes of the forsaid bolynbroke wer content and confyrmable to Abyde all suche order as then was taken, then the said prestes of Lowtheske as this deponent saythe he harde yt openly spoken ... that they wold nott be so orderyd ne yet axamyned of ther Abillyte in lerninge or otherwyse in kepying of cure of Soule.[99]

Examinations to enable clerks to compete for fewer benefices threatened the clergy. Nor were the implications of losing one benefice and having to find another lost on them. The full horror of the statute for first-fruits and tenths had reached them: the rector of Conisholm was reported to have said 'They will deprive us of our benefices because they would have the first fruits, but rather than I will pay the first fruits I had liever lose benefice and all.'[100] Nor was this the only difficulty which confronted the unbeneficed. As the hammers demolished Legbourne, it cannot have escaped the notice of some clerks that the route by which they had come to a benefice in the past would not be available in the future. Of thirty-two parochial clergy known to have taken a prominent part in the rising, at least one third owed their benefice to a religious house which was either suppressed or awaiting suppression or which was itself involved in the rising.[101] Nine more owed their patronage to houses or corporations whose loyalty was doubtful, like the college of Tattershall, which was said to have assisted the rebels.[102] Five more owed their livings to gentlemen who were directly involved in the rising.[103] As they gathered at Louth on 2 October, the priests of the deanery of Loutheske were exchanging rumours and fears and were all too ready to go back and raise their parishes by ringing the bells.[104] They saw exactly how they were affected by the Reformation Parliament and were in no mood to accept its legislation without a murmur.

They were assisted by the religious and the commons, who clearly took the view that church plate was at risk and believed that the legacies of their ancestors were about to be carried off to the Tower for the king's use. Philip Trotter reported 'that the beginnynge of thys mater was by Reason of a noyse that the Ornamentes of theyr churchys shuld be taken from them by the kinges commandemente'.[105] The plea to save the jewels of the church came not only from Trotter at Horncastle but from the commons of Louth, who in the recent past had given so much to the rebuilding of the spire of their church and refurbishing its linen and plate.[106]

Very early in the Lincolnshire rising, Cromwell was appraised of some of the grievances of the rebels; they appear to have wanted holy days as before, and that 'all religious husses beyng suppresyd may stand',[107] and this agrees with the testimony of Nicholas Leche, rector of Belchford, who stated that among the early attempts to draw up a list of their 'greffes' was a clause asking the king to let the 'abbays stande'.[108] George Huddiswell, one of the commons from Caistor, said they would take the king to be Supreme Head of the Church, but he should suppress no more abbeys.[109] That the commons were concerned about holy days is not surprising. Obviously they would have more opportunity to work and earn, at least in the summer, but the loss of festivities which marked these days would rid the village of much of its life and entertainment and an opportunity to indulge, at the expense of a nearby gentleman, in free ale and delicacies such as cakes and roasted meat.[110] They may also have perceived that the loss was of a piece with the Ten Articles and marked an attempt to focus their attention on God and his Son rather than on the saints – a point particularly stressed in the injunctions.[111] The concern for monasteries exhibited by the Lincolnshire rebels did not go to the extreme of actually re-instating the religious as it did later in the East Riding of Yorkshire and in Lancashire.[112] It probably owed a lot to the fact that tithe relations with the religious in Lincolnshire were at least amicable enough to produce no lawsuits;[113] but, additionally, it may have been appreciated by clergy and laity alike, that the return of monasticism would have the effect of removing from the shire religious who not only now wandered about the villages near their former houses, but also held 'capacities' which allowed them to compete for benefices on the same footing as seculars. Monks with capacities but no pension were a threat to the secular clergy, as the case of William Morland indicates. Morland had, after the dissolution of Louth Park, chosen to take a capacity and turn his back on the religious life, and he was at Keddington, where he lodged, when news of Kendall's sermon reached him. On 2 October he went to Louth to hear the gossip from a butcher related to another monk of Louth Park.[114] It was not long before Morland was involved – at first as a moderating influence. He initially tried to protect John Frankish, the bishop's registrar, and to save his papers, but he alleged that the commons were too strong for him. Thereafter he was one of those who joined up with the rebels in Horncastle and went to Lincoln and played a considerable part in leading them. His reasons were largely selfish. He hoped that if the bishop's vicar general deprived rectors and vicars of their benefices he would get a benefice himself.[115]

Other religious who were still in their houses also supported the rebels. The abbot of Barlings sent food to them,[116] and monks from Barlings, Kirkstead, Vaudey and Bardney were implicated in the rising.[117] Unlike the clergy, the commons and the ex-religious, these monks left no reasons for their dangerous participation in the rebellion. The abbot of Barlings tried to make out that he was forced to join the rebels.[118] But it would seem that the larger religious houses, quite as much as the small, were expecting dissolution or plunder even as early as 1536, and were envisaging being put in the same position as Morland. In any event the abbot of Barlings was quietly sending plate from his monastery, and the vicar of Scothern was looking after £100 of it for him. He also had £20 worth of plate belonging to Welbeck, and his sister had more; a priest in Lincoln was also storing a hamper of plate sent to him from Barlings.[119] The religious perhaps saw the rebellion as one desperate gamble to save their houses.

The gentry, like the religious, were also playing a dangerous game. Lord Hussey and Thomas Moigne were as deeply committed as the abbot of Barlings, and the Dymocks, Skipwiths and Ayscoughs, while alleging that they were intimidated into joining, had at best put up a token resistance and were ready enough to support and ultimately to lead the rebels.[120] As a result of their participation, grievances touching taxation and the statute of uses, both of them of no interest at all to the commons, religious, clergy or ex-religious, came to figure in the rebels' list of complaints.[121]

Though the gentry and the religious contributed to the Lincolnshire Rising, it was the priests who seem to have been at its centre, supported by their congregations. There is no suggestion of anticlericalism closely resembling tithe riots which occurred when the Pilgrimage of Grace was well under way in Westmorland,[122] nor was there any suggestion amongst the commons of rack renting, or unscrupulous enclosures which were a feature of the North-West, especially on the Earl of Cumberland's estates.[123] Lincolnshire sported no Protestants like Sir Francis Bigod.[124] Along with the desire to return to the old order with its holy days and monasteries, Kendall when examined said he had no desire but to establish the faith, and put down English books.[125] This was what the great number of clergy and people thought they were doing. When the bells were rung to raise the village of Alford, all took an oath to be true to the faith,[126] and when the rebels were not preceded by the emblem of the cross, they had the Sacrament before them.[127] Few saw the faith as involving the pope, though Kendall certainly did,[128] and the parson of Farforth made the first Sunday after the rebellion the occasion to pray for the pope and the cardinals.[129] In this, Lincolnshire differed from Beverley and the North-East, where books on the supremacy were said to be circulating.[130] Priests and people in Lincolnshire wanted the clock put back to 1534, not to 1529.

The protest was directed particularly not against the king but against those who had been instrumental in bringing novelty to their doors. Cromwell, the archbishop of Canterbury, and the bishop of Lincoln were especially hated. Longland's desire to be seen as the source of ecclesiastical authority in his own see, and his perhaps premature enactment of business, cost him the affection and respect of Lincolnshire. His people did not know that his aims were so close to their own, that he was concerned to keep out Protestantism and that he controlled preaching and searched out books. They did not know it because in the last week of September Longland was at Biggleswade. His preference for his manor of Wooburn in Buckinghamshire, which was in part necessitated by his duties at court, meant that he probably never preached about the supremacy in his cathedral church, as did Cuthbert Tunstall.[131] This did not mean that he emerged from the rebellion as a highly respected courtier bishop. He did not. Neither side trusted him, and by 1538 he was required to give his views over the supremacy.[132] He was at least alive to do so. The rebels, especially the priests, paid dearly for their involvement: of those priests originally put in prison (approximately seventy-nine[133]), not a single one whose participation is well authenticated was pardoned. This was not because all priests were as active as Thomas Kendall; it is hard to believe that a blind priest of Sotby who had been indiscreet enough to call Cromwell rude names really constituted a threat to the Tudor state – but he was executed all the same.[134] The anticlericalism so significantly absent in Lincolnshire was ruthlessly present in the king.[135]

APPENDIX: TEXT OF ORDER TO DECLARE SUPREMACY

Register 26, fo. 260v.

Ye shall understande that the unlawful jurisdiction, power and aucthoryte of longe tyme usurped by the bysshope of rome, in this realme, who then was called pope, is nowe by gods lawe, iustely lawfully and upon good groundes reasons and causes by aucthorite of parliament and by and with the hole consent and agrement of all the bisshops, prelates and bothe the unniversities of oxforthe and Cambridge and also the hole clergie of the realme extincte and ceased for ever and of [no] streng[t]he, value or effecte, in this realme of Englande. In wiche realme the sayd hole clergie, Bisshops, prelates, and either of the convocacions of both provinces with also the universities of oxforthe and Cambridge, have accordyng to godes lawes, and upon good and lawfull reasons and groundes, knowledged the kinges highnes to be supreme hede in erthe immedyatly undre god of the chirche of Englande, which there knowledge confessed beyng nowe by Parliament establisshed and by gods lawe justifiable to be iustely executed. Soo ought every true chisten subiecte of this realme not oonly to knowledge and obedyently to recognise the kynges highnes to be supreme hede in erthe of the churche of England but also to speke, publisshe and teache there children and servantes the same and to shewe unto them howe that the sayd bisshope of Rome hath hertofore usurped not onlye upon god, but also upon princes of this realme and there progenitors. Wherefore and to thentent (fo. 261) ye shold the better beleve me and take and receve the truthe as ye ought to do I declare this unto you not onely of my seffe which I know to be true but also declare unto you thathe same is certified to me from the mowthe of myn ordinary the bisshope of Lincoln undre his seale. Whiche I have here redy to shewe you.

IV

1538–47:
THE BATTLE FOR THE CONSCIENCES OF ENGLISHMEN

The aftermath of the Pilgrimage of Grace and that small initial part of it known as the Lincolnshire rebellion proved in every way difficult for John Longland. To the rebels he, quite as much as Cranmer and Cromwell, had provoked the rebellion.[1] To those suppressing it, notably Cromwell and Charles Brandon, Duke of Suffolk, he was a lot nearer to the church of Rome than they would like a bishop of such a large diocese to be. To add to Longland's difficulties he had lost a good vicar general in Dr Rayne; the rebellion was also at its most dangerous in his nephew's archdeaconry of Lincoln, and it is hard to suppose that the bishop had much sympathy and understanding for the problems which prompted the unrest of the secular clergy and the religious: the former had rarely received the benefit of his attention and the latter were the subject of his pained correction. The proper course on which to set his diocese after so dramatic an upheaval (which called into question such fundamental issues affecting this life if not the world to come) should also have concerned him. Longland kept his nerve and, for good or ill, exhibited few signs of dissenting from the outward policy of his king even though he was not afraid to take issue with his vicegerent. As his intransigent policy grew more marked, it led inevitably to an increasing personal and national isolation, and in late 1536 this was acute.

The immediate problem was one of personnel; who should be vicar general, and should he hold the post permanently or only in Longland's absence? At first it was given to Robert Cliffe,[2] but within a year to Anthony Draycott, an Oxford canon lawyer who had also served briefly as commissary general.[3] Draycott seems to have held his post on a permanent basis, though his commission does not survive. By 1537 he was as pervasive as Rayne had been, and his activity in the church in the diocese spanned the reigns of Edward VI and Mary and only faltered

4. The manor of Liddington

under Elizabeth. She had him confined to the Fleet and he died in 1571.[4] For Longland in the earlier years, this meant that he was free to be at court or in the diocese as he chose. It would appear that he visited some archdeaconries in 1543 in person, notably that of Buckingham, which was nearest to his favourite residence of Wooburn. We know that he visited his cathedral in 1539,[5] and that when the king and queen visited the city, they were received into the close by the bishop, who celebrated high mass to mark the occasion.[6] But he seems, partly through age and partly through inclination, to have preferred to stay at Holborn or Wooburn and to direct his deputies, notably his vicar general, from there.[7] His concern for the reform of the church had largely been overtaken by events: the plea for a close adherence to the rule could now only fall on ruined cloisters, and both he and Tunstall must have reflected ruefully on their protests to Erasmus on pilgrimages and fasts; Cranmer and Cromwell and even the king himself had put an end to much of that.

It was less easy to dispel doubts about Longland's own personal loyalty. It was curious that he was not appointed to the groups of scholars who were to scan the translation of the Old and New Testaments. In view of his theological knowledge and his position as chancellor of the university of Oxford, this must have been a calculated snub by his fellow bishops.[8] Longland continued to remind Cromwell that his nephew Richard Pate needed money, but the ultimate defection of Pate once again raised questions of the family's allegiance.[9] Longland's papers were searched in 1541, but nothing incriminating appears to have been found. Longland seems to have been genuinely committed to a royal supremacy 'under God', and was too experienced an observer of the court scene to have left around anything incriminating – even supposing there was any evidence of that kind. He seems to have realised, somewhat late, that ecclesiastical conservatism or reform were no longer within the power of the bishops and convocations, but that the king in Parliament was the important means of change. In consequence of his perception of this fact, we find him personally attending the House of Lords and convocation much more regularly than he had in his early years as a bishop and more regularly than most of his fellow bishops.[10]

But what of his theological view-point? What did Longland make of the Ten Articles, the Bishops' Book and the Six Articles? Early in 1536, he had on Good Friday preached before the king at Greenwich and his theme was, as ever, designed to rouse his audience to acknowledge their sins, do penance and follow Christ. But he also urged his congregation to submit themselves to the sacraments of the church:

For undre this manner, it besemeth us to fulfyll all justice, *id est humilitate* al humylite. Here christe taught all ye worlde humblye to submytee themselves unto the sacramentes of hys churche, whate degree so ever they be of.[11]

The Ten Articles which came out after this sermon did not mention three of the sacraments, and within a few months of his preaching, the question of the number of sacraments had become a crucial one. By 1537, Longland, as a signatory to the *Institutions of a Christian Man*, subscribed to the preface which explained: 'we have intreated of the institution the vertue and right use of the seven sacraments',[12] and to the explicit assumption that confirmation, marriage and unction were among them.[13] The *Institutions* signed by the bishops were a statement of the faith which became known as the Bishops' Book and which the king ordered to be promulgated in churches for three years. In 1538 the second set of royal injunctions were issued, and they included much of concern to the clergy and laity alike. They included the requirement that a Bible in English was to be placed in every church and no one was to be prevented from reading it; parishioners were to be taught the Our Father, the Creed and the Ten Commandments in English and were to be examined upon them in the confessional. Superstitious ceremonies were to be condemned and lights were only to be burned in the rood loft, before the Sacrament, and before the sepulchre in the church. Non-resident absentees were responsible for seeing that their curates read and acted on these injunctions, but only licensed preachers were to expound them. Parish registers were to be kept and fast days were not to be altered without permission. The bell for the *Ave* after mass was to be abandoned and the suffrages *Parce nobis Domine* and *Libera nos Domine* were to be preferred to *Ora pro nobis* which was so obviously addressed to the saints rather than to God.[14]

For a bishop whose diocese had rebelled at the curtailment of holy days and whose clergy disliked being examined, these requirements would smack of radical Protestantism, and the problem of enforcement would be exceedingly great. Cromwell appreciated this, and in returning to Longland and to other bishops their rights of visitation he had transferred the main brunt of enforcement to them.[15] Cromwell had had the royal injunctions printed, and Longland appears to have let them go out without embellishment. In 1543, in his personal visitations, he tested whether the clergy had complied with the requirements, but there were a number of questions which the injunctions raised for Longland himself. The most pressing of these was whether he thought it wise or right to have an English Bible in each church or whether anyone and everyone should have access to read it. This was a question to which Longland had addressed himself before he was elevated to the episcopate.

In his early sermons, notably that to the monks of Westminster, he had stated that 'scripture is like a nut . . . the rind is bitter, the shell hard, the kernel alone sweet and nourishing'.[16] He was certain that this inner kernel was only reached by those who had the necessary training, which was pre-eminently theological, and those who had the gift of the spirit to understand the mysteries of the spirit. By 1538 he was a lot less certain of this. He seems to have moved closer to his old friend Erasmus; by 1538, preaching before the king, he asked his congregation to consider the fate of Sodom and Gomorrah:

> Why shall it be moore tollerable to the Sodoms and gentyles than to false chrysten people . . . ? Veryly for that they herde never the worde of god declared amonges them. They had never the prophett nor scripture. They had never the gospel taught them. We have Moses and the prophettes. We have olde testamentes and the newe. We have the Gospell and the holy scrypture publysed, taught and preached among us: spoken, opened declared and manifestly showed unto us. We have it in Hebrue, in Greke, in Latyn, and in Englyshe. We have it in our owne mother tongue. We ioye and reiose moche and soo may we, that we soo have it in our own vulgar speche, that we here it, that we reede it, that we have it in our bosomes and hangynge at our gyrdles, and it is dayly preached amonges us. But what shall this profette, yff we lyve not thereafter? Yf we lyve not well and Chrystyanly? What shall we be the better for it if we amende not our lyves . . . Of all the philosophers that ever were, Aristotle lyeth loweste in hell. And why? For he had most knowledge of all philosophers and was dryven by his naturall knoledge, to know *primam causam*, god: and yet worshypped hym not. Soo we chrysten people, we have the bookes and gospell of Chryst. We have all the scrypture in Englyshe, we have knowledge of god and of his lawes; and yet doo not we lyve thereafter wall shall we say to it but that . . . of all the people of the worlde, yf we be dampned, we shall be moost grevously dampned.[17]

In this same sermon he was also addressing himself to the subject of the king as head of the church 'undre god'. It is sometimes suggested that the sermon was delivered under pressure, but since Longland was so regular a preacher this may be doubted. He seems to have taken the headship and the vernacular Bible as part of the necessary reformation. In his change of mind on the subject of scripture, he contrasts notably with Tunstall of Durham; Tunstall, who had expressed similar views on Scripture in the 1520s, kept to them and was deeply dissatisfied with the Great Bible.[18]

Whatever the reasons for Longland's change of mind over the Bible, he perceived with great clarity that the immediate challenge it presented to the pastor was one of interpretation. He needed to secure preachers who would instruct congregations in the precise way in which it supported controversial issues such as transubstantiation or justification. There is considerable evidence to suggest that from 1538 Longland devoted a lot of time and energy to selecting preachers rather than attacking the finer points of translation which might well be over the heads of his people, or looking to the small print of the injunctions which might frighten rather than reassure.

In February 1538, Longland ordered licensed preachers to 'preach in Latin or in English whichever seemed better to them at least four times in a year ... and preach matters which belonged to the true doctrine of the church and not preach on matters which were doubtful and that they should declare the articles recently published by the king and approved by convocation'.[19] These orders show exactly how a conservative bishop could use his episcopal power to advance a conservative cause, or a Protestant bishop could use the same power to achieve the opposite purpose, as Cranmer did in Kent.[20] Longland allows for preaching in Latin, and this would have been accepted procedure in the universities, but a Latin sermon given in the heart of Lincolnshire or Bedfordshire would not stir the congregation from its slumber and could be guaranteed to leave them as theologically ignorant and as practically conservative as they had ever been. On the other hand, the vernacular preacher had to confine himself to uncontentious issues, and these were very difficult to identify, especially in the circumstances of 1539–40 when the Six Articles were thought to contradict the Ten. Who would be the judge of which issues were contentious and which were not? Longland was clear. He was the judge in his own diocese and preachers who deviated from the Six Articles were liable to be silenced with some speed. Longland had reason to believe that Robert Wisdom, the curate of All Hallows, Oxford, was a Protestant. He was forbidden to preach and wrote in complaint to Cromwell:

> forasmuch as I preached Christ and spoke against ungodliness and false doctrine of the papacy, they found means to hunt me thence.[21]

Others who found themselves on the wrong side of the bishop on contentious issues were summarily silenced: Dr Drax of Huntingdon was put in gaol so that he might preach what Longland regarded as heresy to the damp walls.[22] When Longland refused a priest a licence to preach either because the applicant lacked sufficient learning or because he mistrusted his theology, he took care to inform Cromwell so that appeals to the vicegerent by the aggrieved were stopped. In 1539 he wrote to Cromwell: 'There came oon to me callede Curtas to have a lycence to preache within my dioces. Whom I knowe notte be mete for that office as well for lacke of lerninge as of good lyvinge [being noted as] a lighte wylde persone in many thinges.' Longland asked the vicegerent not to licence him.[23] The mutual understanding worked both ways, as the case of the parish priest of Horncastle makes clear. Longland thought that his preaching was rash and insincere; Cromwell examined him and thought his sermons 'proceded of simplicite and Ignorance than of any malice or arragancie'. He thought that the priest had repented and should be absolved.[24]

The care which Longland took over licensing of preachers was not a purely negative exercise with the aim of keeping out Protestant ideas; it was also directed towards the considerable task of making a congregation understand what the church had believed for hundreds of years. It was aimed at defeating heresy by substituting a quasi-Gallican Catholicism which held the hearts and minds of its exponents. And the organisation and the checking of such preaching was carefully watched. Books had to be kept which recorded not only the number of sermons preached in a given parish but also the name of the preacher and occasionally whether his licence came from the bishop or from the archbishop of Canterbury. Some of these books have survived, and they give some idea of the way in which a conservative bishop like Longland could and did use the traditionally Protestant weapon of preaching to advance a Catholicism of the Six Articles. Books of preachers dating from 1538 survive for 313 parishes in Northamptonshire; a very sketchy and difficult record of preaching for the same date has survived for the 109 parishes of the Leicestershire deaneries of Framland, Goscote and Gartree. An exceedingly full book has survived for 118 parishes of the archdeaconry of Bedford in 1541. From this material it looks as though the preaching in the archdeaconry of Bedford was considerably better in terms of the number of sermons preached than that of the archdeaconries of Northampton and Leicester. In Bedford a very high percentage of parishes had four or more sermons in a year; this was not the case in Northampton and Leicester, as Table 24 shows.

There are a number of explanations for the different patterns of preaching which obtained in the archdeaconries of Bedford, of Leicester and of Northampton. The most obvious is date. In 1538 the order to keep books of sermons and the strongly worded order to read the injunctions and to preach, while not new – the clergy had, since the days of

Table 24. *Sermons preached in a year (1538 and 1541), by parish*[25]

Archdeaconry	None	One	Two	Three	Four	More	Not given
Northampton (1538)	42	15	36	62	47	48	63
Leicester (1538)	29	10	12	10	7	11	30
Bedford (1541)	2	0	3	2	84	27	0

Archbishop Pecham, been bound to preach four times in a year – was novel in its emphasis. Moreover, the expectation that sermons would be scripturally based (or as the injunction put it, 'you shall make or cause to be made in the said church, and every other cure you have, one sermon every quarter of the year at the least wherein you shall purely and sincerely declare the very gospel of Christ and in the same exhort your hearers to the works of charity, mercy and faith, specially prescribed and commanded in Scripture')[26] was very new. In the past a preacher might have resort to handbooks of sermons which contained the lives of saints and much apocryphal matter. To preach uncontentiously from the Bible was a wholly new skill for most of the parish clergy and one which they would only gradually learn. At Teigh, Thomas Caslyn claimed in September 1538 that he had preached twenty sermons, but all parishioners were not bombarded in this way. Plague raged at Oakham and explains why there was no preaching there,[27] and the incumbents of Bisbrook, Ryhall, Whisenden and Thistleton were old and frail and could not change their ways; as far as we know they were left in their parishes to die in peace and their parishioners remained ignorant with them.[28] By 1541, when the sermons of the archdeaconry of Bedford were recorded, there had been some attempts to meet the problems of ignorance and old age. A small group of licensed preachers, mainly graduates, undertook all the preaching in the archdeaconry, and this made it easier for Longland to control preaching. Unfortunately we know little about them. In the city of Bedford, as well as in the surrounding country parishes, the most frequent preacher was John Meigote who was rector of St Peter Dunstable in the city and one of the bishop's own chaplains.[29] The city church of St Paul, Bedford, had twelve sermons in a year, of which Meigote preached four and the bishop's vicar general preached at least one.[30] It may be because Bedford was so near to the diocese of Ely and to Cambridge, and so near to the scheming Bishop Goodrich, who regarded the archdeaconry as being very backward, that Longland had ordered the archdeacon himself to preach in the archdeaconry eight times in a year.[31]

The wisdom of keeping the preaching of an area in a few hands and especially of confining it, where possible, to graduates who had a gift for it, as had John Harris who undertook much of the preaching in the deanery of Haddon, comes out more clearly if Bedford is compared with Northampton.[32] One of the most frequent preachers in the archdeaconry of Northampton was a former friar, Stephen Wilson, who preached at one time or another in most of the parishes of Northampton itself.[33] But his activities were brought to a halt when in October 1538 he was accused of heresy. He was alleged to have said that the body of Christ was not contained in the sacrament of the altar and that 'matens and masse was but a babbelyng', and that requiems were designed for the gain of the clergy: 'we have flatered a grette whyle and all for money. We have said for gayne of money that a trentall wolde save a man or woman their soule, and that a masse of *scala celi* would save a soul from hell, and all for money.'[34] Not content with this, Wilson had apparently been apprehended by two sergeants in a lane off the Northampton–Kingsthorpe road having intercourse with a beggar woman.[35] The evidence against Wilson was massive and he was sent for trial at the bishop's consistory court, the papers of which are unfortunately lost; but his defence against the accusation that he had denied that the bread was the body of Christ is so sophisticated that it is clear that both the defence of transubstantiation and the attack upon it were being debated no longer in the simplicity of the Lollard assertions but with the subtlety of university graduates. He was alleged to have been at 'the sign of the Bell' in Northampton when a certain Richard Moreton asked 'how say you by the sacrament of the altar?'. And '... Sir Thomas ... of Brinkton answeryd and said that itt was only god his body. And then ...' Stephen Wilson said,

ye must undrestand the term better, for it is *corpus dominicum* and *corpus christi*; for god of his own kinde and nature is without body, for *verbum carno factum est* for christe is bothe god and man. And his manhood suffered for us. *Hoc est corpus meum quod pro vobis tradetur in remissionem peccatorum.* And in the sacrament of the altar is bothe god and man. And then oon Parker a butcher of Northampton being present said, I saw this day the body of god present betwene a pristes handes. And this respondent answered ne no *unquamvidit deum* [*sic*] No man kan see god with his carnall eyes in this world as god is, in his godly fruition, And in his body gloryfyed but wee see in forme, figure or shappe of brede hym, where as noo brede is, for ther is *accidente sive subiecto*. Therefore the godhede is knyte with the manhode and the manhode with the godhede that they kannot be segregate nor separate asunder. Therefore these passeth mannes capacyte to perceyve by his uttward senses but by beleve in faith which is the inward sign of the godhed.[36]

With talk at the bar attaining that level of sophistication, the battle for the allegiance of parishioners to one set of religious beliefs rather than another was certainly moving deep into difficult theological issues, which it would have been strange to hear in Northampton even ten years before. It was a lesson learned by Longland; in Bedfordshire nine priests delivered most of the sermons, and the only one who may have had Protestant learnings was William Brayse, who had a licence to preach from the archbishop; he may have been the same William Brayse who was deprived of his benefice under Mary because he had married.[37] The hold that Longland tried to keep over preaching in his diocese, and the conservative direction which he insisted it should follow stands out in stark contrast to the efforts of Cranmer in Canterbury.[38] Both men seem to have seen clearly that though the king held the supremacy and though their powers were now described as supported by him, there was still room for individuality and indeed conflicting theology to be exercised in one diocese and not in another.

The control of preaching was one crucial area in which Protestant and conservative fought for supremacy. But the bishops were also charged with the task of enforcing the other injunctions of 1538, as well as the requirement that holy days be limited as in 1536. Furthermore, as though that were not enough, there was the question of the purchase of vernacular Bibles. Full visitation returns for the diocese of Lincoln do not survive for the period 1538–47 and it is therefore difficult to know how diligently Longland or his deputies enquired into the clergy's conformity with the injunctions and with the order for Bibles; but a court of audience book does survive which suggests that Longland asked some searching questions of the clergy of Buckinghamshire and west Bedfordshire – especially in relation to the injunctions of 1538, with their requirement for a parochial register and for the preaching to the parish and teaching the Our Father, the Creed and the Ten Commandments in the vernacular. Longland was unlikely simply to have asked such questions of one set of clergy; in all probability he visited or dealt with the cases arising from a visitation in the southern part of his diocese and he left Draycott to tackle the north. But certainly the cases which came before him in 1543 suggest a thorough and full examination at a visitation of one area of his diocese, and it is improbable that he would have let the matter rest there.

Of the eighteen clergy up before him accused of ignoring either the 1538 injunctions, the Bishops' Book or the Ten Articles, he found that fourteen had failed in their duties in one or more respects, and only four seem to have been cited to appear wrongfully. Their reasons for disobedience were basically of three kinds: the most serious were those which arose because the priest involved disagreed with one or more of the Articles which he was bound to tell his parish, because he was, in all probability, a heretic. The second reason was that of incomprehension accompanied or exacerbated by idleness. The third reason was a bland statement of ignorance of the injunctions which was not as naive as it might appear: William Bolton, vicar of Dorney in Buckinghamshire, claimed he had never heard of the convocation articles or the royal injunctions; yet he had read the Six Articles and he had preached, and he kept a register of births, deaths and marriages, which suggests he knew (albeit unwittingly) something of the royal injunctions of 1538. In all probability his difficulties arose because he did not have a copy of the 1538 injunctions, which were printed,[39] and appear to have cost three pence.[40] Those who had not read the injunctions or acted upon them from incomprehension and idleness were the most numerous. The vicar of Upton, Geoffrey Meredith, was typical of them; he told the bishop he had no idea what was in the convocation articles but he had tried to teach the Pater Noster for three years and had examined his penitents. He had kept a register of preaching but he had not read the king's articles nor was he too clear what they were.[41] The rector of Hitcham had not preached nor read the Six Articles, the Bishops' Book or the royal injunctions and he had not taught the parish the Pater Noster in the mother tongue.[42] He seems to have become confused by all the activity expected of a parish priest and resembles the vicar of Stainton, who apparently commanded 'holy days summe wekes when there is non and sum tyme on a wrong day'.[43] Confusion and ignorance seem to have accounted for the fact that William Wright, vicar of High Wycombe, and his curate had not read the articles of convocation nor the king's book and went on to declare that they thought no curate in the diocese had declared them.[44]

But there were some priests who were more dangerous in the bishop's eyes than those who had adopted the age old adage 'when in doubt, do nowt'. Among the Buckinghamshire and Bedfordshire clergy were a very small group whose disobedience was clearly due to their dissent from the content of the documents which they were being asked to read or act upon. John Carter, vicar of Streatley in Bedfordshire border – appears not merely to have ignored the Six Articles but to have been communicating his parishioners in *both* kinds; sceptically and with a certain coarse ribaldry he told them 'whan thou arte housseld thou doeste take butt thre sippes of wyne of the chalice att the pristes handes for they iid. Where as, thou mightest faare better for thy iid att the tavern. And when thou makest curtesye thre tymes, I cannot tell why thou doeste soo, excepte itt be to the preste orels to the wyne.'[45] There was no merit in attending an early morning mass in Carter's view: 'This daye ye have done nothinge butt disqyted yor selves, and hurted your bodyes with erly rysinge for the twoo masses that ye have harde doeth you noo goode because ye knowe nott the meanying of them.'[46] He was not in favour of good works and told his flock, 'The goode workes that one dothe, dothe nott prouffite for them butt for the faith he doth them on.'[47] The sacrament of unction was in the same category as far as Carter was concerned: 'Whan a man is a dyinge, than they come rennynge to the priste and saynge, come come, he wolbe gone. Where as itt were as goode to anoynte hym with a litle tarre, if he knowe not the meaning of itt.'[48] Carter was well within the spirit of the injunctions in disliking the ceremonies connected with Holy Week; he disapproved of veiling the cross and then unveiling it; the cloth 'signyfyth butt for a nett to catch sparrowes' and 'that thou coudeste nott tell wherefore servede the plucking upp of the clothe before the rode and coveringe of the Images except itt shulde be for wanton children to play pype boo'.[49] His ideas were closer to those of Luther than of Henry VIII or his bishop, and he was duly removed from his cure but not before he had horrified the entire parish by burying a parishioner singing the litany in English as he led the corpse into church, followed by the *Gloria in excelsis*, and interring the corpse to the strains of the *Te Deum*.[50]

Few in the diocese of Lincoln dissented from the royal injunctions of 1538 on grounds of conviction. Nicholas Dere of Hitcham had taken his scriptural exegesis too far by suggesting 'it is nott mencyondde in the scripture that any man is bounde to faste'; he preached in spite of the royal injunctions and had no licence to preach at all.[51] Some held pronounced heretical views, but few others have left signs of ignoring the king or the bishop; at Spalding the curates had failed to instruct the parishioners in the articles of faith,[52] but we have evidence only of the delinquents, and if they represent even one tenth of the number of clergy who disobeyed the king, then the enforcement of these injunctions went forward reasonably smoothly.

The same was not true of the provision of the Bible in every parish church. Problems beset that on every side: not only was there a failure to print the Bible on time, but its price might well put it out of the reach of a poor parish. The royal injunctions of 1538 ordered that a Bible was to be put in each parish, though there is a possibility that an earlier injunction to the same effect had been made since it appears in episcopal injunctions in 1537.[52] In any event an approved test had not appeared by then, and though other texts which relied heavily on Tyndale and Coverdale were published, the Great Bible did not appear until April 1539.[53] Longland did not receive an order to convey to his archdeacons that the churches in his jurisidction should possess an English Bible until May 1541,[54] and it was not until that date that the price of the Bible was limited to ten shillings for an unbound copy and twelve shillings for one 'sufficiently bound, trimmed and clasped' and churches were ordered by proclamation to acquire one before the feast of All Saints 1541.[55] The dean and chapter bought two copies of the Bible for the cathedral at thirteen shillings each between September 1540 and September 1541, and they also bought copies for their appropriated churches.[56] Louth and Amersham had apparently bought a Bible between 1539 and 1540[57] but other churches may not have done so. It was said of the fifty parishes of the deaneries of Horncastle, Hill and Gartree in September 1539 that there were forty Testaments lacking.[58]

In general, there is no way of knowing at what date the parishes of the diocese made their purchase. Certainly by 1548, when inventories of church goods were made, there are occasional mentions of a Bible, but these are so few that it seems more likely that books were not normally included in the inventory than that only two parishes, Ulceby and Maltby, had them.[59] By August 1542 Longland had ordered the reading of Scripture three days a week, on Monday and Wednesday and Friday, for all in holy orders in the cathedral.[60] Only one case survives of a layman being accused of reading it irreverently: he was a tailor of Colnbrook who was said to possess heretical books and was no doubt apprehended primarily for that reason.[61] One ignorant incumbent who was in danger of being deprived of his living for that reason signed a promise to the bishop that he would 'study ancient doctors upon scripture and holy faders admytted by the chirche'.[62] His predicament is a reminder that quite apart from licensing or withholding licences from preachers and checking whether incumbents had complied with royal injunctions or not, a bishop could also limit or accelerate the pace of change in his diocese both by his own patronage and by refusing to admit to a benefice a priest whom he deemed unsuitable.

The problem for a bishop in detecting suspected heretics and refusing to admit them was two-fold. In the first place, if the living was the first the aspirant had ever held or the first he had held within his diocese, the bishop was unlikely to know his affiliations unless he was a well-known Protestant. The second problem was to find the *grounds* on which to refuse admission. If the living was genuinely vacant and the patron was the correct one, grounds had to be found to object to the suitability of the candidate. If he was of age and legitimate birth he could only be refused on educational grounds, as had been the case with candidates before the break with Rome. The oath not to promote Lutheran ideas which Longland had used in the late 1520s and early 1530s would be so outrageous in the eyes of either Cranmer or Cromwell that it might bring down on the bishop more abuse than ever. Ironically, the greatest single factor which helped the bishop to keep Lutherans from the benefices in his diocese was the enormous spread of patronage after the dissolution of the monasteries.

Excluding the king and the bishop himself, only twenty-seven persons or institutions had more than two livings in their gift in the whole diocese between 1536 and the bishop's death in May 1547. This meant that it was extremely difficult for patrons to combine in such a way as to make a given area a Protestant enclave. The two people with obvious power to do so were the king, who exercised just over 20% of the patronage during this period, and the bishop, who exercised just under 5% of it. The only other patrons with a significant amount of patronage were Charles Brandon, Duke of Suffolk and his wife Katherine. The bishop never advanced a committed Protestant; Charles Brandon did, and so did Thomas Goodrich, Bishop of Ely, who presented three candidates for admission to benefices at this time.[63] Brandon gave two of his livings to Alexander Seton,[64] who resided in neither[65] and was busy preaching in London, for which he was apprehended and accused of heresy; he recanted but did not, as far as we know, ever even visit his livings in the diocese of Lincoln.[66] The remaining Suffolk benefices went to priests and ex-religious who exhibited no signs of their patron's Protestant inclinations.

The crucial importance of patronage took some time to grasp, and not surprisingly it was the bishops who were first to perceive it. Longland, like Goodrich, used his patronage to promote graduates of similar sympathies to his own. The valuable living of Goxhill went to a friar from Southampton who had preached in support of the pope but had been let off further process after a long interview with Cromwell.[67]

Longland's chaplains received livings but very few were non-residents: John Meigote resided in the parish of St Peter Dunstable and from there did some useful preaching.[68] Only one of those Longland collated in this period was certainly a non-resident.[69] Royal patronage would appear to have lacked a policy in its application. Many so appointed seem to have been non-resident, and two priests were certainly Protestants and known to be such; but there were a large number whose personal histories are not known to us.[70] Among others presented to livings there would be many who would emerge as Protestants, but there are few means of knowing their convictions on appointment, or of ascertaining the precise moment at which they could be called committed Protestants.

Obviously, if a priest's behaviour attracted enough notice for him to be brought before the bishop, or if he offended against the Treason Act or Act of Six Articles it is possible to see his real convictions. Nine priests from the diocese were attainted between 1538 and 1545[71] and they were found guilty of allegiance to the papacy rather than of any Protestant opinions. One of the most notable was James Mallett who apart from holding many benefices had been in residence in the cathedral at the time of the Pilgrimage of Grace. By 1542 he had been found guilty of treason by words and executed.[72] The defection of the archdeacon of Lincoln to Cardinal Pole was less important in a sense; he had spent most of his time abroad where the lines dividing Catholic from Protestant tended to be more clear cut.[73]

The extreme Protestants seem to have been somewhat more successful at escaping the executioner than their conservative brethren. But William Jerome, who was rector of Heather in 1532, had read theology at Oxford, and was at one time a monk of Christ Church, Canterbury, preached at St Paul's cross in 1540; he was examined after his sermons on his Lutheran views but undeterred he preached again and was attainted by Parliament and burned at Smithfield in July 1540.[74] One other incumbent seems to have been in trouble for his Protestant views: Edward Crone, who was non-resident rector of Swinbrook and vicar general to the bishop of Salisbury, had got married in 1538. Subsequently he preached in London some inflammatory sermons – all in the Protestant cause. But his sail turned to the wind. He surrendered and gave formal obedience to the pope and became Warden of the English College in Rome. The times were attuned to such extremities.[75]

The formal oath renouncing the bishop of Rome, demanded by statute,[76] began to be taken in 1540. The date is curious because it followed naturally from the oaths of 1534–5 denying that the bishop of

Rome had greater authority than any other foreign bishop in England. From 1540, the oath became standard practice at the admission of a candidate to a benefice. It excited no difficulty or fuss.[77] These oaths did not clearly indicate that a priest was a conservative or a Protestant; and the first occasion that we have which may give us some indication at least of what priests did not believe, if not of what they did, is the thoroughly unsatisfactory one of the Marian deprivations.

There is some connection between Protestantism and clerical marriage; but clerks under Mary were deprived for an assortment of reasons of which marriage was only one, albeit the most usual. Professor Dickens summarises the historian's dilemma over the evidence for clerical marriage shrewdly and accurately: 'the assumption that married priests necessarily held "advanced" doctrinal opinions would carry us far beyond the evidence and beyond common sense itself'.[78] Only a tiny handful of clerks got married while Henry VIII was on the throne. Though Cranmer was one of them, the death penalty which was to be inflicted on married clergy resulted in his sending his wife abroad.[79] The majority of the clergy who got married at all did so under Edward VI. It is, therefore, highly dubious to infer from a marriage which could have taken place secretly under Henry VIII or openly under Edward (that is to say some time *before* 1553) a predisposition to Protestantism. What we can say is that a married priest had rejected the discipline but not necessarily the doctrine of the Roman Catholic church, and that this was a step – albeit a first and tentative one – which might end in a wholehearted espousal of Protestantism.

The paucity of the records on the crucial question of theological conviction, and the fact that we really do not know how many priests were Protestant when Longland died, has driven us desperately and reluctantly to the figures for Marian deprivations.

By the time of Mary the diocese of Lincoln had lost Northamptonshire, Rutland and Oxfordshire. It totalled some 1,135 parishes;[80] from these parishes 111 priests were deprived, and this figure *perforce* includes those deprived for reasons other than marriage. In the preceding period they had been very few, but we should recognise that the Marian deprivations are likely to include some whose reasons for deprivation do not survive but were not for marriage. With these limitations in mind, deprivations under Mary were as follows in Table 25. These figures are surprising for a number of reasons; we would have expected that (even if all were deprived for marital reasons) the priests of Buckinghamshire might have modified their attitude to Catholic discipline more markedly in

Table 25. *Marian deprivations*[81]

Archdeaconry	Number of parishes	Percentage of deprivations of incumbents
Buckingham	185	7.56%
Huntingdon	167	7.78%
Leicester	192	4.68%
Bedford	123	13.00%
Lincoln and Stow	468	12.60%

view of the Protestant views circulating in the shire;[82] equally we might have supposed that Lincolnshire, which was reactionary on doctrinal issues in 1536, would be conservative over clerical discipline. But the real interest in these figures is the comparison which arises from them with other parts of the country: in Lancashire only 4% of clerks were deprived; in the diocese of York 10% were deprived, and in Norfolk, Suffolk and Essex a quarter of all clerks were deprived.[83] If we compare these figures, only Leicestershire would appear to vie with Lancashire for the laurels of conservatism in disciplinary matters, but Bedford and Lincolnshire are conspicuous as having more married clergy apparently than York. We might expect Bedfordshire to come under the influence of attitudes prevailing in the diocese of Ely, but we would not have expected Lincolnshire to have done so. But in the six years between Longland's death and the process commencing against Marian clergy, new priests had obviously got livings. To what extent had Longland admitted priests who were to depart from what he would have regarded as an essential point of discipline and to what extent was his successor responsible?

The records of institutions in the period 1547–60 are so poor that it is frequently hard to know exactly when a priest received a living. We do, however, know if he was admitted to it under Longland; only 34 of the 111 deprived were certainly beneficed while Longland was bishop of Lincoln; the remainder owed their cures to a later period. There is no means of knowing if or when these 34 actually got married, but, spread over the diocese, they account for 2.9% of beneficed priests. It does not look as though, on these somewhat shaky figures, the diocese of Lincoln was all set to become Protestant in 1547, but it was not so conscious of Catholic discipline and duty as to be immune from the attractions of Protestant discipline and therefore of Protestant theology.

The laity were a different matter, though Longland clearly thought that if he controlled preaching carefully enough he would keep the laity in the faith in which they had been brought up, even though it had been changed in regard to the headship of the church and more dramatically still with the dissolution of the monasteries. But certain things had not altered. The services were the same, and it was still the formally held view that the Bread and Wine at mass became the Body and Blood of Christ. Certainly the parishioner would have noticed the change in the number of feast days, and, as we have seen, the men of Lincolnshire protested at it. But the central ceremonies which often marked a crucial point in a man's life were there unchanged, and though unction might be ridiculed by the Lutheran, it and the desire for a fitting requiem were common requests at the time of death. Grief could be channelled into prayer in a cycle of requiem masses which the mourner believed would assist the departed, and if the saints could not be prayed to and revered as they had been, yet they still by their merits assisted the penitent sinner on his last journey. The performance of a requiem had often been undertaken by the religious orders, especially if thirty (a trentall) were required, but there were still enough priests ready and able to earn a shilling or two for performing the same office. Had the faith of the parish remained the same in spite of these changes, or had the laity begun to adopt different ideas of purgatory, of the mass and above all of justification by faith?[84]

The same methodological problems beset us in attempting to answer that question as we have noted in attempting to see how far the priests of the diocese had remained as conservative as their bishop. Attempts have been made to infer the loyalties and tenets of the departed from their wills. If testators use a conservative formula at the beginning of the will, this has been taken to indicate a Catholic or conservative faith. The problem about this method of taking the theological temperature of Englishmen is that wills were often written for the dying by scribes who used their own formulae and did not necessarily accept one from the testator. This is especially marked in Lincolnshire. Thus, a shoemaker of Boston named Richard Smith made his will on 5 December 1550. He bequeathed his soul to Almighty God 'trusting faithfylly to be saved by the death and passion of our Saviour Jesus Christ and to be redeemed from all my synnes by the shedding of hys most precious blood'.[85] This was a very different formula from that used by the great majority of testators in the shire, and it would appear that Smith had adopted a more obviously Protestant attitude to the atonement. But the same formula occurs in two other wills, both from persons resident in Boston. It is, therefore, highly probable that there was a scribe in Boston who always used this formula, and subsequent wills from that area confirm that hypothesis.[86]

But if will formulae, however eccentric, are not a reliable guide to the faith of the deceased, some of the *bequests* made in the will may be. Those who bequeathed money for requiems clearly still believed in their value and in the existence of purgatory. Those who left money to the cathedral and to their parish church were more likely to have seen the church militant as a visible body rather than as the invisible body of the elect. Those who left money to the poor often did so because they saw this as a charitable work required by the Gospels. In April 1546 Alice Bronde left the residue of her goods 'to workes of charytie according to the commanmentes of God'.[87] With these considerations in mind, if we look at the pattern of bequests from our sample archdeaconries in 1545 and 1550 and compare them with the earlier patterns of giving, it becomes clear that a change in belief only occurs between 1545 and 1550, and not in the period when Longland was scanning preachers and hunting heretics, (see Table 26, p. 177). It was the arrival of a new king and a new bishop in the diocese of Lincoln that changed or began to change the faith of the ordinary parishioner.[88]

Changes are particularly remarkable in Huntingdonshire; the number of bequests for some form of intercession for the deceased with his family was very high in 1529, and by 1545 it became the lowest of any of our archdeaconries, amazingly, lower than Buckinghamshire where prayer for the dead was conspicuously absent from three quarters of the wills studied. Bequests to the cathedral and to the parish church fell in a similar proportion to those of the archdeaconry of Buckingham and slightly more dramatically than in Lincolnshire; the overriding concern for the men of Huntingdon seems to have been their roads which were benefited by over a fifth of testators. From the Huntingdonshire wills in 1545 there seems to be only one which suggests a Protestant testator: John Fabyan of Therfield bequeathed 'my soul to god, my makere, and redemare, by the merits of whoss passion I trust to have forgiveness of my sinnys'; he left nothing at all for intercession after his decease and nothing at all to the cathedral or parish churches or indeed any pious concern. His family profited from his decease and not the church.[89] In contrast there were a number of testators in Huntingdonshire who were conspicuous for their traditional piety; they embellished the traditional formulae for wills and, as though to underline the sincerity of their meaning, gave generously to the church and to the needy. Thomas Taylor, for example, a husbandman who made his will in April 1545, bequeathed his soul to 'Almighty God and to the intercession of our ladye saynt mary and all the electe and chosyn company of heven and to

Table 26. *Bequests for specific purposes made in three archdeaconries, 1521–50 rendered as a percentage of a sample in 50 wills in each archdeaconry which included bequests to that purpose*

	Arch. of Lincoln				Arch. of Huntingdon				Arch. of Buckingham			
	1530*	1535	1545	1550	1529/30	1535	1545	1550	1521/3	1535/6	1545	1550
Works of the cathedral	(93%)	(86%)	74%	14%	(92%)	(70%)	54%	24%	(98%)	(71%)	56%	Insufficient data available
Other bequests to the cathedral	(25%)	(10%)	0%	0%	(0%)	(0%)	0%	0%	(2%)	(0%)	0%	
Own parish church	(76%)	(80%)	70%	10%	(92%)	(74%)	62%	10%	(86%)	(75%)	64%	
Other parishes	(29%)	(22%)	20%	2%	(24%)	(10%)	2%	0%	(16%)	(11%)	10%	
Religious orders	(11%)	(10%)	N/A	N/A	(8%)	(8%)	N/A	N/A	(0%)	(0%)	N/A	
Friars	(22%)	(14%)	N/A	N/A	(16%)	(6%)	N/A	N/A	(0%)	(0%)	N/A	
Guilds	(14%)	(16%)	10%	0%	(10%)	(16%)	2%	0%	(2%)	(4%)	0%	
Intercession for departed	(22%)	(32%)	28%	0%	(60%)	(42%)	18%	0%	(26%)	(21%)	32%	
Bridges and roads	(0%)	(0%)	4%	2%	(16%)	(4%)	22%	8%	(10%)	(7%)	2%	
Poor	(0%)	(6%)	6%	30%	(2%)	(14%)	2%	30%	(0%)	(0%)	4%	
Orphans and sick	(0%)	(4%)	0%	0%	(0%)	(0%)	0%	0%	(0%)	(0%)	2%	

*For earlier dates, see Table 3, p. 48, and Table 23, p. 148

the suffragys and prayers of the holy and Catholick church of christe'. He left money for the cathedral and the church bells and more to be given to the poor and to those who took part in his burial. In such circumstances the formula seems to suggest the faith of the man because it is of a piece with the rest of his will. A similar will was made by William David, commencing with the bequest of his soul 'unto Allmighty God and to our blessed Lady Saint Mary and to all the blessed company of heaven in full truste and hope to be saved by the merites of christes most glorious passion and also I trust to have our blessed lady saint Mary the mother of our savyour and redeemer Jesu Christ, the most pure and clene queen that ever was to pray for me and also the whole company of heven'. He left money for a requiem and the residue of his estate to deeds of charity.[90]

Buckinghamshire had not been remarkable for its bequests for intercession for the departed, but over Longland's episcopate these increased, and by 1545, at just the moment when the axe would begin to fall on the chantries, 32% of testators left money for some form of intercession for themselves and their families. At the same time, the poor and the orphaned and sick began to impinge on the conscience of Buckinghamshire just as they did in the archdeaconry of Lincoln. The men of Lincolnshire continued to show concern for their parish church and their cathedral and for churches other than their own, like that remembered by John Seyle as 'the church that I was chrystyned in'.[91]

By 1550 there is a marked change in the bequests of the people of the archdeaconry of Lincoln as well as those of Huntingdon. It was no longer possible to leave money for requiems, and the combined effect of the removal by Henry VIII of the jewels of the shrines in the cathedral and the removal by his son of the chantries, many of which were in the parish churches, to say nothing of the militant policy of destroying images especially of the saints, severely restricted the ways in which a testator could help his church without feeling that sooner or later his money would be confiscated by the king. In Buckinghamshire one testator had tried his best to see that his will was not made void or ineffectual by the whim of a king. He had wished for a yearly obit; he stated 'the forseyd house with appurtenances to be made as sure for the performing of the same perpetuall obytt as the lerned shall or can be devysed by the lawe'.[92] Those who lived through the 1530s, and 1540s learned not to put their trust in princes, and the number of bequests which could be confiscated by the monarchy dropped dramatically: less was bequeathed to the cathedral in the archdeaconry of Lincoln than in

Huntingdon, and in both archdeaconries it was the poor who benefited, though the whole level of charitable bequests fell. In the archdeaconry of Lincoln twenty-seven out of fifty testators made no charitable bequests whatsoever, and simply left their goods and estates to their families and friends, while in Huntingdonshire half of the testators studied left nothing to the church or to charity. If Henry VIII's successor and Holbeach, who took over the see of Lincoln after the death of Longland, succeeded in cutting back the traditional Catholic areas of bequest, they certainly did not succeed in encouraging piety which assured men of their likely salvation and manifested itself in good works. By 1550 they had taken away much, and the most obvious beneficiary in these archdeaconries seems to have been the deceased's family.

Longland himself was a victim of the change; his chantry (which still survives in Lincoln cathedral and was restored to use in 1978) was never used for the requiems for which he gave it. His bequest to Henley of a poor house could and did stand, but the poor folk in it were not required to pray for his soul. But as the charity of the years before 1545 gives place to a more obviously inward looking and family centred concern, it cannot be inferred that Englishmen had become Protestants. Deprived of the traditional outlets of Catholic piety they simply gave more to their families and less elsewhere.

The overwhelming evidence of their wills suggests that in 1545 very few in the diocese of Lincoln were Protestants; by 1550 they could not by law exhibit concern for the departed or for many other objects of Catholic piety. But only half of them displayed interest in other works of charity, notably the poor, and concern for them was not the exclusive prerogative of the Catholic church.[93]

The predominantly Catholic and conservative outlook which the people of the diocese of Lincoln display in their wills before 1550 was qualified only by the Protestantism of those small groups of laymen in the diocese whose Lollardy was of long standing: Buckinghamshire continued to trouble the bishop and he did not get any kinder to those found guilty of heresy in his later years than he had in his youth. One of the most bizarre heretics with whom he had to deal was William Cowbridge, whom Foxe described as 'mad and destitute of sense and reason'.[94] His opinions were certainly not in agreement with those of the Lollards, and one suspects that he was nearer to being a deist than a Christian and that this proved an embarrassment for Foxe. A note in Longland's register contains some of his opinions. Cowbridge not only did not believe in auricular confession but he also openly and publicly proclaimed that no pious living, whether by fasting or abstinence, could profit any soul, and that Jesus Christ was not the redeemer of the world but a deceiver, and that the name of Christ should not be called upon in any way as holy. He personally had deleted the name of Christ from his book of offices. He did not believe in hell; and asked what he took to be the meaning of the words 'Take and eat, this is my body', he replied that they meant 'take you and eate, this is the body wherein the people shall be deceyved'.[95] Such sentiments were far from those of Lutherans and Lollards, and the bishop was concerned that anyone should hold such 'strange and heinous' views; but he could not induce him to do penance. Longland wrote to Cromwell about him and kept him in Aylesbury gaol while Cromwell deliberated on what to do with him. He was eventually burned at Oxford in 1538.[96]

In 1541 Longland investigated some more conventional Buckinghamshire heretics. William Fastendich of Wooburn did not believe in the sacrament as the actual body and blood of Christ, and William Har of Great Brickhill was of the same opinion: he was alleged to have told the crowd, 'Thinkest thou that God Almighty will abide over a knave priest's head?' William Garland, like John Carter, did not believe in unction, and Thomas Barnard and James Morton were burned, one allegedly for teaching the Lord's Prayer in English and the other for keeping the Epistle of St James translated into English.[97] As both men were attuned to the spirit of the royal injunctions of 1538, it is hard to believe that this was the sum of their offences.

More serious from Longland's point of view was the presence in Lincolnshire of Suffolk's seat. One aggrieved heretic declared, 'Would God my lord of Suffolk's grace did know the truth of everything with us, and how the most part of us favours the word of God and what a great number favours the Pope's doctrine and especially our priests.'[98] Longland outlived Suffolk and there is no evidence of widespread Protestanism in Lincolnshire. Bishop and people alike were attached to their traditional ways of devotion and it would require a great deal of preaching of the kind which Longland forbade to change their ways. With the death of the king in 1547 and that of Longland just over three months later, the *possibility* of change arose – but it was no more than that.

CONCLUSION

There is much about the diocese of Lincoln, particularly in the 1540s, that we do not know. The long series of episcopal registers, which provide such a useful guide to the clergy of the diocese up to that point, falter after Longland's death, and institutions have to be pieced together from registers which are arranged neither chronologically nor alphabetically and which contain no valuable *memoranda*.[1] The series of court of audience books is interrupted and no proceedings survive for the period 1547–54; a book for 1554–5 is predominantly of instance material.[2] Episcopal visitation records, which provide useful material for Longland's episcopate, cease in 1543 and resume only in 1551.[3] Court material does survive for the archdeaconry of Lincoln, but it is mainly of instance cases; and the visitation books finish in 1538 and are not resumed until 1564.[4] These *lacunae* are indicative of the problems confronting a historian of the diocese in the reigns of Edward VI and Mary. They make it difficult to determine what became of most of those who gained a benefice under Longland. They also make it impossible to compare Longland with his successors or to date with any precision the acceptance of Protestantism under them.

Yet it seems reasonably certain that when Longland died in May 1547, he left a diocese with priests and laity as conservative as he was. The wills studied suggest that many still believed in the efficacy of intercession for the departed, and priests seem to have mistrusted Henry VIII's injunctions and in some cases appear to have ignored them. The part played by Longland personally in keeping so large a diocese on a traditional path cannot be overestimated. It is certainly the case that he preferred to exercise a distant authority rather than undertake the hard riding required for personal visitation. But where he saw a threat to his authority or to what he believed to be the faith of the church, he always acted. He was swift to prosecute or pursue heretics, whether the Lollards of Buckinghamshire or the academic Lutherans of Oxford (of which he remained chancellor, and for many colleges visitor, even after his colleague Robert King took over the new see of Oxford). He took a considerable interest in his cathedral church, which benefited greatly from his generosity. His careful control of preaching and his use of his own patronage meant that if there *were* Protestants, they were unlikely to get either pulpit or parish at his hands; his policy served the conservative cause just as the same policy, differently used, served the opposite one under Cromwell or Cranmer of Canterbury or Goodrich of Ely.[5]

Longland was greatly assisted by the king. The lack of a consistent policy in the exercise of royal ecclesiastical patronage meant that there was not a steady stream of Protestants being presented to livings. Nor was Longland to lose the friendship of Henry VIII in his old age. He must often have wondered whether he would suffer the fate of Wolsey or of Cromwell. But he did not. This was partly because, though often at court, he was not, as far as we know, on the council, nor was he viewed as a minister or diplomat as Stephen Gardiner was. He was essentially a churchman and perhaps could withstand his unpopularity with the Protestant elements at court because he had had (and probably continued to have) Henry as his penitent – a position not accorded regularly to Wolsey and one which Henry's self-deceiving scrupulousness was likely to perpetuate.

Obviously in certain counties outside the diocese, notably in Kent and Gloucester, geography played a significant part in advancing Protestantism.[6] The ports were necessary to book-smugglers, and well-travelled merchants, especially clothiers, appear to have made converts in England whose use in heretical book distribution was great. The diocese of Lincoln had one sea coast in Lincolnshire, but it is striking that it was precisely in that area that the Lincolnshire rising occurred. Neither in Lincolnshire, nor apparently in Lancashire, were the ports a notable means of heretical book smuggling.

Much more important in the diocese of Lincoln was the presence within it, for most of Longland's episcopate, of the university of Oxford, and the very close proximity of Cambridge and the diocese of Ely to the archdeaconry of Huntingdon. That archdeaconry also reached well into Hertfordshire and, as such, was not immune from the gossip or the booksellers of London. Longland's own connections with the university of Oxford which predated his elevation to the bishopric of Lincoln, coupled with a very vigilant commissary in the person of Dr London, meant that the university of Oxford, while not free from heresy, was not free to spread it. Longland also kept a weather eye on Huntingdon and was jealous of any encroachments on to his territory by the Protestant

Goodrich. He did not find grounds to refuse Goodrich's candidates for admission to benefices, but in the wills and in the number of Marian deprivations made in Huntingdonshire, it would not appear that Protestant attitudes had impinged very much.

More dangerous still were the Lollards of Buckinghamshire. We have no indication whether these increased or decreased between 1521 and 1547, but Longland's preference for Wooburn as his residence, and the evidence we have of his personal visitation of the archdeaconry, suggest that he knew all the dark corners of it very well and was too vigilant to allow much proselytising. He asked that the books he possessed of 'the smoler sorte' be 'disturbed emong the parsons and vicars of the cuntrye'* and he gave 'to every parishe church that my body shall goo thrugh and parte of them betwene my house of Wooburne and Eton College begynnyng at Wooburne and endying at Eton oon noble of vis viiid to the mayntenaunce of their chirches'.[7] This would seem to suggest that in his latter years the bishop began to move out and about in Buckinghamshire, and this may account for the seeming conservatism of his clergy in the latter years of his episcopate. It would be helpful to know more of Longland's deputies, not just his vicar general, but little survives of them, and though we can list all the commissaries of his predecessor, Bishop Atwater, even the names of Longland's deputies elude us after 1530. But whether they were the favoured archdeacon of Lincoln or the obstreperous archdeacon of Buckingham, their tasks were usually delegated to an official whose status can have been little more than that of the higher parochial clergy themselves.

Longland was unlikely to have regarded his own episcopate as a success. Starting as he did from ideas of Catholic reform which were primarily monastic-centred, the dissolution of the monasteries left him with a diocese denuded of the centres of prayer and devotion which were his ideal of monasticism – an ideal which he rarely encountered on his visitations but which he held out again and again in his sermons as the way of perfection not only for the religious themselves but for the laity as well. It was to prayer that he saw himself called, and it was prayer which he enjoined on the almsmen of Henley for whose provision he left money in his will. The old and poor were to say at their 'rising ... fyve pater noster, fyve ave maria and oon Credo in the worship of the fyve woundes', and the residentiaries of cathedral and the bishop of Lincoln were solemnly charged 'as they answere unto god at the dradefull day of

* *sic* for 'country'.

judgement' to see that no one was to be admitted who failed to pray in this way and to hear mass daily. His wish that 'every of them be of true pure and syncere Christian faithe not usinge errours or any erronyous opynyons' was to be interpreted differently by bishops for whom daily mass and the worship of the five wounds savoured of superstitious popery.[8] The end of the chantries, signalled in 1545, was for him not only a financial catastrophe after his chantry building at the cathedral, it also marked an end to one of his most profound convictions: the Christian's need to ponder his own end and to pray for all Christian souls in purgatory:

> The body is but earthe, ashes, duste, and wormes meate. Serpentes *hereditabunt illud*. Serpentes shall enheryte thy bodye, as thou doeste naturally enheryte thy fader his landes. Even so serpentis, wormes and toodes, shall enheryte thy bodye. Serpentes, wormes, and toodes, shall naturally ingenre and brede of they bodye. Serpentes, wormes and toodes, shall grewe, eate, and devoure thy beawtyfull face, thy fayre nose, thy clere eyes, thy whyte handes, thy gudly bodye. Remebre this thou lorde and ladye. Remember this thou Chrysten man and woman. Remember this ones a day.[9]

For four and half centuries Longland's chantry remained a broom cupboard, and it has only recently been brought back into use. The epitaph on it, partly from the pun on his name, has been seen by some historians, notably Dr Walker, as an apt one: *Longa terra mensuram ejus Dominus dedit*. His mortal remains and aspirations brought to their proper measure: the meagre measure of a tomb.[10] We have seen that that was not the whole story. Though Longland could not escape the fate of every man, he had strong ideas on how to see that the principles of the church and some of the endowment of his see lasted a little longer. His stand on episcopal authority left the autonomy of the bishop largely intact; his lands and those of the dean and chapter were put beyond the reach of immediate plunder, and his clergy and laity were far from having embraced the tenets of Protestantism.

If the analysis presented here in any way approximates to the truth, then the history of the Reformation must take on a new colour. Since the publication of Professor Dickens' brilliant *English Reformation* and some regional studies (notably by Dr Heal on Ely and Dr Clark on Kent), supported by a number of theses and articles, we have tended to see Protestantism as far advanced by the death of Henry VIII, and the triumphs of Elizabeth (and the failure of Mary) as somewhat inevitable. And so they may have been in those areas. But it now looks as though for Lancashire (studied by Dr Haigh), York, Chichester and the vast area of the diocese of Lincoln the picture is different – not one of Protestant triumph, nor of an inevitable event, nor even of bishops profligate with land and conspicuously lacking in responsibility, but of a hard fight for the consciences of Englishmen, fought not on the battlefields of Europe, but in many hearts and minds of parishioners in the length and breadth of England.[11]

It was precisely because there was no easy Protestant victory in such large parts of England that Elizabeth, who had, with Parker, remained in the country from her birth to her accession, and had felt the change and counter-change, was deeply mistrustful of imposing on her land the ecclesiastical solutions of either Rome or Geneva. The Church of England has been and remains a curious mixture of both insights because its people were only gradually drawn to change and they were reluctant to assign their neighbours to the fires of Smithfield or of hell.

GRAPHS

All are compiled from L.A.O., Register 27. Note that the newly formed diocese of Peterborough removed Northamptonshire and Rutland from the Lincolnshire diocese in October 1541 and that of Oxford removed Oxfordshire in September 1542.

Graph 1 Ordinations

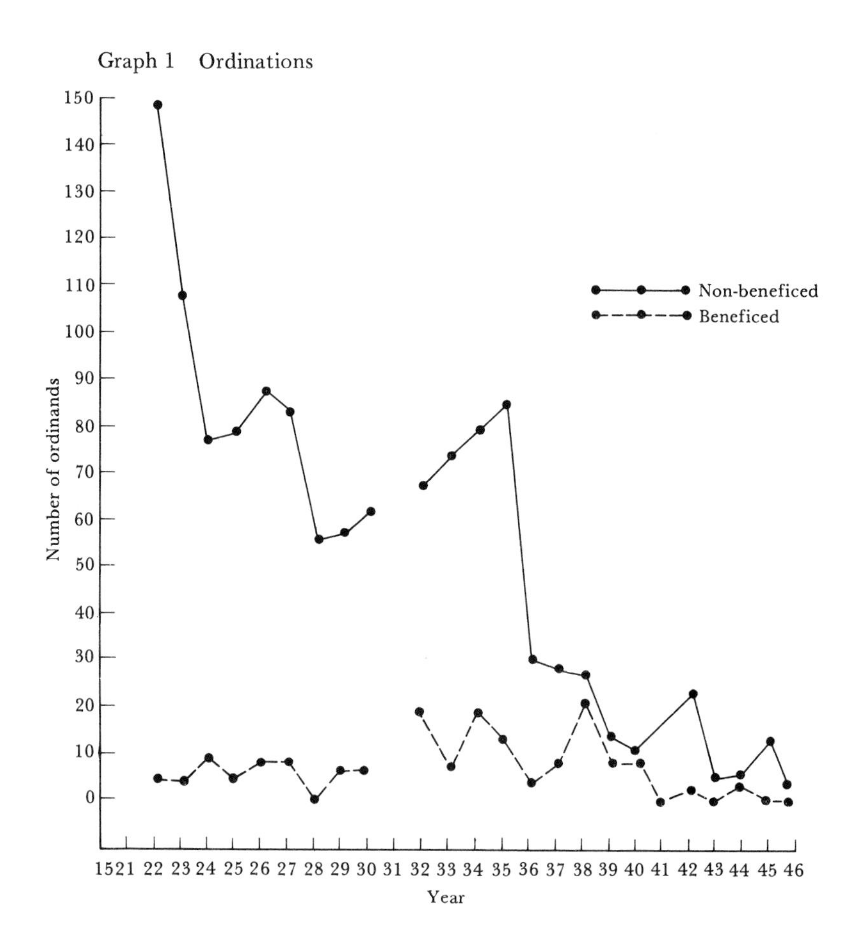

Graph 2 Presentations

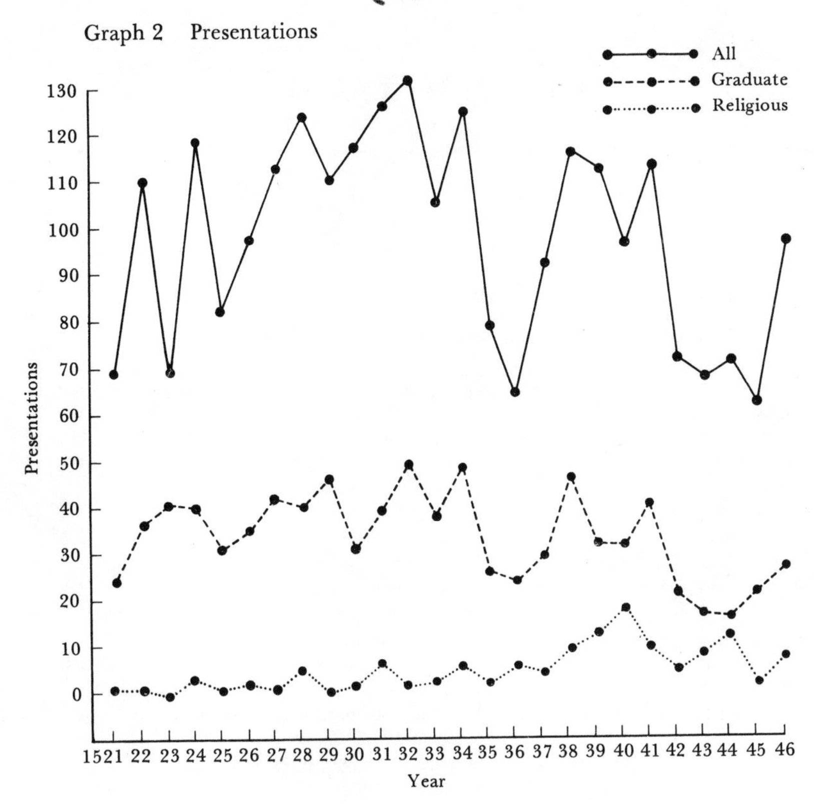

Graph 3 Termination of Incumbency by Death and Resignation, 1522–46/7

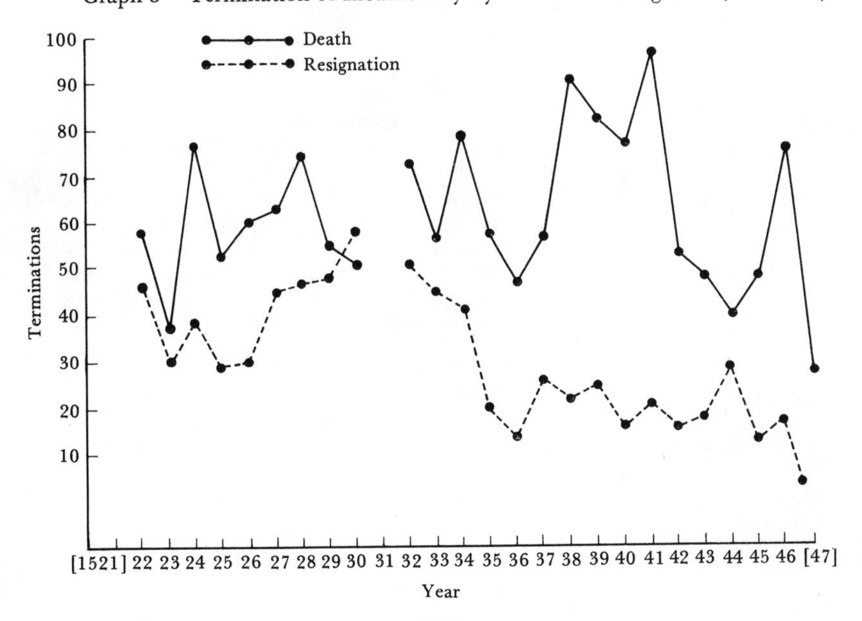

BIBLIOGRAPHY

Unprinted sources

Lincoln Archives Office [The Castle, Lincoln]

Register 25	Bishops Wolsey and Atwater
Register 26	Ordinations and Memoranda Bishop Longland
Register 27	Institutions Bishop Longland
Additional Register 5	Repertorium 1507–8 by Robert Toneys
Additional Register 7	Bishop Fuller's transcripts; sixteenth- and seventeenth-century episcopal accounts
Bishops' Accounts [For. 3]	Episcopal accounts
Subsid. 7–10	Sixteenth-century subsidy books
Glebe Terriers [Ter] Nos. 1 and 2	Vols. I and II, Terriers 1577–80, nos. 1–591
Court Books Cj. 3	1525–62 audience book
4	1527–9 audience book
5	1546 (fragment)
6	1539–40 archidiaconal and commissary court book
Inventories Box 2	1508–50
Visitations Vj. 7, 8, 9	Visitations of parishes and religious houses – printed in *L.R.S.* 33, 35, 37
Vj. 10	Northampton, Leicester and Oxford 1538
Vj. 11	Lincoln and Stow 1539; Bedford, Buckingham and Oxford 1540
Vj. 12	Huntingdon, Bedford, Buckingham 1543

Dean and Chapter Muniments

Bj. 3. 4.	1520–9 accounts of common fund
3. 5.	1529–40 accounts of common fund
Bj. 5. 5.	1538– Receipts
Bj. 5. 12.	1–6 Rough drafts of accounts of common fund
Bj. 5. 16 (3)	Jewels of the shrine of St Hugh
Bj. 5. 19	Fabric accounts 1512–47
Will Book II	Wills, leases and other documents 1530–
A. 4. 3.	Longland's Formulary book
A. 2. 11–16	Inventories of possessions and vestments (partially printed by C. Wordsworth for the Society of Antiquaries 1892)

Archdeaconry of Lincoln

Cij. 1	1536–45 Courts held by official and commissary
Vij. 1	1533–8 Visitations by official
L. C. C. 1521–47	Lincoln Consistory Court Wills

Archdeaconry of Stow

Stow Wills 1521–47	Stow Wills

Bibliography

Buckingham Record Office
Archdeaconry of Buckingham

D/A/Wf. 1	Wills 1506–41

Huntingdon Record Office

Will Registers 1, 2, 3	1536–50

Leicester Museums and Gallery
Department of Archives

ID 41/11/1 /2	Instance Courts 1524–36
ID 41/12/2–4	*Liber Cleri* and visitations 1521, 1525, 1527, 1533, 1535, 1536 (fragmentary)
ID 41/13/1 /2	Correction Courts 1522–38

Northamptonshire Record Office

Court Books 1, 2, 3	1530–40

British Library

MSS. XIX 31998	Churchwardens' accounts for Wing
Add 9822	Sixteenth-century customs of Lincoln diocese
Add MSS. 48022	Copy of selected parts of vicegerential court book
Cleopatra E. VI	Sixteenth-century letters

Lambeth Palace Library

Register of Archbishop Cranmer CM II. 1.	Inhibition of jurisdiction on diocese of Lincoln

Public Record Office

S.P. I S.P. II	State papers
STA C. 2.	26 [224]; 27 [183]; 34 [94] Star Chamber tithe suits
Prob. 11. /31.	Bishop Longland's will
E. 337	Plea roll of first-fruits and tenths
E. 36/118	Depositions of Lincolnshire insurgents

Sermons and early printed books

Bodleian Library Oxford

Arch. A.d.11	*Johannis Longlondi dei gratia Lincolnien' Episcopi, tres conciones*, tr. T. Kay, S.T.C. 1679. [see also Cambridge University Library]

British Library

C. 53. k. 14	*A Sermonde made before King [Henry VIII] An. MDXXXVIII by John Longlande*
C. 53. *bb* 7	*A Sermonde before the King at Greenwich. An. MDXXXVI.*

Cambridge University Library

Sel. 3. 133	Quinque Sermones Johannis Longlandi
SSS. 17. 29	Answere to the Petitions of the Traytours and rebelles in Lincolnshire

Bibliography

Wren Library, Trinity College, Cambridge

C. 7. 79[2] — A Sermonde made be for the kynges hyghenes at Rychemunte upon good fryday, the yere of our lord MCCCCCXXXVI by Johan' Longlond bysshope of Lincoln.

Printed sources

Allen, P. S. and H. M., edd. *Opus Epistolarum Desiderati Erasmi Rotterdami*. Oxford, 1906–48.

Aylmer, G. R., *The King's Servants*. London, 1961.

Bannister, A. J., ed., *Registrum Caroli Bothe, Episcopi Herefordensis, A.D. MDXVI–MDXXXV*. Canterbury and York Society, 1921.

Bennett, H. S., *English Books and Readers 1475–1557*. Cambridge, 1952.

Blench, J. W., *Preaching in England*. Oxford, 1964.

Boulay, F. R. H. du, 'Archbishop Cranmer and the Canterbury Temporalities', *English Historical Review*, LXVII, 1952.

Bowker, M., *The Secular Clergy in the Diocese of Lincoln 1495–1520*. Cambridge, 1968.

— ed., *An Episcopal Court Book. L.R.S.*, 61, 1967.

— 'Some Archdeacons' Court Books and the Commons Supplication Against the Ordinaries', *The Study of Medieval Records*, edd. D. A. Bullough and R. L. Storey, Oxford, 1971.

— 'The Supremacy and the Episcopate: the Struggle for Control, 1534–1540', *Historical Journal*, XVIII, 1975.

— 'Lincolnshire 1536: heresy, schism or religious discontent?', *Studies in Church History*, 9, ed. D Baker. Cambridge, 1972.

Bradshaw, H., and Wordsworth, C., edd., *Lincoln Cathedral Statutes*. Cambridge, 1897.

Brewer, J. S., Gairdner, J. and Brodie, R. H., edd., *Letters and Papers*, London 1862–1910.

Campbell, W. E., ed., *The Dialogue of Sir Thomas More concerning Tyndale*. London, 1927.

Chambers, D., *Faculty Office Registers, 1534–49*. Oxford, 1966.

Chester, A. G., 'Robert Barnes and the Burning of Books'. *Huntingdon Library Quarterly*, 14, 1951.

Chibnall, A. C., ed., *The Certificate of Musters for Buckinghamshire*. London, 1973.

Clark, P., *English Provincial Society from the Reformation to the Revolution: Religion, Politics and Society in Kent, 1500–1640*. Hassocks, 1977.

Clebsch, W. A., *England's Earliest Protestants, 1520–1535*. New Haven and London, 1964.

Cole, R. E. G., ed., *Chapter Acts of the Cathedral Church of St Mary of Lincoln, 1520–36*, 2 vols., *L.R.S.* 12, 13 (1915–17).

Cox, J. E., *The Works of Thomas Cranmer*, 2 vols. Parker Society: Cambridge, 1846.

Cross, C., 'The Economic Problems of the See of York; Decline and Recovery in the Sixteenth Century', *Agricultural History Review*, Suppl., 1970.

Davies, C. S. L., 'The Pilgrimage of Grace Reconsidered', *Past and Present*, XLI, 1968.

Dickens, A. G., *The Marian Reaction in the Diocese of York, Part. I, The Clergy*, St Anthony's Hall Publications, 11, 1957.

— *Lollards and Protestants in the Diocese of York*. Oxford, 1959.

— *The English Reformation*. London, 1964.

Dodds, M. H. and R., *The Pilgrimage of Grace, 1536–7, and the Exeter Conspiracy, 1538*, 2 vols. Cambridge, 1915.

Dudding, R. C., *The First Churchwardens' Book of Louth, 1500–1524*. Oxford, 1941.

Eeles, F. C., ed., *Edwardian Inventories for Buckinghamshire*. Alcuin Club, 1908.

Ellis, H., ed., *Original Letters*, 3 series, 11 vols. London, 1824–46.

Elton, G. R., *Policy and Police*. Cambridge, 1972.

— *Reform and Renewal*. Cambridge, 1973.

— *Reform and Reformation*. London, 1977.

Elvey, E. M., *The Courts of the Archdeaconry of Buckingham, 1483–1523*. Buckinghamshire Record Society, 19, 1975.

Emden, A. B., *A Biographical Register of the University of Oxford to A.D. 1500*, 3 vols. Oxford, 1957–9.

— *A Biographical Register of the University of Oxford 1501–1540*. Oxford, 1974.

— *A Biographical Register of the University of Cambridge to A. D. 1500*. Cambridge, 1963.

Frere, W. H. and Kennedy, W. M., *Visitation Articles and Injunctions of the Period of the Reformation 1536–58*. Alcuin Club, 1910.

Foster, C. W., *Lincolnshire Notes and Queries*, v, 1898.

Foster, C. W., ed., *Lincoln Wills, 1505–1530*, 2 vols. *L.R.S.*, 5 (1914), 10 (1918).

— ed., *The State of the Church. L.R.S.*, 23 (1926).

— 'Inventories of Church Goods, 1548', *A.A.S.R.P.*, XXXIV.

— 'Admissions to Benefices and Compositions for First Fruits in the County of Leicester, 1535–1660', *A.A.S.R.P.*, XXXVII.

— 'Institutions to Benefices in the Diocese of Lincoln', *A.A.S.R.P.*, XXXVII.

Foster, C. W., and Thompson A. H., 'The Chantry Certificates of Northamptonshire', *A.A.S.R.P.*, XXXI.

— 'The Chantry Certificates for Lincoln and Lincolnshire Returned in 1548 under the Act of Parliament of I Edward VI', *A.A.S.R.P.*, XXXV, XXXVI.

Gayangas, P. de, ed., *Calender of Letters, Dispatches and State Papers Relating to Negotiations between England and Spain*. Record Publication: London, 1862.

Gee, H., and Hardy, W. J., edd., *Documents Illustrative of English Church History*. London, 1896.

Hamilton, W. D., ed., *A Chronicle of England during the Reigns of the Tudors from 1485–1559, by Charles Wriothesley*. Camden Society, 1875.

Haigh, C., *The Last Days of the Lancashire Monasteries and the Pilgrimage of Grace*. Chetham Society: Manchester, 1969.

— *Reformation and Resistance in Tudor Lancashire*. Cambridge, 1975.

— 'Finance and Administration in a New Diocese: Chester, 1541–1461', in O'Day and Heal, *q.v.*

Hartridge, R. A. R., *A History of Vicarages in the Middle Ages*. Cambridge, 1930.

Heal, F., and O'Day, R., edd. *Church and Society in England*. London, 1977.

Heal, F., 'The Tudors and Church Lands, Economic Problems of the Bishopric of Ely during the Sixteenth Century', *Economic History Review*, XXVI, 1973.

— 'The Economic Problems of the Clergy', in edd., Heal and O'Day, *q.v.*

— 'Clerical Tax Collection under the Tudors', in O'Day and Heal, *q.v.*

Heath, P., *The English Parish Clergy on the Eve of the Reformation*. London, 1969.

— ed., *Bishop Geoffrey Blythe's Visitations, c. 1515–1525*, Staffordshire Record Society, 1973.

Hill, J. W. F., *Tudor and Stuart Lincoln*. Cambridge, 1956.

Hodgett, G. A. J., ed., *The State of the Ex-Religious and Former Chantry Priests in the Diocese of Lincoln, 1547–1584*, *L.R.S.*, 53, 1959.

— *Tudor Lincolnshire*. Lincoln, 1975.

Holderness, B. A., *Pre-Industrial England*. London, 1976.

Hoskins, W. G., 'Harvest Fluctuations and English Economic History, 1480–1619', *Agricultural History Review*, XII, 1964.

Houlbrooke, R., *Church Courts and the People during the English Reformation, 1520–70*. Oxford, 1979.

Hughes, P., *The Reformation in England*, I. London, 1956.

Hughes, P. L., and Larkin, J. F., *Tudor Royal Proclamations, I, The Early Tudors*. New Haven, 1964.

Jack, S., 'Dissolution Dates of the Monasteries Dissolved Under the Act of 1536', *Bulletin of the Institute of Historical Research*, XLIII, 1970.

James, M. E., 'Obedience and Dissent in Henrician England: the Lincolnshire Rebellion, 1536', *Past and Present*, XLVIII, 1970.

— 'The First Earl of Cumberland, 1493–1542, and the Decline of Northern Feudalism', *Northern History*, I, 1966.

Jordan, W. K., *Philanthropy in England, 1480–1660*. London, 1964.

Kitching, C. J., 'The Probate Jurisdiction of Thomas Cromwell as Vicegerent', *Bulletin of Institute of Historical Research*, XLVI, 1973.

Knowles, D., *The Religious Orders in England*, III, *The Tudor Age*. Cambridge, 1959.

Knowles, D., and Hadcock, R. N., *Medieval Religious Houses, England and Wales*. London, 1953.

Lander, S. J., 'Church Courts and the Reformation in the Diocese of Chichester, 1500–1558' in O'Day and Heal, *q.v.*

Lehmberg, S. E., 'Supremacy and Vicegerency: A Re-examination', *English Historical Review*, LXXXI, 1966.

— *The Reformation Parliament, 1529–36*. Cambridge, 1970.

— *The Later Parliaments of Henry VIII, 1536–47*. Cambridge, 1977.

Logan, L. D., 'The Henrician Canons', *Bulletin of the Institute of Historical Research*, XLVII, 1974.

Longden, H. I., *Northamptonshire and Rutland Clergy*, 16 vols. Northampton, 1938–52.

Luxton, I., 'The Reformation and Popular Culture', in Heal and O'Day, *q.v.*

Maddison, A. R., ed., *Lincolnshire Pedigrees*, 4 Vols. Harleian Soc., 1902–6.

Major, K., *Handlist of Lincoln Diocesan Records*. Oxford, 1953.

Martyn, R., *The State of Melford Church and Our Ladies' Chapel, at the East End, As I Did Know It*. 1580.

Mayor, J. E. B., ed., *The English Works of John Fisher*. London, 1876.

McConica, J. K., *English Humanists and Reformation Politics*. Oxford, 1965.

Merriman, R. G., *Life and Letters of Thomas Cromwell*, 2 vols. Oxford, 1902.

Muller, J. A., ed., *The Letters of Stephen Gardiner*. Cambridge, 1933.

O'Day, R., and Heal, F., edd., *Continuity and Change*. Leicester, 1976.

Olin, J. C., ed., *Christian Humanism and the Reformation: Desiderius Erasmus*. New York, 1965.

Orme, N., *English Schools in the Middle Ages*. London, 1973.

Palliser, D. M., 'Popular Reactions During the Years of Uncertainty, 1530–70', in Heal and O'Day, *q.v.*

Perry, G. G., 'Episcopal Visitations of the Austin Canons of Leicester and Dorchester', *English Historical Review*, IV, 1889.

Pill, D. H., 'The Administration of the Diocese of Exeter under Bishop Veysey', *Transactions of the Devon Association* XCVIII, 1966.

Pocock, N., ed., *A Treatise on the Pretended Divorce between Henry VIII and Catherine of Aragon by Nicholas Harpsfield*. Camden Society, 1878.

Powell, K. G., 'The Beginnings of Protestantism in Gloucestershire', *Transactions of the Bristol and Gloucestershire Archaeological Society*, XC, 1971.

— 'The Social Background to the Reformation in Gloucestershire', *Transactions of the Bristol and Gloucestershire Archaeological Society*, XCII, 1973.

Pullan, B., *Rich and Poor in Renaissance Venice*. Oxford, 1971.

Ridley, J., *Thomas Cranmer*. Oxford, 1962.

Salter, H. E., *A Subsidy Collected in the Diocese of Lincoln in 1526*. Oxford Historical Society, vol. 63, 1909.

— *The Churchwardens' Accounts of St Michael's Church, Oxford*, Oxford Archaeological Society, 1933.

Savine, A., 'English Monasteries on the Eve of the Dissolution', in *Oxford Studies in Social and Legal History*, ed. P. Vinogradoff. Oxford, 1909.

Scarisbrick, J. J., *Henry VIII*. London, 1968.

Statutes of the Realm, 11 vols. 1810–28.

Stone, L., ed., *The University in Society*, 2 vols. Princeton, 1975.

Strype, J., *Ecclesiastical Memorials relating chiefly to Religion and the Reformation of it under King Henry VIII, King Edward VI and Queen Mary*, 3 vols. 1822.

Sturge, C., *Cuthbert Tunstal.* London, 1938.

Sylvester, R. S., and Harding, D. P., edd., *The Life and Death of Cardinal Wolsey by George Cavendish.* New Haven, 1962.

Thompson, A. H., ed., *Visitations in the Diocese of Lincoln 1517–1531*, 3 vols. *L.R.S.*, 33, 1940; 35, 1944; 37, 1947.

— *The History of the Hospital and the New College of the Annunciation of St Mary in the Newarke, Leicester.* Leicester, 1937.

— 'The Chantry Certificates of Northamptonshire', *A.A.S.R.P.*, XXXI.

— 'Pluralism in the Medieval Church', *A.A.S.R.P.*, XXXIII.

Thompson, E. P., 'Time Work Discipline in Industrial Capitalism', *Past and Present*, XXXVIII, 1967.

Thomson, J. A. F., *The Later Lollards, 1414–1520.* Oxford, 1965.

Townsend, G., ed., *Acts and Monuments of John Foxe.* London, 1846.

Ullmann, W., 'This Realm of England is an Empire', *Journal of Ecclesiastical History*, XXX, 1979.

Valor Ecclesiasticus, 6 vols. 1810–28.

Venn, J. and J. A., *Alumni Cantabrigienses*, Part I, 4 vols. Cambridge, 1922–7.

Wharhirst, G. E., 'The Reformation in the Diocese of Lincoln and Illustrated by the Life and Work of Bishop Longland, 1521–47', *A.A.S.R.P.*, I.

Wilkins, D., *Concilia Magnae Britanniae et Hiberniae*, 4 vols. London, 1733, 1739.

Wordsworth, C., 'Inventories of Plate, Vestments, etc., Belonging to the Cathedral Church of the Blessed Mary of Lincoln', *Archaeologia*, LIII, 1892.

Wright, T., ed., *Letters Relating to the Suppression of Monasteries*, Camden Society, old series XXVI, 1842.

Youings, J., *The Dissolution of the Monasteries.* London, 1971.

Zell, M. L., 'The Personnel of the Clergy in Kent in the Reformation Period', *English Historical Review*, LXXXIX, 1974.

Unpublished dissertations

Brigden, S. E., 'The Early Reformation in London, 1520–1547: The Conflict in the Parishes', Cambridge Ph.D., 1979.

Heal, F., 'The Bishops of Ely and their Diocese during the Reformation Period, 1515–1600', Cambridge Ph.D., 1972.

Hodgett, G. A. J., 'The Dissolution of the Monasteries in Lincolnshire', London M.A., 1947.

Lander, S. J., 'The Diocese of Chichester, 1508–1558: Episcopal Reform under Robert Sherburne and its Aftermath', Cambridge Ph.D., 1974.

Scarisbrick, J. J., 'The Conservative Episcopate in England, 1529–1535', Cambridge Ph.D., 1956.

Walker, R. B., 'A History of the Reformation in the Archdeaconries of Lincoln and Stow, 1534–94', Liverpool Ph.D., 1959.

NOTES

Introduction

1. Knowles, *The Religious Orders in England*, III, *The Tudor Age.*
2. Dickens, *The English Reformation.*
3. Scarisbrick, *Henry VIII.*
4. Elton, *Policy and Police; idem, Reform and Renewal; idem, Reform and Reformation.*
5. Haigh, *Reformation and Resistance in Tudor Lancashire*; Clark, *English Provincial Society from the Reformation to the Revolution*; *Religion Politics and Society in Kent 1500–1640*; Powell, 'The Beginnings of Protestantism in Gloucestershire'; *idem*, 'The Social Background to the Reformation in Gloucestershire'; Heal, 'The Bishops of Ely and their Diocese during the Reformation Period 1515–1600'.
6. Haigh, *Tudor Lancashire.*
7. Many such studies are in thesis form but their authors have published some of their findings in *Continuity and Change*, edd. O'Day and Heal; *Church and Society in England*, edd. Heal and O'Day; Lander, 'The Diocese of Chichester 1508–1558; Episcopal Reform under Robert Sherburne and its Aftermath'; Brigden, 'The Early Reformation in London, 1520–1547. The Conflict in the Parishes'.
8. *Diocesan Visitations*, ed. A. H. Thompson, 3 vols. (*L.R.S.* 33 (1940), 35 (1944), 37 (1947)) – hereinafter *sub LR.S.*
9. *The State of the Ex-Religious and Former Chantry Priests in the Diocese of Lincoln 1547–1574*, ed. Hodgett.
10. Walker, 'A History of the Reformation in the Archdeaconries of Lincoln and Stow 1534–94'. For a smaller work which is concerned to portray Longland but neglects L.A.O. Register 27, his sermons and the dean and chapter material, see Wharhirst, 'The Reformation in the Diocese of Lincoln and Illustrated by the Life and Work of Bishop Longland 1521–47'.
11. Bowker, *The Secular Clergy in the Diocese of Lincoln 1495–1520.*
12. Heath, *The English Parish Clergy on the Eve of the Reformation.*

I: The diocese of Lincoln: the inheritance of a new bishop

1. Hughes, *The Reformation in England*, I, pp. 32–5.
2. Hill, *Tudor and Stuart Lincoln*, pp. 1–6.
3. Holderness, *Pre-Industrial England*, pp. 10–17.
4. Hodgett, *Tudor Lincolnshire*, pp. 189–99; cf. *The State of the Church*, ed. Foster, pp. 442 ff.
5. Bowker, *Secular Clergy*, pp. 85–154.
6. *ibid.* pp. 110–54; Haigh, *Tudor Lancashire*, p. 50; Heath, *English Parish Clergy*, pp. 104–8.
7. Bowker, *op. cit.*, p. 38–60; Heath, *op. cit.*, pp. 70–104; Haigh, *op. cit.*, pp. 42 ff.
8. Bowker, *op. cit.*, pp. 137–49; Heath, *op. cit.*, pp. 135–74; Haigh, *op. cit.*, pp. 26 ff.

9. Bowker, *op. cit.*, p. 126.
10. Bowker, *op. cit.*, pp. 149–54; Heath, *op. cit.*, pp. 148–58; Haigh, *op. cit.*, p. 62.
11. Bowker, *op. cit.*, pp. 152–4; Haigh, *op. cit.*, pp. 79–86 suggests a similar picture for Lancashire; see also Thomson, *The Later Lollards 1414–1520*, pp. 237–8.
12. Bowker, *Secular Clergy*, pp. 155–79.
13. *ibid.*, p. 172.
14. Bodl. Libr. Arch. A.d.11., *Tres conciones*, I, fos. 9–10.
15. Scarisbrick, 'The Conservative Episcopate in England 1529–1535', p. 2.
16. Bowker, *op. cit.*, p. 16.
17. Emden, *Oxford*, II, pp. 1160 ff.
18. P.R.O., Prob. 11/13.
19. Bodl. Libr. Arch. A.d.11., *Quinque Sermones*, IV, fo. 88v.
20. Emden, *Oxford*, II, pp. 1160 ff.
21. *L.P.*, II, ii, p. 1477; *L.P.*, III, ii, pp. 1533, 1539, 1540, 1546.
22. *L.P.*, III, i, no. 704.
23. *ibid.*, no. 1008.
24. Emden, *Oxford*, II, p. 1161; cf. *L.P.*, II, ii, no. 4340.
25. *L.P.*, IV, i, no. 481.
26. The theologians were Blythe and Fisher, the doctor of medicine Sherburne of Chichester. Two sees were held by Wolsey, those of Winchester and Bath and Wells.
27. *L.P.*, III, i, no. 567.
28. *Opus Epistolarum Desiderati Erasmi Rotterdami*, edd. P.S. and H. M. Allen, VI, p. 1; VII, p. 429.
29. *ibid.*, VI, pp. 332, 440; VII, p. 531; VIII, p. 167; XI, p. 300.
30. *Christian Humanism and the Reformation: Desiderius Erasmus*, ed. Olin pp. 92–106; cf. *The Dialogue of Sir Thomas More concerning Tyndale*, ed. Campbell, *passim.*
31. *Opus*, edd. Allen, VII, pp. 460–1.
32. Quoted in Blench, *Preaching in England*, p. 233.
33. *ibid.*, p. 22.
34. *ibid.*, pp. 22–8.
35. Bodl. Libr. Arch. A.d.11., *Tres conciones*, I, fo. 21.
36. B. L. C. 53. k. 14, *A Sermonde made before King* [*Henry VIII*] *An. MDXXXVII by John Longlande*, p. 10.
37. Blench, *op. cit.*, p. 136.
38. *Opus*, edd. Allen, VII, p. 147.
39. Blench, *op. cit.*, pp. 75–6; Walker, 'A History of the Reformation', p. 67.
40. Bodl. Libr. Arch. A.d. 11., *Tres conciones* I, fo. 7v.
41. L.A.O., Register 26, fos. 206–206v.
42. *Bishop Geoffrey Blythe's Visitations c. 1515–1525*, ed. Heath.
43. Lander, 'The Diocese of Chichester 1508–1558', *passim*; Heal, 'The Bishops of Ely and the Diocese, pp. 7–12, 43–64.
44. B.L., C. 53. k. 14., p. 16.
45. *Chapter Acts of the Cathedral Church of St Mary of Lincoln 1520–1536*, ed. Cole. (L.R.S. vol. 12), pp. 9–11, 30–1.
46. *L.P.*, III, ii, no. 2288 (1) and (2).
47. *ibid.*, nos. 2956, 3013.
48. *L.P.*, IV, i, no. 481.
49. *ibid.*, no. 1142.
50. *ibid.*, no. 1412.
51. Ellis, *Original Letters Illustrative of English History* III, i, pp. 251–4. The letter is undated.
52. *L.P.*, IV, i, no. 1082; p. 864; nos. 2101, 2192.
53. *L.P.*, IV, ii, no. 2391.
54. *L.P.*, IV, ii, no. 2564.

55. *The Life and Death of Cardinal Wolsey by George Cavendish*, edd. Sylvester and Harding, p. 87.
56. *A Treatise on the Pretended Divorce between Henry VIII and Catherine of Aragon by Nicholas Harpsfield*, ed. Pocock, p. 176.
57. *Calendar [of Letters, Dispatches and State Papers relating to negotiations between England and] Spain*, ed. de Gayangas, vol. IV, pt. ii, nos. 27, 598.
58. *L.P.*, IV, iii, nos. 5613, 5694.
59. *ibid.*, no. 5751.
60. *ibid.*, no. 6306.
61. *Calendar Spain*, ed. de Gayangas, p. 475; *L.P.*, IV, iii, no. 6308.
62. *L.P.*, V, no. 1272; L.A.O. Register 26, fos. 229–229v.
63. *L.P.*, V, Appendix 33; Lehmberg, *The Reformation Parliament 1529–1536*, p. 163, n. 2.
64. Lehmberg, *op. cit.*, p. 87.
65. *ibid.*, pp. 109–16.
66. *ibid.*, pp. 142–52.
67. *L.P.*, IV, i, no. 1412. (The letter actually has no date; see n. 51, above.)
68. *Acts and Monuments of John Foxe*, ed. Townsend, V, Appendix: Letter to Wolsey, 3 March 1528.
69. *ibid.*, V, Appendix: 1 April 1528.
70. *ibid.*, V, Appendix: 8 April 1528.
71. Bowker, *Secular Clergy*, pp. 18–30.
72. L.A.O. Register 26, fo. 94.
73. L.A.O. Register 26, fo. 101.
74. Trinity College, Cambridge, C. 7, 79². *A sermonde made be for the kynges hyghenes at Rychemunte* ... 1536, unpaginated.

II 1521–30: A time for reform?

1. The monasteries

1. Genesis 18:18.
2. Bodl. Libr., Arch. A. d. 11. *Tres conciones*, I, fos. 8–8v.
3. *ibid.*, fo. 9.
4. *ibid.*, fo. 9v.
5. *ibid.*, fos. 10–10v.
6. Savine, 'English Monasteries on the Eve of the Dissolution', pp. 280–1.
7. Knowles and Hadcock, *Medieval Religious Houses, England and Wales.*
8. Hodgett, 'The Dissolution of the Monasteries in Lincolnshire', p. 124.
9. Rayne's commission is not extant though that of his successor has survived; L.A.O. Register 26, fo. 274. Morgan's commission also survives; *ibid.*, fo. 190.
10. Emden, *Oxford*, n.s., p. 477.
11. *L.R.S.*, 35, pp. 87–91.
12. *L.R.S.*, 35 and 37, *passim.*
13. *L.R.S.*, 35, p. 92.
14. *ibid.*, p. 98.
15. *ibid.*, p. 105.
16. *L.R.S.*, 37, pp. 27, 29, 105.
17. *L.R.S.*, 35, pp. 174 ff.
18. *ibid.*, pp. 88 ff.
19. *L.R.S.*, 37, pp. 119 ff.
20. *L.P.*, IV, ii, no 2367.
21. *Bishop Geoffrey Blythe's Visitations c. 1515–1525*, ed. Heath, p. lii.
22. L.A.O., Cj. 4, fo. 46.

23. L.A.O., Register 26, fos. 164–164v.
24. L.A.O., Register 26, fos. 170–1. These are printed: see Perry, 'Episcopal Visitations of the Austin Canons of Leicester and Dorchester', pp. 310–13.
25. Knowles, *Religious Orders*, III, p. 66: 'we may even suppose that the whole framework of the horarium had been broken down'.
26. L.A.O., Register 26, fos. 170–1.
27. *L.R.S.*, 35, pp. 115–22.
28. *L.R.S.*, 37, pp. 18–27.
29. *ibid.*, p. 24.
30. L.A.O., Register 26, fo. 212.
31. *ibid.*, fos. 212–13.
32. *L.R.S.*, 35, pp. 183–6.
33. L.A.O., Register 26, fos. 226–7; Perry, 'Episcopal Visitations', pp. 303–9. Both Professors Knowles and Hamilton Thompson have assumed that Longland visited Leicester before Rayne (Knowles, *Religious Orders*, III, p. 67). Consultation with the original documents suggests that this cannot have been the case. The later date of 1531 for Longland's injunctions is also in keeping with the spate of letters which date from 1532 and show the bishop attempting to deprive the abbot.
34. L.A.O., Register 26, fo. 227.
35. *L.P.*, V, no. 1158; P.R.O., S.P., I, 70, fo. 171.
36. *L.P.*, V, no. 1175. It is clear that the abbot had appeared before the council and had done his best to undermine Longland's authority.
37. *L.P.*, VII, no. 579.
38. *L.R.S.*, 35, pp. 155 ff.
39. *Bishop Geoffrey Blythe's Visitations c. 1515–1525*, ed. Heath, p. lii; Knowles, *Religious Orders*, III, pp. 223 ff.
40. *L.R.S.*, 37, pp. 94 ff.
41. *ibid.*, pp. 83–9.
42. *L.R.S.*, 35, pp. 167 ff.
43. *ibid.*, p. 173.
44. *ibid.*, p. 153, n. 2.
45. L.A.O., Register 26, fos. 101v–102.
46. L.A.O., Register 26, fo. 152.
47. *L.R.S.*, 37, pp. 7–8.
48. *L.R.S.*, 37, pp. 107–11.
49. L.A.O., Register 26, fos. 179v–180v.
50. *L.R.S.*, 35, pp. 124–6.
51. L.A.O., Register 26, fos. 177–8.
52. *L.R.S.*, 35, pp. 127–8.
53. *ibid.*, pp. 129–30.
54. *ibid.*, pp. 130–2.
55. See above, p. 26.
56. For Littlemore, see *An Episcopal Court Book*, ed. Bowker, pp. 50–1.
57. L.A.O., Register 26, fos. 101v–102. The case is discussed in detail in Knowles, *Religious Orders*, III, pp. 70–2, and in *L.R.S.*, 35, pp. 209–10.
58. P.R.O., S.P., I, 52, fos. 157–157v; *L.P.*, IV, iii, no. 5189.

2. The secular colleges

1. Bowker, *Secular Clergy*, p. 155. The bishop was the visitor of a number of colleges which served an educational purpose, among them Eton; King's College, Cambridge; Oriel, Lincoln and Brasenose Colleges in Oxford. These have been omitted from the present study since, in a sense, their connection was not part of Longland's diocesan duties and their conduct belongs to the history of the two universities.

2. *L.R.S.*, 12, p. 107.
3. *L.R.S.*, 33, 35, 37; A. H. Thompson recorded the history of some of these colleges but he was unaware of material about them surviving after 1538.
4. See below, pp. 29 ff.
5. *L.R.S.*, 12, p. 47.
6. These are now in the custody of the Lincolnshire Archives Office. I have distinguished the archives pertaining to the dean and chapter from those of the diocese.
7. Bowker, *Secular Clergy*, pp. 171–3.
8. L.A.O., D and C, Bj. 3. 4 (no foliation) *sub Curialitates.*
9. Bowker, *Secular Clergy*, p. 20; *L.R.S.*, 12, p. 20.
10. L.A.O., D and C, A.2.10 (8): this document shows Longland's own marginalia. These are labelled A and B in the printed form: see *Lincoln Cathedral Statutes*, edd. Bradshaw and Wordsworth, II, pp. 559–63.
11. *L.R.S.*, 12, p. 128.
12. For a prebendal court book see L.A.O., Cj. 1.
13. L.A.O., Register 26, fo. 95.
14. *ibid.*, fo. 95v.
15. *L.R.S.*, 12, p. 94.
16. Emden, *Oxford*, n.s., pp. 280–1.
17. P.R.O., S.P., I, 49, p. 119 (*L.P.* IV, ii, no. 4527).
18. *L.R.S.*, 12, pp. 102, 105–6.
19. *ibid.*, p. 137.
20. L.A.O., D and C, A.3.3. fos. 21v and 222v.
21. *L.R.S.*, 12, p. 104; see also Emden, *Oxford*, I, p. 543.
22. *L.R.S.*, 12, pp. 111–12.
23. *ibid.*, pp. 116–17.
24. Italics mine; *ibid.*, p. 117.
25. *ibid.*, p. 119.
26. *ibid.*, p. 120.
27. *ibid.*, pp. 126–7.
28. *ibid.*, pp. 139–40.
29. L.A.O., D and C., Bj. 3. 4 (unfoliated). Emden, *Oxford*, I, p. 543.
30. Bowker, *Secular Clergy*, p. 157.
31. Thompson, *The History of the Hospital and the New College of the Annuciation of St Mary in the Newarke, Leicester*, pp. 1–10.
32. *L.R.S.*, 37, pp. 1–4.
33. The text of Longland's injunctions is in L.A.O., Register 26, fos. 47–50. A translation is in Thompson, *St Mary in the Newarke*, pp. 184–96. Rayne's subsequent visitation, which Thompson thought was the last, is printed in *L.R.S.*, 37, p. 4. Later visitations of the college which Thompson did not include are in L.A.O., Vj. 10, fos. 69v, 70v; Cj. 3, fo. 51.
34. L.A.O., Vj. 10, fo. 64v; *L.R.S.*, 35, p. 172.
35. *ibid.*, pp. 147–51.
36. *ibid.*, pp. 145 ff.

3. The clergy

1. Thomson, *The Later Lollards*, pp. 237–8.
2. Brigden, 'The Early Reformation in London', pp. 26, 33.
3. Scarisbrick, *Henry VIII*, pp. 163–240.
4. L.A.O., Register 26, fos. 1–26v, 130. The suffragans in the diocese, in addition to John, bishop of Mayo, included Robert King, abbot of Bruern and then Thame (see p. 28, above) who was given particular responsibility for the archdeaconries of Oxford,

Buckingham, Huntingdon and Bedford (L.A.O., Register 26, fo. 135v); Roger, bishop of Lydda (Bowker, *Secular Clergy*, p. 24); John Young, bishop of Gallipoli (L.A.O., Register 26, fos. 10v, 14, 17); William Duffield, a friar minor and bishop of Ascolensis (L.A.O., Register 26, fos. 30, 32, 33); and Matthew Mackerell, abbot of Barlings and bishop of Chalcedon (L.A.O., Register 26, fos. 32, 208v, 225v).

5. For Dorchester, see above, pp. 22 ff.
6. 24 September 1524, L.A.O., Register 26, fo.10.
7. L.A.O., Register 27, fos. 231v, 237.
8. L.A.O., Cj. 3 *passim*; Cj. 4 *passim.*
9. L.A.O., Cj. 3, fos. 21, 34v.
10. Bowker, *Secular Clergy*, p. 41.
11. L.A.O., Register 26, fos. 17–18.
12. L.A.O., Register 26, fos. 32 ff.
13. Wilkins, *Concilia*, III, p. 719; Lehmberg, *Reformation Parliament*, pp. 142–3.
14. L.A.O., Register 25, fos. 111–136v; Register 26, fos. 1–67.
15. Brigden, 'The Early Reformation in London', p. 38.
16. Bowker, *Secular Clergy*, pp. 42 ff.
17. L.A.O., Register 26, fos. 3 ff.
18. L.A.O., Register 27, fo. 21v.
19. *A Subsidy Collected in the Diocese of Lincoln in 1526*, ed. Salter, p. 159.
20. *ibid.*, p. 108.
21. L.A.O., Register 27, fo. 160.
22. For a discussion of titles, see Bowker, *Secular Clergy*, pp. 61–4; Heath, *English Parish Clergy*, p. 17.
23. L.A.O., Register 26, fos. 1–67.
24. Zell, 'The Personnel of the Clergy in Kent in the Reformation Period', pp. 518 ff.
25. L.A.O., Register 27, fos. 117v, 147, $154v^2$, 155^3, 156^2, 156v, 158^2, 262v, 263.
26. *Subsidy*, ed. Salter, 102, 112, 115; cf. L.A.O., Register 27, fo. 155^2.
27. Leics. R. O., ID/41/12/3, fo. 63v, cf. Emden, *Cambridge*, p. 277.
28. Leics. R. O., ID/41/12/3, fo. 58v.
29. *Subsidy*, ed. Salter, p. 115.
30. Leics, R. O., ID/41/12/2, 3 and 4, *passim*; ID/41/11/1 and 2 *passim.*
31. *Subsidy*, ed. Salter, *passim*, cf. *The Certificate of Musters for Buckinghamshire*, ed. Chibnall, pp. 12–13.
32. Brigden, *The Early Reformation in London*, p. 62.
33. Zell, 'The Personnel of the Clergy in Kent', p. 532.
34. Heal, 'The Bishops of Ely', p. 50.
35. Haigh, *Tudor Lancashire*, p. 29.
36. Bowker, *Secular Clergy*, pp. 91–7.
37. cf. Zell, 'The Personnel of the Clergy of Kent', p. 524.
38. Salter, *Subsidy*, *passim.*
39. L.A.O., Register 27, fos. 21, 31v, 60v, 111v, 112v, 113, 117, 177, 180, 181v, 201, 203, 232; cf. Salter, *Subsidy*, 10, 16, 57, 76, 135, 150, 152, 167, 173, 219, 228, 258, 273. The parishes concerned were Mumby, Quarrington, Hitcham, Middleton Stoney, Marsworth, Wheathampstead, Thenford, Stanton St John, Stretton Magna, Northampton St John, Eydon, Bulwick, Waterperry.
40. L.A.O., Register 27, fo. 232v; *Subsidy*, ed. Salter, p. 173.
41. *L.P.* IV, i, no. 481.
42. L.A.O., Register 27, fos. 184v, 192, 234; Vj. 11, fos. 82, 96; *Subsidy*, ed. Salter, pp. 184, 261, 272.
43. L.A.O., Register 27, fos. 175, 177, 187; cf. *Subsidy*, ed. Salter, pp. 184, 261, 262.
44. L.A.O., Register 27, *passim.*
45. Knowles, *Religious Orders*, III, pp. 225 ff.
46. L.A.O., Register 27, fos. 235v, 255v; cf. *Subsidy*, ed. Salter, p. 173.

47. *L.R.S.*, 35, p. 15.
48. Leics. R.O., ID/41/12/3, fo. 79.
49. L.A.O., Register 27, fos. 44v, 46v, 158, 178v, 194^2, 202, 219v.
50. L.A.O., Register 26, fo. 208v; Vj. 11, fo. 65.
51. L.A.O., Register 27, fo. 44v.
52. L.A.O., Register 27, fos. 178v, 184, 188, 189v, 191v, 193^2, 195, 216v.
53. B.L., C. 53, k. 14, unpaginated. 'Confirm' is used in a general and not a technical sense.
54. L.A.O., Register 26, fos. 94–94v.
55. L.A.O., Register 27, fo. 181v.

4. The laity and the church

1. Trinity College, Cambridge, Wren Library, C.7, 79^2, p. 1.
2. Luxton, 'The Reformation and Popular Culture' pp. 57–77.
3. *The Courts of the Archdeaconry of Buckingham 1483–1523*, ed. Elvey, p. 391.
4. Jordan, *Philanthropy in England 1480–1660*, pp. 322 ff.
5. *Lincoln Wills*, ed. Foster, II, pp. 170–210. Elvey, *op.cit.*, pp. 371 ff. Huntingdonshire Record Office, Will Register 3, *passim*, cf. pp. 212, 215 below.
6. Huntingdonshire Record Office, Will Register 3, fos. 90v, 96, 99, 108, 109v.
7. Jordan noted Buckinghamshire's lack of 'religious' bequests; see *Philanthropy in England*, p. 302.
8. *Lincoln Wills*, ed. Foster, II, p. 189.
9. 'The Chantry Certificates for Lincoln and Lincolnshire under the Act of Parliament – Edward VI'. edd. Foster and Thompson, no. 131, pp. 258–9.
10. Huntingdonshire Record Office, Will Register 3, fos. 90v, 94, 94v, 98^2, 108, 109, 109v, 111v.
11. *ibid.*, fos. 102v, 104.
12. E. P. Thompson, 'Time Work Discipline in Industrial Capitalism', pp. 56 ff.
13. *L.R.S.*, 33, p. 26.
14. *An Episcopal Court Book*, ed. Bowker, p. 63.
15. Elvey, *op cit.*, pp. 128, 161, 163, 175, 288, 289, 292.
16. Bowker, *Secular Clergy*, pp. 127 ff.
17. Bucks, R. O., D.A.V.1, fos. 6, 6v, 9v^3, 17^2, 21v; D A We, fos. 72av, 85v, 100, 111, 111v^2, 112, 143v, 145v, 146^2, 160, 188, 194, *L.R.S.*, 33, pp. 37, 39^3, 40, 42^3, 43, 46^2, 48, 49^2, 50^2, 51, 53. See also Bowker, *Secular Clergy*, p. 127.
18. L.A.O., Vj. 5, fos. 22–100; cf. Vij. 1, fos. 8 ff.
19. L.A.O., Vj. 5, fo. 29; cf. Vij. 1, fo. 138.
20. L.A.O., Vj. 5, fo. 37; cf. Vij. 1, fo. 154.
21. L.A.O., Vj. 11 and 12, both contain Buckinghamshire material, but it relates exclusively to the church personnel and not to the fabric.
22. *An Episcopal Court Book*, ed. Bowker, *passim.*
23. L.A.O., Cj. 3, fos. 21, 22, 34v.
24. *S.R.*, III, 21 Henry VIII, c.5.
25. Elvey, *op. cit.*, pp. 322–414; *Lincoln Wills*, ed. Foster, II, pp..155–85.
26. Lander, 'The Diocese of Chichester 1508–1558', p. 86; Houlbrooke, *Church Courts and the People during the English Reformation 1520–1570*, p. 96.
27. Houlbrooke, *op. cit.*, p. 95.
28. Bowker, 'Some Archdeacons' Court Books', pp. 298–301.
29. Kitching, 'The Probate Jurisdiction of Thomas Cromwell as Vicegerent', pp. 208–9.
30. Leics. R.O., ID/41/11/2, fos. 1–2, cf. ID/41/13/2, fo. 7. For the vicegerent's court, see below, pp. 76 ff.
31. Houlbrooke, *op. cit.*, p. 95.
32. Leics. R.O., ID/41/11/2, fos. 59–103v.

33. See below for instance cases in the 1530s and 1540. A few were heard in the court of audience.
34. Elvey, *op. cit.*, pp. 23–4, 71, 89, 105, 161.
35. L.A.O., Register 26, fos. 130–6.
36. L.A.O., Register 26, fos. 124v, 129v, 130.
37. *ibid.*, fo. 124v.
38. L.A.O., Register 26, fo. 132.
39. Houlbrooke, *Church Courts*, pp. 46–7.
40. Elvey, *op. cit.*, pp. 138, 178, 199, 215.
41. Leics. R.O., ID/41/11/2, *passim*; ID/41/13/2, *passim.*
42. *An Episcopal Court Book*, ed. Bowker, p. xxii.
43. L.A.O., Cj. 3, fo. 46.
44. L.A.O., Cj. 4, fo. 46; *Lincolnshire Pedigrees*, ed. Maddison, III, p. 775.
45. See above, pp. 15 ff.

5. The challenge of heresy

1. Dickens, *English Reformation*, p. 36; see also Dickens, *Lollards and Protestants in the Diocese of York.*
2. *The English Works of John Fisher*, ed. Mayor, pt. I, pp. 311–45.
3. Bodl. Libr. Arch. A.d.11, fo. 44.
4. Clebsch, *England's Earliest Protestants 1520–1535*, p. 12.
5. *Tudor Royal Proclamations*, I, *The Early Tudors*, edd. Hughes and Larkin, p. 133.
6. L.A.O., Register 26, fo. 101.
7. *Acts and Monuments of John Foxe*, ed. Townsend, IV, p. 219.
8. Trinity College, Dublin, MS. 775, fos. 128v ff. I am indebted to the Librarian for his transcript of this entry.
9. *Acts and Monuments of John Foxe*, ed. Townsend, IV, pp. 219–20.
10. *ibid.*, p. 245.
11. P.R.O., C. 85, no. 13.
12. Clebsch, *England's Earliest Protestants*, pp. 26, 258–70.
13. Ellis, *Original Letters*, I, i, pp. 180–4. This letter has been re-dated to 5 January 1526 by Chester, 'Robert Barnes and the Burning of Books', pp. 211 ff.
14. L.A.O., Cj. 3, fo. 21v.
15. L.A.O., Register 26, fo. 140.
16. Ellis, *Original Letters*, III, i, p. 247.
17. *ibid.*, p. 252.
18. *Acts and Monuments of John Foxe*, ed. Townsend, V, Appendix I.
19. *ibid.*, Appendix VI.
20. *ibid.*, Appendix VI, Letter 2.
21. Ellis, *Original Letters*, III, ii, p. 77, (cf. *L.P.* IV, ii, no. 4004); Clebsch, *England's Earliest Protestants*, p. 80.
22. L.A.O., Register 27, fos. 27, 52v, 93, 125, 150v, 189v, 191, 207, 216, 216v; cf. Heal, 'The Bishops of Ely', pp. 60–1.
23. L.A.O., Cj. 3, fos. 21v–22.
24. Lehmberg, *The Reformation Parliament*, p. 100.

III. 1530–40: Reform in head and members?

1. The supremacy and the bishopric

1. Wilkins, *Concilia*, III, p. 717; Lehmberg, *Reformation Parliament*, pp. 99–101: Logan, 'The Henrician Canons', pp. 99 ff.

2. Lehmberg, *op. cit.*, pp. 100–1.
3. *L.P.*, VII, no. 541; XIII, i, no. 811; XVI, no. 1334.
4. Scarisbrick, *Henry VIII*, pp. 273–5.
5. *ibid.*, p. 275; Lehmberg, *op. cit.*, pp. 108, ff.
6. See above, pp. 24 ff.
7. A fuller version of the argument expounded here may be found in Bowker, 'The Supremacy and the Episcopate: The Struggle for Control 1534–1540', pp. 227 ff. I had not then seen the significance of the second licence for jurisdiction (p. 242); see above, p. 111.
8. Lehmberg, *Reformation Parliament*, pp. 106–16.
9. *ibid.*, pp. 109–16; *S.R.*, III, 22 Henry VIII, c.15.
10. Ullmann, 'This Realm of England is an Empire', pp. 183, 203.
11. The text of the supplication is found in *Documents Illustrative of English Church History*, edd. Gee and Hardy, pp. 145–53; for a study of the significance of these grievances see my 'Some Archdeacons' Court Books and the Commons Supplication Against the Ordinaries of 1532', pp. 282–316.
12. *Documents*, edd. Gee and Hardy, pp. 154–76; Ullmann, *op. cit.*, p. 203.
13. Wilkins, *Concilia*, III, p. 749; Lehmberg, *op. cit.*, pp. 148–53.
14. Lehmberg, *op. cit.*, pp. 76–160.
15. *Dowments*, ed. Gee and Hardy, pp. 187–95.
16. Ullmann, *op. cit.*, p. 195.
17. *Documents*, edd. Gee and Hardy, pp. 243–4.
18. *L.P.*, VIII, no. 190.
19. *ibid.*, no. 600.
20. *L.P.*, VII, no. 14.
21. B.L., C. 53.k.14. *A Sermonde made before King* [*Henry VIII*], *An. MDXXXVIII by John Longlande*, pp. 7–10.
22. Italics mine. L.A.O., Register 27, fos. 73, 73v.
23. L.A.O., Register 26, fos. 250v–253v.
24. *S.R.*, III, 25 Henry VIII, c.19.
25. Ridley, *Thomas Cranmer*, p. 79.
26. L.A.O., D and C, Wills, II, fo. 10v.
27. *ibid.*, fo. 5; *L.P.*, VII, no. 1044.
28. L.A.O., D and C, Wills, II, fo. 10v.
29. *The Letters of Stephen Gardiner*, ed. Muller, p. 56.
30. *L.P.*, VII, no. 689.
31. *L.P.*, VII, no. 872.
32. Lander, 'The Diocese of Chichester 1508–1558', p. 46.
33. L.A.O., D and C, Accounts; Bj. 3. 5. (no foliation), *sub Curialitates.*
34. L.A.O., Bishop Fuller's transcripts, fo. 17.
35. L.A.O., Register 25, fos. 18v–19; D and C, Dvj. 26.
36. L.A.O., Register 26, fos. 40v–1.
37. See for example L.A.O., Register 27, fos. 58v, 135v, 136v, 161v, 162, 243v. These admissions all date from June 1534 to December 1534.
38. L.A.O., Register 27, fo. 266.
39. Elton, *Policy and Police*, p. 227.
40. It was not until 1539 that letters patent were recognised by Parliament as sufficient ground for the appointment of bishops, *S.R.*, III, 31 Henry VIII, c.9.
41. Lehmberg, 'Supremacy and Vicegerency: A Re-examination', pp. 225 ff.
42. Lehmberg, 'Supremacy and Vicegerency', p. 227. Professor Lehmberg did not, however, notice the connection with Cranmer's visitation.
43. Strype, *Ecclesiastical Memorials*, I, ii, pp. 216–18.
44. Notably over the question of holy days; see above, p. 150.
45. Strype, *op. cit.*, I, ii, p. 216.
46. Wilkins, *Concilia*, III, 797.

47. B.L., Cottonian MSS, Cleopatra F, ii, fo. 130.
48. *ibid.*
49. *S.R.*, III, 37 Henry VIII, c.17.
50. B.L., Cottonian MSS, Cleopatra F, ii, fos. 130–130v.
51. L.A.O., Register 26, fos. 261–3.
52. *ibid.*, fos. 286v ff.
53. L.A.O., D. and C, Wills, fos. 1–1v, (second numeration).
54. L.A.O., D and C, Accounts, Bj. 3. 8, unfoliated *sub Curialitates* and Bj. 3. 5. (unfoliated) *sub Custos Placitorum* and *Procurationes.*
55. [This section was written before the publication of Heal's *Of Prelates and Princes: A Study of the Economic and Social Position of the Tudor Episcopate* (Cambridge, 1980).] The comparative table of episcopal incomes as given in the *Valor Ecclesiasticus* is found in Strype, *Annals*, II, i, pp. 575–6.
56. *L.P.*, VII, nos. 322, 541; XIX, i, no. 80 (33).
57. His will in particular shows this: he is meticulous in his list of debts and debtors. P.R.O., Prob. 11/31.
58. See above, p. 9.
59. *L.P.*, VII, no. 541.
60. *L.P.*, VIII, no. 169; X, no. 1257.
61. P.R.O., Prob. 11/31, *passim.*
62. L.A.O., Additional Register 7, fo. 16 (pagination from back).
63. L.A.O., Subsid. 1/7b.
64. L.A.O., Bishops Accounts/Misc/18, fo. 1.
65. Heal, 'The Bishops of Ely', p. 185.
66. *L.P.*, XIII, i, no. 29.
67. *L.P.*, X, no. 1267.
68. *L.P.*, XVI, no. 190; P.R.O., S.P., I, 163, fo. 150.
69. Heal, 'The Tudors and Church Lands; Economic Problems of the Bishopric of Ely during the Sixteenth Century', p. 208.
70. *Valor Ecclesiasticus*, IV, p. 6.
71. Heal, 'The Bishops of Ely', p. 165.
72. *ibid.*, pp. 165 ff.
73. F. Heal, 'The Economic Problems of the Clergy', p. 107; 'spiritual sources of income ... helped, in theory, to give the bishops *the same revenue as before the Reformation*' (italics mine). But this was not so.
74. L.A.O., Bishop Fuller's Transcripts, fo. 2.
75. L.A.O., Bishops Accounts, Rentals, I, fo. 11v.
76. *L.P.*, XII, ii, 780.
77. Strype, *Ecclesiastical Memorials*, I, ii, pp. 275–8.
78. L.A.O., Bishops Accounts, Rentals, I, fos. 6, 12.
79. P.R.O., Prob. 11/31.
80. L.A.O., Register 26, fo. 144v.
81. *L.P.*, XVII, 881, no. 3
82. *Valor Ecclesiasticus*, IV, p. 7. Unfortunately, procurations are not separately listed.
83. Major, *Handlist of Lincoln Diocesan Records*, p. 105.
84. *Valor Ecclesiasticus*, IV, p. 4; L.A.O., Bishop Fuller's Transcripts, fo. 239v; *L.R.S.*, 13, pp. 139–41.
85. *Valor Ecclesiasticus*, IV, p. 5; L.A.O., Bishop Fuller's Transcripts, fo. 239; *L.R.S.*, 12, pp. 175–7.
86. *L.P.*, VII, no. 1232; VIII, no. 583; IX, no. 553.
87. *Valor Ecclesiasticus*, IV, p. 2; L.A.O., Bishop Fuller's Transcripts, fo. 239v; *L.R.S.*, 13, pp. 108–11.
88. *L.R.S.*, 13, pp. 108–11.
89. *L.R.S.*, 12, pp. 153–5; 13, pp. 122–3.

90. *Valor Ecclesiasticus*, IV, p. 6; L.A.O., Bishop Fuller's Transcripts, fo. 236.
91. *L.R.S.*, 13, pp. 106–8.
92. *ibid.*, pp. 142–3.
93. *L.R.S.*, 12, p. 54; 13, p. 137–40; cf. *Valor Ecclesiasticus*, IV, pp. 4–5.
94. *L.R.S.*, 13, pp. 104–5, 106–8, 130, 139; cf. *Valor Ecclesiasticus*, IV, pp. 2, 3, 6. cf. L.A.O., Bishop Fuller's Transcripts, fos. 236, 238v, 239.
95. P.R.O. Prob. 11/9.
96. *Registrum Caroli Bothe, Episcopi Herefordensis AD. MDXVI–MDXXXV*, ed. Bannister, VII, pp. 149, 285. I am grateful to Dr Lander for this reference.
97. Lander, 'The Diocese of Chichester 1508–1558', p. 109; Heal, 'The Bishops of Ely', p. 111.
98. Haigh, 'Finance and Administration in a new diocese: Chester 1541–1641', p. 153.
99. du Boulay, 'Archbishop Cranmer and the Canterbury Temporalities', pp. 25–8, 34; and Cross, 'The Economic Problems of the See of York: Decline and Recovery in the Sixteenth Century', pp. 69–72.
100. *L.R.S.*, 12, pp. 47–8; 13, pp. 132–3.
101. *Valor Ecclesiasticus*, IV, p. 5.
102. *L.R.S.*, 13, pp. 135–7; see above, p. 82.
103. Aylmer, *The King's Servants*, pp. 96 ff.
104. *L.R.S.*, 13, pp. 135–7.
105. *L.R.S.*, 13, pp. 132–3.
106. *L.R.S.*, 12, pp. 188–9; L.A.O., Register 26, fos. 277v–278.
107. *L.R.S.*, 13, pp. 135–7.
108. L.A.O., Register 26, fo. 217.
109. L.A.O., Register 26, fos. 170, 263, 267v[2].
110. L.A.O., Register 26, fos. 174–174v, 179a.
111. *L.R.S.*, 13, pp. 150–2.
112. Houlbrooke, *Church Courts*, *passim.*
113. Leics. R. O., ID 41/11, 2; ID 41/13, 1 and 2.
114. L.A.O., Cj. 6: Northampton R.O., Books 1–3.
115. L.A.O., Cij. 1, fos. 1–13.
116. L.A.O., Cij. 1 fos. 222–257v; Haigh, *Tudor Lancashire*, p. 59.
117. Lander, 'Church Courts and the Reformation in the diocese of Chichester 1500–1558', pp. 230–1.
118. *ibid.*, p. 232; Houlbrooke, *Church Courts*, pp. 278–81.
119. Houlbrooke, *Church Courts*, pp. 273–4.
120. See above, pp. 135 ff.
121. L.A.O., Cij. 1, fo. 98.
122. Northampton R.O., Book 1, p. 31.
123. Houlbrooke, *Church Courts*, pp. 55–88; *S.R.*, III 32 Henry VIII c.38.
124. L.A.O., Cj. 3, fos. 50–192v. See also above, pp. 167 ff.
125. Houlbrooke, *Church Courts*, *passim.*

2. The secular colleges and the monasteries

1. L.A.O., D and C, Bj.3.5 (unfoliated).
2. *L.R.S.*, 13, p. 9.
3. *ibid.*, 12, p. 146.
4. L.A.O., D and C, Wills, II, fos. 9, 11v (second numeration): abbreviations indicate where the page is torn.
5. L.A.O., D and C, Bj. 3. 5 *sub Curialitates.*
6. *ibid.*
7. *ibid.*

8. L.A.O., D and C, Wills, II, fo. 33v (second numeration), for inhibition; fo. 1–1v, for licence.
9. L.A.O., D and C, Wills, II, fos. 25–37; Stow Wills 1530–52, fos. 21–2.
10. L.A.O., L.C.C. Wills 1535–7, fos. 60–1.
11. *L.P.*, VIII, no. 582.
12. L.A.O., D and C, Wills, II, fos. 35–35v. Peter's pence were discontinued in 1533 (Bj. 3. 4, *sub Procurationes*).
13. *L.R.S.*, 13, p. 24.
14. *L.R.S.*, 13, pp. 27–31; Lander, 'The Bishops of Chichester 1508–1558', p. 145.
15. See above, p. 31.
16. *S.R.*, III, 21 Henry VIII, c.13.
17. *L.R.S.*, 13, p. 8.
18. *ibid.*, p. 13.
19. *ibid.*, pp. 16^2, 17.
20. See above, p. 33, *L.R.S.*, 12, pp. 62, 119, 120.
21. *L.R.S.*, 13, pp. 29–30.
22. *L.R.S.*, 12, p. 52; 13, pp. 27, 31.
23. L.A.O., D and C, Fabric Accounts, Bj. 5/19, fos. 148–172v.
24. L.A.O., D and C, Bj. 3. 2. *sub Aperture.*
25. L.A.O., D and C, Bj. 3. 4. (unfoliated), *sub Aperture.*
26. L.A.O., D and C, Bj. 3. 5. (unfoliated).
27. L.A.O., D and C, Bj. 3. 4. (unfoliated).
28. L.A.O., D and C, Bj. 3. 4, and Bj. 3. 5 (unfoliated). The accounts follow a pattern annually, but the new financial year commenced in September. The decline in offerings can be traced by following the annual entry of *Aperture.*
29. *L.R.S.*, 12, pp. 7–8.
30. 'Inventories of Plate, Vestments, etc., belonging to the Cathedral Church of the Blessed Mary of Lincoln', collected and translated by Christopher Wordsworth, pp. 12 ff.
31. *ibid.*, p. 40.
32. *L.R.S.*, 13, pp. 35–6.
33. *L.P.*, XV, nos. 772, 809.
34. *L.R.S.*, 13, pp. 55–6.
35. L.A.O., D and C, A.2/11–16.
36. P.R.O., Prob. 11/31.
37. *L.R.S.*, 12, pp. 157–8.
38. Walker, 'A History of the Reformation in the Archdeaconries of Lincoln and Stow', p. 438. It is clear from a lease book dating mainly from Chaderton's episcopate that one lease was made of the rectory of Wigtoft in 1525 with a reversion, but this is the only such lease to survive L.A.O., 2, CC. 33.
39. Youings, *The Dissolution of the Monasteries*, pp. 145–7.
40. L.A.O., D and C, Wills, II, *passim*; *L.R.S.*, 13, *passim*; L.A.O., Register 26, *passim.* See also n. 38 above.
41. See above, pp. 83 ff.
42. L.A.O., Register 26, fos. 282–282v.
43. *ibid.*, fos. 299v–300.
44. *L.R.S.*, 13, pp. 119–20.
45. *ibid.*, 12, pp. 186–8; L.A.O., D and C, Wills, II, fo. 25.
46. L.A.O., D and C, Wills, II, fo. 49v.
47. The monasteries just before dissolution appear to have adopted a policy of high entry fines and lower rents; see Haigh, *The Last Days of the Lancashire Monasteries and the Pilgrimage of Grace*, pp. 108–9.
48. L.A.O., Register 26, fos. 282v–3; D and C, Wills, II, fo. 75v; *Valor Ecclesiasticus*, IV, p. 19. Dr Walker in his thesis (see above, n. 38) suggested that this lease was never

confirmed by the dean and chapter (p. 148). The appearance of a dean and chapter will book which contains much extraneous material has come to light since his researches. Additionally, I have dated grants according to their indenture date and not according to the date of last approval, whether by dean and chapter or by bishop. Hence there is some difference between Dr Walker's figures and my own.

49. L.A.O., Register 26, fos. 299v–300.
50. *L.R.S.*, 13, pp. 119–20.
51. *ibid.*, 12, pp. 186–8.
52. L.A.O., Register 26, fos. 302v–303.
53. L.A.O., D and C, Wills, II, fo. 25; Register 26, fos. 119–20, 283–4, 299v–300, 307–8; *L.R.S.*, 13, pp. 58–60.
54. L.A.O., Register 26, fos. 282–282v.
55. *L.R.S.*, 13, p. xxiii.
56. Walker, *op. cit.*, p. 66.
57. *L.R.S.*, 12, pp. 160–70.
58. *L.R.S.*, 13, p. 116.
59. L.A.O., Register 26, fos. 237v–238; *L.R.S.*, 12, pp. 145–6. Richard Pate and John Barker were combined in the grant of Caistor with the earl.
60. L.A.O., Register 26, fo. 260v.
61. *ibid.*, fos. 278v, 291v.
62. *ibid.*, fo. 297.
63. *L.R.S.*, 13, pp. 129, 132, 141[2]. L.A.O., Register 26, fos. 276v, 280v, 281v, 285.
64. Notably, Aylesbury, Brampton, Caistor, Empingham, and St Margaret, Leicester.
65. *L.R.S.*, 13, p. 20.
66. *L.P.*, XIV, i, no. 213.
67. *L.R.S.*, 13, p. viii.
68. *ibid.*, pp. 23, 125.
69. *ibid.*, p. 91.
70. *ibid.*, p. 65.
71. *ibid.*, p. 29.
72. L.A.O., D and C, Bj. 3. 5. *sub Curialitates.*
73. L.A.O., D and C, Wills, II, fo. 7v (second numeration).
74. *L.R.S.*, 13, p. 195.
75. *ibid.*, p. 196.
76. Dickens, *English Reformation*, pp. 207–8.
77. *Subsidy*, ed. Salter, pp. 3, 11, 14, 36; Foster and Thompson, 'The Chantry Certificates for Lincoln and Lincolnshire Returned in 1548 under the Act of Parliament of I Edward VI', II, p. 3.
78. Foster and Thompson, 'The Chantry Certificates of Northamptonshire', pp. 87, 92–3; *Subsidy*, ed. Salter, pp. 131, 136; for the treatment of one college as though a monastery, see above, p. 102.
79. Foster and Thompson, 'The Chantry Certificates for Lincoln and Lincolnshire', pp. 3, 11. The dean of the cathedral was master of the college.
80. L.A.O., Vj. 10, fos. 69v; Thompson, '*A History ... of St Mary in the Newarke*, pp. 208–9. Professor Thompson was not aware of the visitations of the college contained in L.A.O. Vj. 10 and his account of the college does not quite cover its last years.
81. *L.P.*, IX, no. 1005.
82. Thompson, *A History ... of St Mary in the Newarke*, *passim*; L.A.O., Vj. 10, fos. 69v–71v.
83. *L.P.*, VII, nos. 921, 1024.
84. *ibid.*, nos. 1121, 1216.
85. Knowles, *Religious Orders*, III, pp. 228 ff., 373.
86. *L.P.*, XIII, i, 981 (1).
87. *ibid.*, 981 (2); S.P., I, 132., fos. 76ff.

88. *L.P.*, XIII, i, 981 (5): S.P., I, 132, fo. 81v.
89. *L.P.*, XIII, i, 981 (2:1).
90. *ibid.*, 981 (2:16).
91. Knowles, *Religious Orders*, III, pp. 373 ff.
92. *S.R.*, III, 27 Henry VIII, c.28.
93. Knowles, *Religious Orders*, III, p. 286.
94. *ibid.*, p. 271.
95. *L.P.*, IX, no. 1005.
96. *An Episcopal Court Book*, ed. Bowker, pp. 49–51.
97. *L.R.S.*, 35, pp. 91, 155, 159.
98. *L.P.*, IX, no. 1005.
99. *ibid.*
100. *L.P.*, X, no. 364.
101. Knowles, *Religious Orders*, III, p. 48.
102. *L.R.S.*, 35, p. 159.
103. Knowles, *Religious Orders*, III, p. 481.
104. *L.P.*, IX, no. 457.
105. *L.R.S.*, 35, p. 107.
106. *L.P.*, IX, no. 457.
107. *L.R.S.*, 35, p. 81.
108. See above, pp. 23ff.
109. Youngs, *The Dissolution of the Monasteries*, p. 151.
110. *L.P.*, IX, no. 375; Knowles, *Religious Orders*, III, p. 336; P.R.O., S.P., I, 96.
111. *S.R.*, III, 27 Henry VIII, c.28.
112. Youings, *op. cit.*, pp. 47–8.
113. Savine, 'English Monasteries on the Eve of the Dissolution', pp. 270 ff.
114. *Letters Relating to the Suppression of Monasteries*, ed. T. Wright, pp. 116–17.
115. Jack, 'Dissolution dates of the Monasteries Dissolved under the Act of 1536', p. 173.
116. *Letters*, ed. Wright, p. 129.
117. *L.R.S.*, 35, p. 103.
118. *Letters*, ed. Wright, p. 136.
119. See above, p. 20.
120. *Letters*, ed. Wright, pp. 173–4.
121. Jack, *op. cit.*, pp. 173, 175.
122. Jack, *op. cit*; Hodgett, *Tudor Lincolnshire*, p. 25.
123. Hodgett, *Tudor Lincolnshire*, p. 25.
124. Hodgett, 'The Dissolution of the Monasteries in Lincolnshire', p. 43.
125. *ibid.*, p. 46.
126. Bodl. Libr. Arch. A. d. 11, *Tres conciones*, I, fo. 11. The contrast in attitude is marked in comparison to Lancashire, see Haigh, *Tudor Lancashire*, pp. 125 ff.
127. Hodgett, 'The Dissolution of the Monasteries in Lincolnshire', p. 42.
128. *Letters*, ed. Wright, pp. 192–3.
129. *ibid.*, p. 151.
130. *L.P.*, XIII, i, no. 196; L.A.O., Register 27, fo. 247v.
131. L.A.O., Register 27, fo. 268; Chambers, *Faculty Office Registers, 1534–49*, p. 137.
132. See below, p. 187; cf. Haigh, *The Last Days of the Lancashire Monasteries*, pp. 112 ff.
133. Hodgett, 'The Dissolution of the Monasteries in Lincolnshire', p. 45.
134. L.A.O., Register 26, fo. 287.
135. L.A.O., Vj. 12, fos. 4v–6v. This is a clergy list from which it is hard to be exact: deaths can be shown by crossing out but sometimes the details of the new incumbent are not given.
136. L.A.O., Vj. 12, fos. 5v, 6.
137. *ibid.*, fo. 5; Chambers, *op. cit.*, p. 79.
138. L.A.O., Vj. 12, fo. 5; Chambers, *op. cit.*, p. 207.

139. *ibid.*
140. L.A.O., Vj. 12, fo. 7.
141. See below, p. 186.
142. Hartridge, *A History of Vicarages in the Middle Ages*, p. 204.
143. Lander, 'The Bishops of Chichester', p. 276; Haigh, *Tudor Lancashire*, p. 61.
144. See above, p. 133.

3. The secular clergy.

1. Lehmberg, *The Reformation Parliament*, pp. 81–9.
2. Bowker, *Secular Clergy*, pp. 56 ff.
3. Orme, *English Schools in the Middle Ages*, p. 195. Bennett, *English Books and Readers 1475–1557*, pp. 65–70.
4. *Tudor Royal Proclamations*, I, edd. Hughes and Larkin, pp. 181–93; Lehmberg, *op. cit.*, pp. 117 ff.
5. *S.R.*, III, 21 Henry, c.13.
6. A. H. Thompson, 'Pluralism in the Medieval Church', pp. 35–73; Bowker, *Secular Clergy*, pp. 85 ff.
7. The evidence is largely contained in the visitation returns of 1530; *L.R.S.*, 35, ed. A. H. Thompson. But the material for the archdeaconry of Lincoln is in L.A.O., Vij. 1, *passim*, which is mainly for 1533–8. There are scant visitation returns for the archdeaconry of Northampton but nothing survives with which to compare them (*L.R.S.*, 35, pp. 24–31), and there is no complete material for the archdeaconry of Leicester *after* the act, though some material survives indicating the rate of absenteeism and the vigilance of the authorities between 1520 and c. 1528, notably Leics. R.O., ID/41/11 and ID/41/13.
8. Haigh, *Tudor Lancashire*, p. 27.
9. See above, pp. 43 ff.
10. *L.R.S.*, 33, *passim.*
11. *L.R.S.*, 35, *passim*; L.A.O., Vij. 1, *passim.*
12. L.A.O., Vj. 11, *passim.*
13. L.A.O., Vj. 12, *passim.*
14. Sources as in nn. 10, 11, 12, 13, above.
15. Leics. R.O., ID/41/12/2 fo. 22; ID/41/12/3 fos. 15, 37.
16. Zell, 'The Personnel of the Clergy in Kent in the Reformation Period', p. 532.
17. L.A.O., Register 27, fos. 188, 216v; Vj. 11, fo. 72v.
18. Bowker, *Secular Clergy*, p. 131.
19. See above, pp. 132 ff.
20. L.A.O., Vj. 12, fos. 37 ff.
21. *Subsidy*, ed. Salter, p. 203.
22. L.A.O., Register 27, fo. 269; Vj. 11, fo. 33v; Vj. 12, fo. 25.
23. *Subsidy*, ed. Salter, p. 197; L.A.O., Register 27, fo. 264; Vj. 11, fo. 32; Vj. 12, fo. 31.
24. L.A.O., Register 27, fos. 180v, 237.
25. *L.P.*, VII, ii, Appendices 40, 41; Merriman, *Life and Letters of Thomas Cromwell*, II, no. 210, p. 78; *L.R.S.*, 35, p. 23; L.A.O., Vj. 12, fo. 4.
26. L.A.O., Register 27, fo. 246; Chambers, *Faculty Registers*, p. 244.
27. Bowker, *Secular Clergy*, p. 91.
28. The livings were Hertford St Nicholas, Paxton Parva, Throcking, Radwell. For their valuation see *Subsidy* ed. Salter, pp. 173, 178, 179, 188. Gibson, *Codex Juris Ecclesiastici Anglicani*, (Oxford 1761), vol. II, Tit. XXXVII, cap. i, p. 906, gloss z, suggests that benefices below £8 were exempt from the operation of the statute but not from existing canon law; accordingly they would have been deemed void if another benefice

were accepted. This interpretation makes nonsense of the rest of the statute and does not appear to accord with early sixteenth-century practice.

29. Zell, *op. cit.*, pp. 529 ff.
30. L.A.O., Register 25, fo. 57; Vj. 12, fo. 8.
31. L.A.O., Register 25, fo. 57; Vj. 12, fo. 16v.
32. Zell, *op. cit.*, p. 519, remarks on the longevity of the clergy of Kent.
33. Bowker, *Secular Clergy*, p. 96; Haigh, *Tudor Lancashire*, pp. 29–30.
34. *Subsidy*, ed. Salter, pp. 62, 259, 264.
35. See above notes for sources.
36. Haigh, *Tudor Lancashire*, p. 29.
37. L.A.O., Vj. 11, *passim*; Vj. 12, *passim.*
38. *The University in Society*, ed. Stone, I, p. 91; unfortunately we have not got comparable figures for Cambridge until 1550; *ibid.*, p. 92.
39. See below, pp. 163 ff.
40. L.A.O., Register 26, fo. 60.
41. *ibid.*, fo. 62.
42. *ibid.*, fo. 61.
43. *ibid.*, fo. 61v.
44. Bowker, *Secular Clergy*, pp. 61 ff.
45. Knowles, *Religious Orders*, III, p. 265.
46. Livings in Oxfordshire and Northamptonshire have been omitted so as not to distort the figures by the over-all loss in patronage that the new dioceses of Peterborough and Oxford represented. L.A.O., Register 27, *passim.*
47. L.A.O., Register 27, fos. 139, 163, 165v, 166v, 267v. *Subsidy*, ed. Salter, p. 154.
48. L.A.O., Register 27, fo. 221; Vj. 11, fo. 75.
49. L.A.O., Register 27, fo. 268; Emden, *Cambridge*, p. 126, *sub* Cotton alias Bronde; Knowles *op. cit.*, p. 26.
50. L.A.O., Register 27, fos. 44, 100, 214v.
51. L.A.O., Register 26, fos. 1v–66v.
52. L.A.O., Register 27, *passim.*
53. Zell, 'The Personnel of the Clergy in Kent', pp. 513 ff.
54. *Subsidy*, ed. Salter, pp. 170 ff. L.A.O., Vj. 12, *passim.*
55. L.A.O., Register 26 and 27, *passim.*
56. Hughes, *The Reformation in England*, I, p. 53, n.1. Pill, 'The Administration of the Diocese of Exeter under Bishop Veysey', pp. 269–71. Brigden, 'The Early Reformation in London', p. 38.
57. Hodgett, *Tudor Lincolnshire*, p. 42.
58. L.A.O., Register 25, 26, 27, *passim.*
59. Zell, *op. cit.*, pp. 529 ff.
60. *Subsidy*, ed. Salter, *passim*; cf. L.A.O., Vj. 12, *passim.*
61. L.A.O., Vj. 12, *passim.*
62. Zell, *op. cit.*, pp. 529–31.
63. Those ordained before 1521 were likely to be well into their forties by 1540: the canons governing entry to the priesthood normally required an ordinand to be in his twenty-fifth year – that is, 24. Bowker, *Secular Clergy*, p. 41.
64. *L.P.*, IX, no. 453; P.R.O., S.P., I, 97, fo. 24.
65. *L.P.*, IX, no. 20; PRO., S.P., I, 95, fo. 10.
66. L.A.O., Register 27, fo. 227v: Chambers, *Faculty Registers*, p. 244.
67. Bucks R.O. D/A/We/2, fo. 75.
68. L.A.O., Inventories, Box 18, no. 96.
69. L.A.O., Inventories, Box 15, no. 218.
70. L.A.O., L.C.C. Wills 1545–6, Box I, fo. 20.
71. L.A.O., Register 27, fos. 118v, 139; Longden, XI, pp. 191, 257.
72. *The State of the Church*, ed. Foster, pp. xviii-xix.

73. *ibid*., p. 456.
74. These are given in percentages even when, as in the case of Lee, only one priest was involved, for the purpose of comparison.
75. See above, p. 152.
76. Lander, 'The diocese of Chichester 1508–1558', p. 342.
77. *S.R.*, III, 26 Henry VIII, c.3; for Atwater's attempts to augment vicarages, Bowker, *Secular Clergy*, pp. 143–4.
78. *S.R.*, III, 27 Henry VIII, c.8.
79. Dr Lander's findings rest on comparison of the *Valor*, the taxation of Nicholas IV in 1291 and any other available evidence, see *op.cit*., pp. 387 ff. See also Heal, 'Economic Problems of the Clergy', p. 104.
80. Hodgett, *Tudor Lincolnshire*, p. 67.
81. L.A.O., Glebe Terriers, I, fo. 169.
82. *Subsidy*, ed. Salter, p. 18.
83. *Valor Ecclesiasticus*, IV, p. 56.
84. L.A.O., Glebe Terriers, I, no. 35.
85. Savine, 'English Monasteries on the Eve of the Dissolution', p. 171.
86. *Subsidy*, ed. Salter, p. 17. For the importance of glebe see Heal, 'Economic Problems of the Clergy' p. 104.
87. *Valor Ecclesiasticus*, IV, p. 54.
88. L.A.O., Vij. 1, fos. 163 ff.
89. L.A.O., Register 27, fo. 44v; Venn, *Alumni*, C.I, p. 170.
90. Brigden, 'The Early Reformation in London', p. 94.
91. Haigh, *Tudor Lancashire*, pp. 23–4.
92. Heath, *Parish Clergy*, p. 173.
93. Walker, 'A History of the Reformation in Lincoln and Stow', p. 357.
94. *Subsidy*, ed. Salter, pp. 3, 6; cf. *Valor Ecclesiasticus*, IV, pp. 46–7.
95. L.A.O., Glebe Terriers, I, no. 64.
96. *Valor Ecclesiasticus*, IV, p. 138.
97. Lander, *op. cit*., p. 317.
98. L.A.O., Glebe Terriers, I, 1–316.
99. Lander, *op. cit*., p. 257.
100. L.A.O., Subsid. 1/7b/8 (4).
101. L.A.O., Subsid. 1/7b/6.
102. Heal, 'Clerical Tax Collection under the Tudors', pp. 100 ff.
103. P.R.O., Prob. 11/31, p. 7.
104. Sherburne certainly did so; see Lander, *op. cit*., pp. 342 ff.
105. L.A.O., Cij. 1, fos. 225v-257; Houlbrooke, *Church Courts*, p. 144.
106. Heal, 'Economic Problems of the Clergy', p. 109.
107. See above, p. 138.
108. L.A.O., Cj. 3, fos. 57v ff.
109. L.A.O., Cj. 3, fo. 61, Houlbrooke, *op. cit.* p. 134.
110. L.A.O., Cij. 1, fo. 127v.
111. *S.R.*, IV, 2 & 3 Edward VI c.13; Houlbrooke, *op. cit*., p. 145.

4. *Reform and reaction in the parishes*

1. Elton, *Policy and Police*, pp. 229 ff.
2. Haigh, *Tudor Lancashire*, p. 113.
3. *ibid*., p. 109.
4. L.A.O., Register 27, fos. 232, 265v; Emden, *Oxford*, n.s., p.1.
5. *S.R.*, III, 25 Henry VIII, c. 12.
6. McConica, *English Humanists and Reformation Politics*, p. 128.
7. Emden, *Oxford*, n.s., p. 1.

8. *S.R.*, III, 25 Henry VIII, c.12; *L.P.*, VII, nos. 70, 238; L.A.O., Register 27, fo. 161.
9. L.A.O., Register 27, fo. 260; *L.P.*, VI, nos. 154, 1571.
10. Emden, *Oxford*, n.s., pp. 373–4; L.A.O., Register 27, fo. 24; *L.R.S.*, 12, p. 1.
11. *L.P.*, VII, no. 1025.
12. See above, pp. 148 ff.
13. L.A.O., Register 27, fo. 183.
14. *L.P.*, XIII (ii), no. 986 (13); L.A.O., Register 27, fo. 183.
15. L.A.O., Register 27, fos. 52v, 63v.
16. L.A.O., Register 26, fos. 32 ff; *L.P.* XI, no. 1137; Knowles, *Religious Orders*, III, p. 494.
17. L.A.O., Register 27, fo. 109v; McConica, *op. cit.*, p. 265; Brigden, 'The Early Reformation in London', p. 315.
18. Emden, *Oxford*, III, p. 1475; n.s., p. 435; L.A.O., Register 27, fos. 150v, 169v, 197, 199.
19. L.A.O., Register 27, fos. 48v, 64, 64v^2, 74, 76v, 79, 87v, 96v, 97v, 169v, 197, 199, 246v.
20. Elton, *Policy and Police*, p. 387.
21. *L.P.*, XII, ii, Appendix 40; Merriman, *Life and Letters of Thomas Cromwell*, II, 78; L.A.O., Register 27, fo. 23.
22. Elton, *Policy and Police*, p. 344; *L. P.*, VII, nos. 449, 472, 982; L.A.O., Register 27, fo. 73.
23. L.A.O., Register 27, fo. 149; Chambers, *Faculty Registers*, p. 312; *L.P.*, VIII, nos. 406, 589.
24. L.A.O., Register 27, fo. 176v; *L.P.*, XII, ii, no. 998; XIX, i, no. 1035 (140).
25. L.A.O., Register 27, fo. 158; *L.P.*, XI, no. 44; Elton, *Policy and Police*, p. 342.
26. L.A.O., Register 27, fo. 229v; *L.P.*, XII, i, no. 182; Emden, *Oxford*, n.s., p. 295; P.R.O., S.P., I, 114, fo. 226.
27. L.A.O., Register 27, fo. 135v.
28. *L.P.*, XII, i, 126; Elton, *Policy and Police*, p. 10.
29. L.A.O., Vj. 11, fos. 102 ff.
30. L.A.O., Register 27, fo. 163; *L.P.*, XII, i, no. 384.
31. *L.P.*, V, no. 631; X, no. 14; Elton, *Policy and Police*, p. 236; L.A.O., Register 27, fo. 135v; Vj. 11, fos. 102 ff.
32. McConica, *op. cit.*, p. 162.
33. *L.P.*, IX, no. 661; P.R.O., S.P., I, 98, fo. 48.
34. *L.P.*, IV, iii, no. 6176; L.A.O., Register 27, fo. 141.
35. Elton, *Policy and Police*, pp. 255–6; *L.P.*, IX, no. 84; L.A.O., Register 27, fo. 238.
36. Brigden, *op. cit.*, p. 140; Haigh, *Tudor Lancashire*, pp. 118 ff.
37. *L.P.*, VI, nos. 1541, 1571.
38. Haigh, *op. cit.*, p. 109.
39. Brigden, *op. cit.*, pp. 239 ff.
40. *L.P.*, VII, no. 463.
41. *The Works of Thomas Cranmer*, ed. Cox, pp. 460–1.
42. L.A.O., Register 26, fo. 266v.
43. Ellis, *Original Letters*, III, ii, pp. 335–6; another copy of the letter is in Strype, *Ecclesiastical Memorials* I, ii, p. 206.
44. Strype, *op cit.*, p. 213.
45. For a detailed discussion of the possible text see Elton, *Policy and Police*, pp. 232–6. It is quite clear that Longland's register does *not* contain a copy of 'articles for priests unlearned' and is, in a slightly modified form, Cromwell's circular letter to bishops.
46. L.A.O., Register 26, fo. 260v.
47. *The Works of Thomas Cranmer*, ed. Cox, p. 460.
48. *L.P.*, VIII, no. 105.
49. L.A.O., Register 26, fo. 26.
50. Emden, *Oxford*, n.s., p. 506.
51. *L.P.*, XI, nos. 136, 137.
52. *L.P.*, XII, ii, no. 374.
53. *L.P.*, XI, no. 138; P.R.O., S.P., I, 105, fo. 104.
54. *L.P.*, X, nos. 804, 850.

55. *ibid.*, no. 891; P.R.O., S.P., I, 103, fo. 302.
56. Register 26, fo. 266v.
57. *L.P.*, IX, no. 611.
58. *L.P.*, X, no. 267.
59. Thomson, *Later Lollards*, pp. 90–2; L.A.O., Register 26, fos. 201v, 228, 228v.
60. *Acts and Monuments of John Foxe*, ed. Townsend, IV, p. 580.
61. *ibid.*, pp. 581 ff.; L.A.O., Register 26, fos. 171, 180v, 205v.
62. *L.P.*, IX, no. 20; P.R.O., S.P., I, 95, fo. 10.
63. L.A.O., Register 26, fo. 267.
64. Clark, *English Provincial Society from the Reformation to the Revolution*, p. 47.
65. L.A.O., Vij. 1, fo. 222.
66. L.A.O., Register 26, fo. 225v; Clebsch, *England's Earliest Protestants*, pp. 80 ff.
67. cf. Clark, *op. cit.*, p. 58.
68. L.A.O., L.C.C., Box 4, fos. 105–128; Bucks R.O., D/A/We (unfoliated); Huntingdon R.O., Will Register 5, fos. 1 ff.
69. Hodgett, *Tudor Lincolnshire*, p. 25.
70. Haigh, *Tudor Lancashire*, p. 123.
71. L.A.O., Cij. 1, fos. 2v-16; cf. Davies, 'The Pilgrimage of Grace Reconsidered', p. 66.
72. See above, pp. 77 ff.
73. L.A.O., Vij. 1, fos. 96, 154–5v.
74. Cambridge University Library, SSS. 17. 29, 'Answere to the Petitions of the Traytours and rebelles in Lyncolneshyre'.
75. *The First Churchwardens' Book of Louth 1500–1524*, ed. Dudding, *passim.*
76. Davies, *op. cit.*, James, 'Obedience and Dissent in Henrician England: The Lincolnshire Rebellion 1536', pp. 3 ff.
77. *Letters relating to the Suppression of the Monasteries*, ed. Wright, pp. 116–17.
78. M. H. and R. Dodds, *The Pilgrimage of Grace 1536–7 and the Exeter Conspiracy 1538*, I, pp. 90–1.
79. Hoskins, 'Harvest Fluctuations and English Economic History 1480–1619', pp. 28 ff.
80. L.A.O., L.C.C., fos. 166v–170.
81. L.A.O., Vij. 1, fos. 81, 96, 154^2.
82. *Documents*, edd. Gee and Hardy, p. 269.
83. Wilkins, *Concilia*, III, pp. 823–4.
84. L.A.O., Register 26, fo. 276.
85. *The Works of Thomas Cranmer*, ed. Cox, p. 470.
86. L.A.O., Register 26, fo. 275v–276.
87. L.A.O., Register 25, fo. 76v.
88. *L.P.*, XI, no. 970.
89. Wilkins, *Concilia*, III, p. 803.
90. *A Chronicle of England during the Reigns of the Tudors from 1485–1559 by Charles Wriothesley*, ed. Hamilton, I, p. 55.
91. *L.P.*, XI, no. 1110; Elton, *Policy and Police*, p. 251.
92. *L.P.*, XII, i, no. 70; P.R.O., E/36/119, pp. 1 ff.
93. P.R.O., E/36/118, fo. 4.
94. Dodds, *The Pilgrimage of Grace*, I, pp. 101–2.
95. *ibid.*, p. 92.
96. Page torn.
97. P.R.O., E36/118, fo. 4; *L.P.*, XI, no. 975.
98. *L.P.*, XI, nos. 970, (6), 973.
99. P.R.O., E/36/118, fo. 4v; *L.P.*, XI, 975.
100. *L.P.*, XII, (i), no. 481.
101. Alford, Cockerington, Elkington, Gaiton, Halington, Saleby, Snelland, Scothern, Sotby, North Somercotes, Welton, L.A.O., Register 23, fos. 67, 126, 128, 130, 130v, 146v, 148v; Register 27, fos. 21v, 59v, 83v, Vij. 1, fo. 149v.

102. Biscethorpe, Donington on Bain, Hainton, Hatton, Lowth, Miningsby, Rothwell, Tetney, Nether Toynton. L.A.O., Register 23, fos. 36, 91, 103, 143v; Register 25, fos. 16, 23; Register 27, fos. 51, 53, 59.
103. Belchford, Beaulieu, Conisholm, Farforth, Harrington, L.A.O., Register 27, fos. 25, 46v, 55v, 57v, 60v.
104. *LP*., XI, no. 967.
105. P.R.O., S.P., I, 109, fo. 2; *L.P*., XI, no. 828 (2).
106. *L.P*., XI, nos. 853, 854; *The First Churchwardens' Book of Louth*, ed. Dudding, *passim.*
107. *L.P*., XI, no. 553; P.R.O., S.P., I, 106, fo. 270.
108. *L.P*., XII, no. 70 (XI); P.R.O., E/36/119, fos. 15v–16.
109. *L.P*., XI, 853; P.R.O., E/36/119, fo. 8v.
110. See especially Roger Martyn's *The State of Melford Church and Our Laides Chapel, at the East end, as I did know it* (1580).
111. *Documents*, edd. Gee and Hardy, p. 271.
112. *L.P*., XI, no. 1319; Haigh, *Tudor Lancashire*, p. 129.
113. L.A.O., Cij. 1, *passim*; Cj. 3. *passim*; Cj. 4 *passim.*
114. Dodds, *The Pilgrimage of Grace*, I, pp. 92–3.
115. *L.P*., XII, i, 380.
116. *L.P*., XI, nos. 805, 827, 828, 853, 967, 975; *L.P*., XII, (1), no. 70; P.R.O., E/36/118, fo. 1.
117. *L.P*., XI, no. 828; XIV, ii, no. 509.
118. *L.P*., XI, no. 805.
119. *L.P*., XII, i, no. 702.
120. James, 'Obedience and Dissent in Henrician England: The Lincolnshire Rebellion', p. 9.
121. *L.P*., XI, no. 553; XII, i, 70.
122. *L.P*., XI, no. 1080.
123. James, 'The first Earl of Cumberland 1493–1542 and the Decline of Northern Feudalism'.
124. Dickens, *Lollards and Protestants in the Diocese of York*, pp. 106 ff.
125. *L.P*., XI, 970.
126. *LP*., XI, 967.
127. *L.P*., XI, nos. 828, 975; P.R.O., E/36/118, fo.10.
128. *L.P*., XII i, 70.
129. *L.P*., XI, no. 975; P.R.O., E/36/118, fo. 4.
130. *L.P*., XII, i. no. 370.
131. Strype, *Ecclesiastical Memorials*, I, ii, p. 207.
132. *Acts and Monuments of John Foxe*, ed. Townshend, V, p. 171.
133. This figure only relates to one set of prisoners; there were possibly others, *L.P*., XI, no. 827.
134. *L.P*., XII, i, 581 (2).
135. See especially *L.P*., XII, i, no. 380.

IV: The battle for the consciences of Englishmen

1. *L.P*., XII, i, 70.
2. L.A.O., Register 26, fo. 55v.
3. L.A.O., Cj. 4, fo. 22v.
4. Emden, *Oxford*, n.s., p. 176.
5. For visitations of Buckingham, see L.A.O., Cj.3, *passim*; Citations episcopal, Box 81, number 1–32. For his visitation of the cathedral, see above, pp. 90 ff.
6. L.A.O., Lincoln City MSS, Entries of the Common Council L/1/1/1/1, fo. 286v.
7. The practice of amalgamating the offices of archdeacon's official with bishop's commissary seems to have continued during Longland's episcopate. The paucity of

material for the 1540s, makes it impossible to compile a list of these all-important deputies.

8. Wilkins, *Concilia*, III, p. 861.
9. *L.P.*, XII, i, no. 29.
10. Lehmberg, *The Later Parliaments of Henry VIII, 1536–47*, p. 13.
11. B.L., C. 53.b.b.7, pp. 14–15.
12. Wilkins, *Concilia*, III, p. 831.
13. *L.P.*, XII, ii, no. 403.
14. *Documents*, edd. Gee and Hardy, pp. 275–81.
15. Elton, *Policy and Police*, pp. 254–5.
16. Bodl. Libr. Arch. A.d.11, fo. 50.
17. B.L., C. 53, k. 14.
18. Sturge, *Cuthbert Tunstal*, pp. 125, 226 ff.
19. L.A.O., Register 26, fo. 278.
20. Clark, *English Provincial Society*, p. 47.
21. Emden, *Oxford*, n.s., p. 633.
22. *L.P.*, XIII, ii, no. 135.
23. *L.P.*, XIV, i, no. 238; P.R.O., S.P., I, 163, fo. 21.
24. Merriman, *Life and Letters of Thomas Cromwell*, II, no. 326, p. 241.
25. L.A.O., Vj. 10, fos. 1–6v, 41–43; Vj. 11, fos. 166–178v.
26. *Documents*, edd. Gee and Hardy, p. 277.
27. L.A.O., Vj. 10. fos. 4, 4v.
28. *ibid.*, fos. 2v, 3, 4v[2].
29. Chambers, *Faculty Registers*, p. 255.
30. L.A.O., Vj. 11, fo. 166.
31. L.A.O., Register 26, fo. 278; for Goodrich's attempt to plant a preacher in Somersham, see Elton, *Policy and Police*, p. 213.
32. L.A.O., Register 27, fo. 119; Vj. 10, fo. 28; Harris also possessed a good library of theological books see Longden, VI, p. 159.
33. L.A.O., Vj. 10, fos. 30–31v.
34. L.A.O., Vj. 10, fos. 79, 83.
35. *ibid.*, fos. 77v, 82v.
36. *ibid.*, fo. 77v.
37. L.A.O., Vj. 11, fos. 166–178v.
38. Clark, *English Provincial Society*, pp. 60 ff.
39. L.A.O., Cj. 3, fo. 68.
40. *The Churchwardens' Accounts of St Michael's Church, Oxford*, ed. Salter, p. 212.
41. L.A.O., Cj. 3, fo. 69.
42. *ibid.*, 77v.
43. L.A.O., Vij. 1, fos. 81 ff.
44. L.A.O., Cj. 3, fo. 66v.
45. *ibid.*, fo. 74.
46. *ibid.*, fo. 74v.
47. *ibid.*, fo. 74v.
48. *ibid.*, fo. 75.
49. *ibid.*, fos. 73v, 75.
50. *ibid.*, fo. 70v; cf. Brigden, 'The Early Reformation in London', p. 209.
51. L.A.O., Cj. 3, fo. 72.
52. *Documents*, edd. Gee and Hardy, p. 275; cf. Frere and Kennedy, *Visitation Articles*, pp. 1–11.
53. Dickens, *The English Reformation*, pp. 129–35.
54. L.A.O., Register 26, fo. 291v; cf. Wilkins, *Concilia*, III, p. 856.
55. Hughes and Larkin, *Tudor Proclamations*, p. 296.

56. L.A.O., D and C, Bj. 3.5, unpaginated *sub Curialitates; Edwardian Inventories for Buckinghamshire*, ed. Eeles, p. 1.
57. Walker, 'A History of the Reformation in the Archdeaconries of Lincoln and Stow', p. 106.
58. *L.P.*, XIV, ii, no. 214.
59. Foster, 'Inventories of Church Goods 1548', pp. 27–46.
60. L.A.O., D and C, Wills, II, fo. 7b (second foliation).
61. L.A.O., Cj. 3, fo. 78v.
62. *ibid.*, fo. 83.
63. L.A.O., Register 27, fos. 244, 244v, 250v.
64. L.A.O., Register 27, fos. 69v, 78.
65. L.A.O., Vj. 11, fo. 20^2.
66. Brigden, 'The Early Reformation in London', p. 240.
67. L.A.O., Register 27, fo. 73; *L.P.*, VII, no. 982; Elton, *Policy and Police*, p. 344.
68. L.A.O., Register 27, fos. 267v, 271; see also above p. 165.
69. Robert Beste, chaplain to the Earl of Rutland and collated to Woolsthorpe. L.A.O., Register 27, fo. 63v; vj. 11, fo. 18.
70. John Taylor was a Protestant and a later bishop of Lincoln. He was presented to S. Somercotes. L.A.O., Register 27, fo. 73; Venn, IV, p. 205. Also John Redmayne, who helped with the compilation of the Prayer Book; L.A.O., Register 27, fo. 224 and Venn, II, p. 430.
71. L.A.O., Register 27, fos. 76v, 79, 82v, 96v, 97, 147v, 197, 199, 246v.
72. Emden, *Oxford*, n.s. 373–4; see above, p. 138.
73. Emden, *Oxford*, III, p. 1475.
74. L.A.O., Register 27, fo. 159v; Emden, *Oxford*, n.s. pp. 316–17.
75. L.A.O., Register 27, fos. 125, 189v; Emden, *Oxford*, n.s., pp. 103–4.
76. *S.R.*, III, 28 Henry VIII, c.10.
77. For examples of the oath see Register 27, fos. 71v, 72, 197v, 223v, 247, 269v.
78. Dickens, *The Marian Reaction in the Diocese of York*, Part I, The Clergy, p. 16.
79. Ridley, *Thomas Cranmer*, pp. 146–8.
80. *The State of the Church*, ed. Foster, pp. 442 ff.
81. Foster, *Lincolnshire Notes and Queries*, V, pp. 129–44; *idem*, 'Admissions to Benefices and Compositions for First Fruits in the County of Leicester 1535–1660'; *idem*, 'Institutions to Benefices in the Diocese of Lincoln', II, pp. 459–544.
82. Dickens, *English Reformation*, p. 36.
83. Haigh, *Tudor Lancashire*, pp. 180–1 has an excellent discussion of the problems posed by the deprivation figures, and his notes refer the reader to the literature on the subject.
84. Dickens, *The English Reformation*, p. 207. Clark, *English Provincial Society*, pp. 58 ff. Palliser, 'Popular Reactions during the Years of Uncertainty 1530–70'; I. Luxton, 'The Reformation and Popular Culture'.
85. L.A.O., L.C.C. Wills 1549–1550, Box 2, fo. 9.
86. *ibid.*, fos. 10, 104.
87. Bucks. R.O., D/A/We, 3, fos. 14–14v.
88. The sources for these tables are: L.A.O., L.C.C. Wills 1545–6, Book 1 and 2; 1549–50, Box 1 and 2. Bucks. R.O., D/A/We, *passim*; Huntingdonshire R.O., Will Registers 7 and 8.
89. Huntingdonshire R.O., Will Register 7, fo. 179v.
90. *ibid.*, fos. 173, 184.
91. L.A.O., L.C.C., Wills, Book 1, fo. 33v.
92. Bucks. R.O., D/A/We, fos. 21v–22.
93. Pullan, *Rich and Poor in Renaissance Venice*, pp. 11 ff.
94. *Acts and Monuments of John Foxe*, ed. Townsend, V, p. 252.
95. L.A.O., Register 26, fos. 284v–285.

96. *Acts and Monuments* of John Foxe, ed. Townsend, v, p. 253.
97. *ibid.*, pp. 453–4.
98. *L.P.*, XIV, ii, no. 214.

Conclusion

1. Major, *Handlist*, pp. 14–15.
2. *ibid.*, p. 56.
3. *ibid.*, p. 76.
4. *ibid.*, pp. 84, 92.
5. Clark, *Provincial Society*, pp. 50 ff. Heal, 'The Bishops of Ely', pp. 72 ff.
6. Clark, *op. cit.*, p. 11. Powell, 'The Social Background of the Reformation in Gloucestershire', p. 119.
7. P.R.O., Prob. 11/31.
8. *ibid.*
9. B.L. C. 53. K. 14, p. 34.
10. Walker, 'A History of the Reformation in Lincoln and Stow', p. 66.
11. See above, pp. 158 ff. and notes.

INDEX

The following abbreviations have been used:

A	Augustinian Canons	KH	Knights Hospitallers
AB	Bonshommes	KT	Knights Templars
B	Black Monks, Benedictine	NA	Augustinian Canonesses
BC	Cluniac	NB	Benedictine Nuns
C	Cistercian Monks	NBC	Cluniac Nuns
CA	Carthusians	NBr	Bridgettines (Double Order)
FA	Friars, Austin	NC	Cistercian Nuns
FC	Carmelite	ND	Dominican Nuns
FCr	Crutched	NF	Franciscan Nuns
FD	Dominican	NG	Gilbertine (Double Order)
FF	Franciscan	NP	Premonstratensian Canonesses
FFO	Franciscan Observant	P	Premonstratensian Canons
G	Gilbertine Canons	S	Secular College (Collegiate)
H	Hospital		

Index

Index

Index